JUMBO BIBLE WORD GAMES

VOL. 2

BARBOUR BOOKS

An Imprint of Barbour Publishing, Inc.

© 2001 by Barbour Publishing, Inc.

ISBN 1-58660-235-7

All Scripture quotations, unless otherwise noted, are taken from the King James Version of the Bible.

Scripture quotations marked niv are taken from the HOLY BIBLE, NEW INTERNATIONAL VERSION®. NIV®. Copyright © 1973, 1978, 1984 by International Bible Society. Used by permission of Zondervan Publishing House. All rights reserved.

Scripture quotations marked NKJV are taken from the New King James Version. Copyright © 1979, 1980, 1982 by Thomas Nelson, Inc. Used by permission. All rights reserved.

Published by Barbour Books, an imprint of Barbour Publishing, Inc., P.O. Box 719, Uhrichsville, Ohio 44683 www.barbourbooks.com

ecpa Member of the
Evangelical Christian
Publishers Association

Printed in the United States of America.

JUMBO BIBLE WORD GAMES

VOL. 2

INTRODUCTION

Welcome to *Jumbo Bible Word Games Volume 2!* Here are more than four hundred pages of challenging and fun word games, all based on the greatest book of all time—the Bible. Featuring traditional crossword puzzles, word searches, acrostics, "CryptoScriptures," anagrams, and more, you'll have hours of enjoyment and edification.

Eleven types of word games are mingled throughout the pages of this book. Instructions, along with the names of contributors, are on the first page of each section—please be sure to look them over before you launch into the puzzles. Answers begin on page 413.

Pencils ready? Then put your skills to the test with *Jumbo Bible Word Games Volume 2!*

Drop Two Puzzles

by Dorothy Pryse

Remove two letters from each seven-letter word in the left-hand column to create a new five-letter word (you may need to rearrange the remaining letters). Put the two dropped letters into the spaces to the right of the blanks. Then use these letters to spell out a phrase or sentence from the Bible.

REVELATION

ANTIQUE	Silent	*quiet*	1.	_A_ _N_
NODDING	Acting	*doing*	2.	_N_ _D_
AVERAGE	Serious	*grave*	3.	_A_ _E_
WESTERN	Change	*reset*	4.	_W_ _N_
HELICES	Pie serving	*slice*	5.	_H_ _E_
CHOWDER	Musical tones	*Chord*	6.	_W_ _E_
MEDIATE	Measured speed	*timed*	7.	_A_ _E_
CANVASS	Browses	*Scans*	8.	_V_ _A_
PRELATE	Home base	*plate*	9.	_R_ _E_
NASTIER	Pay hike	*raise*	10.	_N_ _T_
SPANISH	Whirls	*spins*	11.	_A_ _H_

A N E W H E A V E N A
N D A N E W E A R T H

1 2 3 4 5 6 7 8 9 10 11

EZEKIEL

BLANKLY	Skinny	_____	1. ___ ___
LOCATED	Military trainee	_____	2. ___ ___
PRESENT	Exhausted	_____	3. ___ ___
SLAVERY	Disentangle	_____	4. ___ ___
DESPOIL	Heaped	_____	5. ___ ___
FREAKED	Gathered leaves	_____	6. ___ ___
TRASHED	Clip sheep	_____	7. ___ ___
BEARISH	Uplift	_____	8. ___ ___
BEREAVE	Daring	_____	9. ___ ___
AILMENT	N. E. state	_____	10. ___ ___
ALCOHOL	Nearby	_____	11. ___ ___
BOARDER	Wide	_____	12. ___ ___
SINGLED	Paper guides	_____	13. ___ ___

— — — — — — — — — — — — — —

— — — — — — — — — — — — — —

1   2   3   4   5   6   7   8   9   10   11   12   13

JEREMIAH

EARTHLY	Pumping organ	_____	1. ___ ___
WHERETO	Pitched	_____	2. ___ ___
AFFABLE	Fictional tale	_____	3. ___ ___
SCARLET	Fish skin	_____	4. ___ ___
CHASTEN	Social class	_____	5. ___ ___
NEITHER	Belongs to them	_____	6. ___ ___
DEBORAH	Staff of life	_____	7. ___ ___
FROSTED	Model T's	_____	8. ___ ___
BRAVEST	Speech parts	_____	9. ___ ___
STEALTH	Smallest	_____	10. ___ ___
HECTARE	Copy	_____	11. ___ ___
WEIGHTS	Vision	_____	12. ___ ___
CHAPMAN	Winner	_____	13. ___ ___

___ ___ ___ ___ ___ ___ ___ ___ ___ ___ ___ ___ ___

___ ___ ___ ___ ___ ___ ___ ___ ___ ___ ___ ___ ___

1 2 3 4 5 6 7 8 9 10 11 12 13

ROMANS

FRESHEN	Transparent	_____	1. ___ ___
NOTEPAD	Framed glass	_____	2. ___ ___
BREADTH	Restrained	_____	3. ___ ___
GRANITE	Concede	_____	4. ___ ___
LODGING	Leaving	_____	5. ___ ___
FORSAKE	Flatware	_____	6. ___ ___
SHALLOW	Angels' wear	_____	7. ___ ___
INBOARD	Trademark	_____	8. ___ ___
GRAFTED	Graded	_____	9. ___ ___
GUSHING	Utilizing	_____	10. ___ ___
TOPMOST	Walk heavily	_____	11. ___ ___
CITADEL	Sports shoe	_____	12. ___ ___

— — — — — — — — — — — —

— — — — — — — — — — — —

1   2   3   4   5   6   7   8   9   10   11   12

EZRA

GRAFTED	Wind	_____	1. ___ ___
SIGNORA	Wheat	_____	2. ___ ___
INBOARD	Songbird	_____	3. ___ ___
WEALTHY	Tool	_____	4. ___ ___
HEATHER	Not here	_____	5. ___ ___
FEATHER	Anesthetic	_____	6. ___ ___
BLATANT	Trite	_____	7. ___ ___
ESSENCE	View	_____	8. ___ ___
REBIRTH	Roman river	_____	9. ___ ___
ARBITER	Thorn	_____	10. ___ ___
PLANISH	Aches	_____	11. ___ ___
STENCIL	Pennies	_____	12. ___ ___
WRESTED	Prevent	_____	13. ___ ___

__ __ __ __ __ __ __ __ __ __ __ __ __

__ __ __ __ __ __ __ __ __ __ __ __ __

1   2   3   4   5   6   7   8   9   10   11   12   13

JOB

OCTOPUS	To lower	_____	1. __ __
COLONEL	Violin-like instrument	_____	2. __ __
MANTELS	Slants	_____	3. __ __
STARDOM	Small missiles	_____	4. __ __
GUILDER	Reigned	_____	5. __ __
DETROIT	Attempted	_____	6. __ __
DAMPING	Mimicking	_____	7. __ __
WORLDLY	Humorous	_____	8. __ __
CLAMOUR	Wall art	_____	9. __ __
UNAIDED	Ate	_____	10. __ __
UNCLOSE	Ice cream holders	_____	11. __ __
SCALDED	Image for transfer	_____	12. __ __
MILEAGE	Small light	_____	13. __ __

_ _ _ _ _ _ _ _ _ _ _ _ _

_ _ _ _ _ _ _ _ _ _ _ _ _

1 2 3 4 5 6 7 8 9 10 11 12 13

Ruth

SCARLET	Loves	_____	1. ___ ___
NIGHTLY	Knotting	_____	2. ___ ___
BLARNEY	Discover	_____	3. ___ ___
PLEASES	Gross receipts	_____	4. ___ ___
INFLAME	Last	_____	5. ___ ___
ALIMONY	Italian city	_____	6. ___ ___
PROPHET	Spasm	_____	7. ___ ___
MISDEAL	Female servants	_____	8. ___ ___
COASTER	Vehicles	_____	9. ___ ___
SPARING	Corn	_____	10. ___ ___
SHINGLE	Burn	_____	11. ___ ___
EATABLE	Sheep sound	_____	12. ___ ___

— — — — — — — — — — — —

— — — — — — — — — — — —

1   2   3   4   5   6   7   8   9   10   11   12

GALATIANS

BEATLES	Rent	_____	1. ___ ___
HECKLER	Salesperson	_____	2. ___ ___
ANTIQUE	One of five	_____	3. ___ ___
REDRESS	Plant starters	_____	4. ___ ___
STYGIAN	Goliath	_____	5. ___ ___
BEDSIDE	Agreed with	_____	6. ___ ___
ONEROUS	Sleep noise	_____	7. ___ ___
REGNANT	Representative	_____	8. ___ ___
SWARMED	Heats	_____	9. ___ ___
ANOTHER	Brier	_____	10. ___ ___
NOCTURN	Woo	_____	11. ___ ___
ONWARDS	Sketched	_____	12. ___ ___

__ __ __ __ __ __ __ __ __ __ __ __

__ __ __ __ __ __ __ __ __ __ __ __

1   2   3   4   5   6   7   8   9   10   11   12

JOHN

CORONET	Sing	_____	1. ___ ___
HABITED	Decreased	_____	2. ___ ___
ANDIRON	Deplete	_____	3. ___ ___
CAPTURE	Prank	_____	4. ___ ___
HOMERIC	Felony	_____	5. ___ ___
BEATING	Human	_____	6. ___ ___
SLAVISH	Closed vessels	_____	7. ___ ___
TENSILE	Clothes ropes	_____	8. ___ ___
SWARMED	Imagine	_____	9. ___ ___
COASTER	Grocery helps	_____	10. ___ ___
REDSKIN	Glided over snow	_____	11. ___ ___
LAMBERT	Dark yellow	_____	12. ___ ___
MILDEST	Set of steps	_____	13. ___ ___

__ __ __ __ __ __ __ __ __ __ __ __ __

__ __ __ __ __ __ __ __ __ __ __ __ __

1   2   3   4   5   6   7   8   9   10   11   12   13

TITUS

CHEETAH	Instruct	_____	1. ___ ___
FLOATER	Another time	_____	2. ___ ___
LEATHER	Not here	_____	3. ___ ___
DIEHARD	Listened	_____	4. ___ ___
DIALECT	Woven	_____	5. ___ ___
HARMONY	City official	_____	6. ___ ___
FREIGHT	Not our	_____	7. ___ ___
FEARFUL	Beacon	_____	8. ___ ___
CAPITOL	Theme	_____	9. ___ ___
SWARMED	Fantasize	_____	10. ___ ___
ENDMOST	Darns	_____	11. ___ ___
STEWART	Refuse	_____	12. ___ ___
DOLTISH	Works	_____	13. ___ ___

___ ___ ___ ___ ___ ___ ___ ___ ___ ___ ___ ___ ___

___ ___ ___ ___ ___ ___ ___ ___ ___ ___ ___ ___ ___

1   2   3   4   5   6   7   8   9   10   11   12   13

GENESIS

GRADING	1,000	_____	1. ___ ___
VENISON	Climbing plants	_____	2. ___ ___
HUNDRED	Below	_____	3. ___ ___
CLAIMED	Award of honor	_____	4. ___ ___
FARMERS	Skeleton	_____	5. ___ ___
ELATION	Romance language	_____	6. ___ ___
AWARDED	Fear	_____	7. ___ ___
WRITTEN	Correspond	_____	8. ___ ___
MISSILE	Becomes slender	_____	9. ___ ___
DAMMING	Urchin	_____	10. ___ ___
ABDOMEN	Studied	_____	11. ___ ___
EGGHEAD	Encircle	_____	12. ___ ___
NEAREST	Look fixedly	_____	13. ___ ___

__ __ __ __ __ __ __ __ __ __ __ __ __

__ __ __ __ __ __ __ __ __ __ __ __ __

1 2 3 4 5 6 7 8 9 10 11 12 13

JOSHUA

GRAFTED	Swap	_____	1. ___ ___
PLATOON	Shrub	_____	2. ___ ___
DEAREST	Pester	_____	3. ___ ___
MARTIAL	Warning	_____	4. ___ ___
REFRESH	Allude	_____	5. ___ ___
WEATHER	Organ	_____	6. ___ ___
LITERAL	Not now	_____	7. ___ ___
STATION	Smooth cloth	_____	8. ___ ___
THROUGH	Strong	_____	9. ___ ___
TRACKED	Squeak	_____	10. ___ ___
FRESHET	Releases	_____	11. ___ ___
MESSIAH	Not right	_____	12. ___ ___
ELYSIAN	Murdered	_____	13. ___ ___

__ __ __ __ __ __ __ __ __ __ __ __ __

__ __ __ __ __ __ __ __ __ __ __ __ __

1 2 3 4 5 6 7 8 9 10 11 12 13

ZECHARIAH

Word	Clue		#	
ISHMAEL	Food times	____ ____	1.	____ ____
OVERSAW	Relish	____ ____	2.	____
ALIFORM	Plants	____ ____	3.	____
BOILING	Game	____ ____	4.	____
PEDICLE	A portion	____ ____	5.	____
MADNESS	Titles	____ ____	6.	____
FITCHEW	Leader	____ ____	7.	____
POACHER	To dry	____ ____	8.	____
HERSELF	Transparent	____ ____	9.	____
SHALLOT	Sandbar	____ ____	10.	____
ETHICAL	Shoe grip	____ ____	11.	____
REAGENT	Large	____ ____	12.	____ ____
DEEPEST	Hasten	____ ____	13.	____ ____

— — — — — — — — — — — — —

— — — — — — — — — — — — —

1 2 3 4 5 6 7 8 9 10 11 12 13

HAGGAI

ANEROID	Bee	_____	1. ___ ___
IMPASTO	Jazz dance	_____	2. ___ ___
MIGRANT	Wood fiber	_____	3. ___ ___
WEATHER	Consumer	_____	4. ___ ___
INDITED	Supped	_____	5. ___ ___
CHAPLET	Put	_____	6. ___ ___
HYDRATE	Late	_____	7. ___ ___
LEPROSY	Literary medium	_____	8. ___ ___
ROOTAGE	Rasp	_____	9. ___ ___
TOURISM	Damp	_____	10. ___ ___
SHORTED	Pain	_____	11. ___ ___

— — — — — — — — — — —

— — — — — — — — — — —

1   2   3   4   5   6   7   8   9   10   11

LUKE

MICHAEL	Blood sucker	_____	1. ___ ___
ARCHAIC	Official seat	_____	2. ___ ___
GRENADE	Incline	_____	3. ___ ___
ASHTRAY	Waste	_____	4. ___ ___
FASTEST	Banquet	_____	5. ___ ___
HEATHEN	Devoured	_____	6. ___ ___
AVARICE	Slice turkey	_____	7. ___ ___
LARGEST	Elaborate	_____	8. ___ ___
BEASTLY	Leaven	_____	9. ___ ___
REPLICA	Arrange	_____	10. ___ ___
ENSURED	Sand hills	_____	11. ___ ___
JESTING	Scorch	_____	12. ___ ___
DEBOUCH	Diced	_____	13. ___ ___

__ __ __ __ __ __ __ __ __ __ __ __ __

__ __ __ __ __ __ __ __ __ __ __ __ __

1   2   3   4   5   6   7   8   9   10   11   12   13

HEBREWS

NESTLED	Horse	_____	1. ___ ___
CLOAKED	Encrusted	_____	2. ___ ___
LAWLESS	Bargains	_____	3. ___ ___
ATTIRED	Tire mark	_____	4. ___ ___
SEVENTH	Nervous	_____	5. ___ ___
FEELING	Throw	_____	6. ___ ___
JOBLESS	Bottoms	_____	7. ___ ___
PIOUSLY	Ruin	_____	8. ___ ___
FELSITE	Choice	_____	9. ___ ___
PAINTED	Yearned	_____	10. ___ ___
APHESIS	Form	_____	11. ___ ___
BROTHER	Shipworm	_____	12. ___ ___
ASHAMED	Women	_____	13. ___ ___

___ ___ ___ ___ ___ ___ ___ ___ ___ ___ ___ ___ ___

___ ___ ___ ___ ___ ___ ___ ___ ___ ___ ___ ___ ___

1 2 3 4 5 6 7 8 9 10 11 12 13

MALACHI

REFRACT	Respond	_____	1. ___ ___
EARSHOT	Garbage	_____	2. ___ ___
OURSELF	Bad person	_____	3. ___ ___
HOLBEIN	Aristocrat	_____	4. ___ ___
NEPOTIC	Theme	_____	5. ___ ___
SALIENT	Angle	_____	6. ___ ___
RASPING	Mimicking	_____	7. ___ ___
MILDEST	Kept watch	_____	8. ___ ___
DEFICIT	Quoted	_____	9. ___ ___
IRKSOME	Code	_____	10. ___ ___
SPRAYER	Beseeches	_____	11. ___ ___
PAINTER	Block letters	_____	12. ___ ___

— — — — — — — — — — — —

— — — — — — — — — — — —

1 2 3 4 5 6 7 8 9 10 11 12

1 CORINTHIANS

CREATED	Step	_____	1. ____ ____
SPRIGHT	Seizes	_____	2. ____ ____
HEARTED	Cornered	_____	3. ____ ____
WESTERN	Sugary	_____	4. ____ ____
NAIROBI	Intellect	_____	5. ____ ____
TRANSIT	Pours	_____	6. ____ ____
YORKIST	Big bird	_____	7. ____ ____
THRIVED	Employed	_____	8. ____ ____
ANGELUS	Thrust	_____	9. ____ ____
UNAIRED	Draw off	_____	10. ____ ____
NET BALL	Furniture	_____	11. ____ ____
FITNESS	Trigometric formulas	_____	12. ____ ____

__ __ __ __ __ __ __ __

__ __ __ __ __ __ __ __ __

1 2 3 4 5 6 7 8 9 10 11 12

MARK

GERMANE	Combine	_____	1. ___ ___
ENDLESS	Snow vehicles	_____	2. ___ ___
DROWNED	Buzzing sound	_____	3. ___ ___
HEALING	Ascertain	_____	4. ___ ___
SWATTER	Scatter	_____	5. ___ ___
VARNISH	Pours down	_____	6. ___ ___
DIETARY	Unclean	_____	7. ___ ___
PLANTER	Future	_____	8. ___ ___
COOLEST	Clusters	_____	9. ___ ___
ANALECT	Scrub	_____	10. ___ ___
CHAMFER	Set up	_____	11. ___ ___
DEVOTEE	Chose	_____	12. ___ ___
ENDORSE	Compact	_____	13. ___ ___

___ ___ ___ ___ ___ ___ ___ ___ ___ ___ ___ ___ ___

___ ___ ___ ___ ___ ___ ___ ___ ___ ___ ___ ___ ___

1   2   3   4   5   6   7   8   9   10   11   12   13

1 JOHN

TRASHED	Cut off	_____	1. ___ ___
EUCHRED	Healed	_____	2. ___ ___
NEAREST	Trap	_____	3. ___ ___
TEACHER	Touch	_____	4. ___ ___
RAMBLER	Point finger	_____	5. ___ ___
UNEARTH	Valentine	_____	6. ___ ___
ASPIRED	Falls in drops	_____	7. ___ ___
GHASTLY	Hurriedly	_____	8. ___ ___
OCULATE	Sharp	_____	9. ___ ___
DEALING	Gather grain	_____	10. ___ ___
FEARING	Rule	_____	11. ___ ___
NASCENT	Bare	_____	12. ___ ___

__ __ __ __ __ __ __ __ __ __ __ __

__ __ __ __ __ __ __ __ __ __ __ __

1   2   3   4   5   6   7   8   9   10   11   12

DECODER PUZZLES

by Christy Barritt

Using the decoder grid, uncover a Bible verse for each puzzle. For each two-digit number in the puzzle, find a corresponding letter by matching the first number with the vertical column and the second number with the horizontal row. Place all letters above their corresponding numbers, and the verse will appear.

PSALM 4:8

	1	2	3	4	5
1	T	U	G	W	P
2	L	J	Z	D	V
3	E	F	B	M	Q
4	K	H	Y	S	C
5	A	N	I	O	R

53   14-53-21-21   33-54-11-42   21-51-43   34-31

24-54-14-52   53-52   15-31-51-45-31,   51-52-24

44-21-31-31-15:   32-54-55   11-42-54-12,

21-54-55-24,   54-52-21-43   34-51-41-31-44-11

34-31   24-14-31-21-21   53-52   44-51-32-31-11-43.

1 CORINTHIANS 9:27

	1	2	3	4	5
1	T	U	G	W	P
2	L	J	Z	D	V
3	E	F	B	M	Q
4	K	H	Y	S	C
5	A	N	I	O	R

33-12-11   53   41-31-31-15   12-52-24-31-55   34-43

33-54-24-43,...21-31-44-11   11-42-51-11   33-43

51-52-43   34-31-51-52-44,   14-42-31-52

53   42-51-25-31   15-55-31-51-45-42-31-24   11-54

54-11-42-31-55-44,   53   34-43-44-31-21-32

44-42-54-12-21-24   33-31   51

45-51-44-11-51-14-51-43.

Psalm 7:17

	1	2	3	4	5
1	T	U	G	W	P
2	L	J	Z	D	V
3	E	F	B	M	Q
4	K	H	Y	S	C
5	A	N	I	O	R

53   14-53-21-21   15-55-51-53-44-31   11-42-31

21-54-55-24   51-45-45-54-55-24-53-52-13   11-54

42-53-44   55-53-13-42-11-31-54-12-44-52-31-44-44:

51-52-24   14-53-21-21   44-53-52-13

15-55-51-53-44-31   11-54   11-42-31   52-51-34-31

54-32   11-42-31   21-54-55-24   34-54-44-11

42-53-13-42.

ECCLESIATES 1:9

	1	2	3	4	5
1	T	U	G	W	P
2	L	J	Z	D	V
3	E	F	B	M	Q
4	K	H	Y	S	C
5	A	N	I	O	R

11-42-31   11-42-53-52-13   11-42-51-11   42-51-11-42

33-31-31-52, 53-11 53-44 11-42-51-11 14-42-53-45-42

44-42-51-21-21   33-31:   51-52-24   11-42-51-11

14-42-53-45-42 53-44 24-54-52-31 53-44 11-42-51-11

14-42-53-45-42   44-42-51-21-21   33-31   24-54-52-31:

51-52-24   11-42-31-55-31   53-44   52-54   52-31-14

11-42-53-52-13   12-52-24-31-55   11-42-31   44-12-52.

PSALM 20:7

	1	2	3	4	5
1	P	V	Q	C	R
2	W	D	M	S	O
3	G	Z	B	Y	I
4	U	J	F	H	N
5	T	L	E	K	A

24-25-23-53   51-15-41-24-51   35-45

14-44-55-15-35-25-51-24,   55-45-22   24-25-23-53

35-45   44-25-15-24-53-24:   33-41-51   21-53

21-35-52-52   15-53-23-53-23-33-53-15   51-44-53

45-55-23-53   25-43   51-44-53   52-25-15-22

25-41-15   31-25-22.

PHILIPPIANS 4:13

	1	2	3	4	5
1	P	V	Q	C	R
2	W	D	M	S	O
3	G	Z	B	Y	I
4	U	J	F	H	N
5	T	L	E	K	A

35   14-55-45   22-25   55-52-52   51-44-35-45-31-24

51-44-15-25-41-31-44   14-44-15-35-24-51

21-44-35-14-44   24-51-15-53-45-31-51-44-53-45-53-51-44

23-53.

MATTHEW 5:44

	1	2	3	4	5
1	P	V	Q	C	R
2	W	D	M	S	O
3	G	Z	B	Y	I
4	U	J	F	H	N
5	T	L	E	K	A

52-25-12-53   34-25-41-15   53-45-53-23-35-53-24,

33-52-53-24-24   51-44-53-23   51-44-55-51

14-41-15-24-53   34-25-41,   22-25   31-25-25-22

51-25 51-44-53-23 51-44-55-51 44-55-51-53 34-25-41,

55-45-22   11-15-55-34   43-25-15   51-44-53-23

21-44-35-14-44   22-53-24-11-35-51-53-43-41-52-52-34

41-24-53   34-25-41,   55-45-22

11-53-15-24-53-14-41-51-53   34-25-41.

PROVERBS 30:5

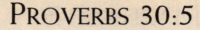

	1	2	3	4	5
1	P	V	Q	C	R
2	W	D	M	S	O
3	G	Z	B	Y	I
4	U	J	F	H	N
5	T	L	E	K	A

53-12-53-15-34   21-25-15-22   25-43   31-25-22

35-24   11-41-15-53:   44-53   35-24   55

24-44-35-53-52-22   41-45-51-25   51-44-53-23

51-44-55-51   11-41-51   51-44-53-35-15

51-15-41-24-51   35-45   44-35-23.

James 1:5

	1	2	3	4	5
1	P	V	Q	C	R
2	W	D	M	S	O
3	G	Z	B	Y	I
4	U	J	F	H	N
5	T	L	E	K	A

35-43   55-45-34   25-43   34-25-41   52-55-14-54

21-35-24-22-25-23,   52-53-51   44-35-23   55-24-54

25-43   31-25-22,   51-44-55-51   31-35-12-53-51-44

51-25   55-52-52   23-53-45   52-35-33-53-15-55-52-52-34,

55-45-22   41-11-33-15-55-35-22-53-51-44   45-25-51;

55-45-22   35-51   24-44-55-52-52   33-53

31-35-12-53-45   44-35-23.

PSALM 5:8

	1	2	3	4	5
1	P	V	Q	C	R
2	W	D	M	S	O
3	G	Z	B	Y	I
4	U	J	F	H	N
5	T	L	E	K	A

52-53-55-22   23-53,   25   52-25-15-22,   35-45

51-44-34   15-35-31-44-51-53-25-41-24-45-53-24-24

33-53-14-55-41-24-53   25-43   23-35-45-53

53-45-53-23-35-53-24;   23-55-54-53   51-44-34

21-55-34   24-51-15-55-35-31-44-51

33-53-43-25-15-53   23-34   43-55-14-53.

1 CORINTHIANS 9:24

	1	2	3	4	5
1	P	V	Q	C	R
2	W	D	M	S	O
3	G	Z	B	Y	I
4	U	J	F	H	N
5	T	L	E	K	A

54-45-25-21   34-53   45-25-51   51-44-55-51

51-44-53-34   21-44-35-14-44   15-41-45   35-45

55   15-55-14-53   15-41-45   55-52-52,   33-41-51

25-45-53   15-53-14-53-35-12-53-51-44   51-44-53

11-15-35-32-53?   24-25   15-41-45,   51-44-55-51

34-53   23-55-34   25-33-51-55-35-45.

ECCLESIASTES 3:1

	1	2	3	4	5
1	P	V	Q	C	R
2	W	D	M	S	O
3	G	Z	B	Y	I
4	U	J	F	H	N
5	T	L	E	K	A

51-25   53-12-53-15-34   51-44-35-45-31

51-44-53-15-53   35-24   55   24-53-55-24-25-45,

55-45-22   55   51-35-23-53   51-25   53-12-53-15-34

11-41-15-11-25-24-53   41-45-22-53-15   51-44-53

44-53-55-12-53-45.

ROMANS 12:10

33-31   21-13-12-44-41-23

11-32-32-31-25-51-13-14-12-31-44   14-12-31   51-14

11-12-14-51-22-31-15   54-13-51-22

33-15-14-51-22-31-15-41-23   41-14-45-31;

13-12   22-14-12-14-52-15

55-15-31-32-31-15-15-13-12-53   14-12-31

11-12-14-51-22-31-15.

ROMANS 12:20

	1	2	3	4	5
1	A	N	I	O	R
2	K	H	Y	S	C
3	E	F	B	M	Q
4	L	J	Z	D	V
5	T	U	G	W	P

51-22-31-15-31-32-14-15-31   13-32   51-22-13-12-31

31-12-31-34-23   22-52-12-53-31-15,   32-31-31-44

22-13-34;   13-32   22-31   51-22-13-15-24-51,

53-13-45-31   22-13-34   44-15-13-12-21:   32-14-15

13-12   24-14   44-14-13-12-53   51-22-14-52

24-22-11-41-51   22-31-11-55   25-14-11-41-24

14-32   32-13-15-31   14-12   22-13-24   22-31-11-44.

PSALM 25:7

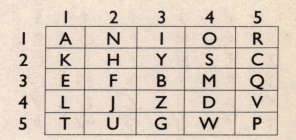

15-31-34-31-34-33-31-15   12-14-51   51-22-31

24-13-12-24   14-32   34-23   23-14-52-51-22,   12-14-15

34-23   51-15-11-12-24-53-15-31-24-24-13-14-12-24:

11-25-25-14-15-44-13-12-53   51-14   51-22-23

34-31-15-25-23   15-31-34-31-34-33-31-15   51-22-14-52

34-31   32-14-15   51-22-23   53-14-14-44-12-31-24-24'

24-11-21-31,   14   41-14-15-44.

Psalm 9:2

	1	2	3	4	5
1	A	N	I	O	R
2	K	H	Y	S	C
3	E	F	B	M	Q
4	L	J	Z	D	V
5	T	U	G	W	P

13   54-13-41-41   33-31   53-41-11-44   11-12-44

15-31-42-14-13-25-31   13-12   51-22-31-31:   13

54-13-41-41   24-13-12-53   55-15-11-13-24-31

51-14   51-22-23   12-11-34-31,   14   51-22-14-52

34-14-24-51   22-13-53-22.

1 CORINTHIANS 3:18

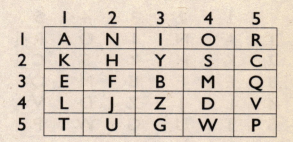

	1	2	3	4	5
1	A	N	I	O	R
2	K	H	Y	S	C
3	E	F	B	M	Q
4	L	J	Z	D	V
5	T	U	G	W	P

41-31-51   12-14   34-11-12   44-31-25-31-13-45-31

22-13-34-24-31-41-32,   13-32   11-12-23   34-11-12.

11-34-14-12-53   23-14-52   24-31-31-34-31-51-22

51-14   33-31   54-13-24-31   13-12   51-22-13-24

54-14-15-41-44,   41-31-51   22-13-34

33-31-25-14-34-31   11   32-14-14-41,   51-22-11-51

22-31   34-11-23   33-31   54-13-24-31-31.

TITUS 3:9

	1	2	3	4	5
1	A	N	I	O	R
2	K	H	Y	S	C
3	E	F	B	M	Q
4	L	J	Z	D	V
5	T	U	G	W	P

33-52-51   11-45-14-13-44   32-14-14-41-13-24-22

35-52-31-24-51-13-14-12-24,   11-12-44

53-31-12-31-11-41-14-53-13-31-24,   11-12-44

25-14-12-51-31-12-51-13-14-12-24,   11-12-44

24-51-15-13-45-13-12-53-24   11-33-14-52-51

51-22-31   41-11-54;   32-14-15   51-22-31-23

11-15-31   52-12-55-15-14-32-13-51-11-33-41-31.

1 TIMOTHY 6:12

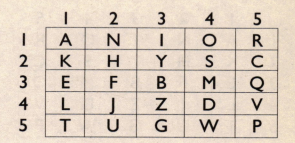

	1	2	3	4	5
1	A	N	I	O	R
2	K	H	Y	S	C
3	E	F	B	M	Q
4	L	J	Z	D	V
5	T	U	G	W	P

32-13-53-22-51 51-22-31 53-14-14-44 32-13-53-22-51

14-32 32-11-13-51-22, 41-11-23 22-14-41-44 14-12

31-51-31-15-12-11-41   41-13-32-31,...11-12-44

22-11-24-51   55-15-14-32-31-24-24-31-44   11

53-14-14-44   55-15-14-32-31-24-24-13-14-12

33-31-32-14-15-31   34-11-12-23

54-13-51-12-31-24-24-31-24.

1 Corinthians 10:26

32-14-15   51-22-31   31-11-15-51-22   13-24

51-22-31   41-14-15-44-'24,   11-12-44   51-22-31

32-52-41-12-31-24-24   51-22-31-15-31-14-32.

ACROSTIC PUZZLES

by Christy Barritt

Read the definition in the left-hand column and write the word it describes in the right-hand column. Then place the coded letters from the right-hand column in the puzzle form following to spell out the Bible verse indicated.

PSALM 18:2

A place of secondary education

u n i v e r s i t y
34 5 17 12 1 29 25 16 42 15

The British spelling of "flavor"

f l a v o u r
18 4 32 24 28 45 43

To move around in a twisting motion

___ ___ ___ ___ ___ ___
11 40 37 23 33 8

A record of days, months, and years

c a l e n d a r
9 26 13 30 20 41 38 3

The process of returning to health

r e c o v e r y
19 6 35 2 21 14 27 44

A location for buying or selling

___ ___ ___ ___ ___ ___
10 31 39 7 36 22

22-34-8   4-28-27-41   40-1   10-44   39-42-35-7,

31-20-41   10-44   18-42-43-22-39-14-1-1,   32-20-41

10-44   41-30-33-40-21-6-19-36-27;   10-44

23-16-41,   10-44   1-22-3-30-20-17-22-12,   40-20

11-25-2-10   5   11-5-13-15   22-39-45-1-22.

PSALM 2:11

Fairness

$$\overline{33}\ \overline{37}\ \overline{8}\ \overline{21}\ \overline{25}\ \overline{15}\ \overline{3}$$

Bodily equilibrium

$$\overline{24}\ \overline{16}\ \overline{32}\ \overline{35}\ \overline{1}\ \overline{22}\ \overline{9}$$

Special treats

$$\overline{23}\ \overline{36}\ \overline{7}\ \overline{29}\ \overline{17}\ \overline{26}$$

Broken

$$\overline{11}\ \overline{2}\ \overline{14}\ \overline{19}\ \overline{6}\ \overline{27}\ \overline{39}$$

To dry or shrivel

$$\overline{18}\ \overline{4}\ \overline{31}\ \overline{10}\ \overline{5}\ \overline{13}$$

Not singular

$$\overline{30}\ \overline{12}\ \overline{34}\ \overline{28}\ \overline{20}\ \overline{38}$$

26-9-17-7-3   31-10-5   12-29-28-11   18-4-31-10

23-9-36-17,   35-1-39   13-5-33-29-4-22-27

18-4-31-10   21-17-9-14-24-32-25-1-6.

PSALM 3:7

A tiny, brightly colored tropical fish

$$\overline{} \ \overline{} \ \overline{} \ \overline{} \ \overline{}$$
6 23 30 1 14

Easy to love

15 43 38 3 32 21 13

The year of school before first grade

7 24 33 8 31 41 16 44 35 22 37 26

The study of the stars

34 12 39 2 29 18 45 4 28

A professional cook

10 17 40 5

To appoint to an office

9 42 20 19 11 36 25 27

36-2-24-12-13,   29   15-45-41-8;   12-34-38-27

4-37,   42   4-28   6-43-8:   5-29-35   22-17-43-23

17-44-12-39   12-20-19-39-22-27-11   3-15-21

20-19-9-13   37-26-27-20-24-13-12   23-30-43-33

25-17-40   10-17-13-31-7   32-42-18-13.

PSALM 19:14

Land on which crops and/or animals are raised

$$\overline{11}\ \overline{27}\ \overline{34}\ \overline{4}$$

A perforated pan to drain off liquids

$$\overline{13}\ \overline{39}\ \overline{36}\ \overline{5}\ \overline{26}\ \overline{12}\ \overline{41}\ \overline{21}$$

Vacation of a newly married couple

$$\overline{6}\ \overline{43}\ \overline{15}\ \overline{42}\ \overline{22}\ \overline{10}\ \overline{28}\ \overline{16}\ \overline{3}$$

A maze

$$\overline{9}\ \overline{32}\ \overline{19}\ \overline{14}\ \overline{29}\ \overline{23}\ \overline{2}\ \overline{30}\ \overline{18}$$

Motion pictures where parental guidance is suggested

$$\overline{40}\ \overline{44}\ \overline{31}\ \overline{1}\ \overline{45}\ \overline{38}\ \overline{24}\ \overline{37}$$

To become too large for

$$\overline{7}\ \overline{25}\ \overline{17}\ \overline{33}\ \overline{20}\ \overline{35}\ \overline{8}$$

36-42-30   17-18-24   8-7-20-12-37   39-11   10-22

31-28-25-17-18,   32-3-12   17-6-42

10-41-12-23-17-5-17-38-1-26   43-11   31-14

6-24-5-21-17,   19-42   32-13-13-41-40-17-5-19-9-42

38-26   17-18-22   37-38-33-18-17,   16

36-35-20-12,   4-14   37-30-21-24-2-33-30-6,

27-15-12   31-14   29-24-12-42-41-31-24-34.

Philippians 4:6

The ocean along the west coast of America

$\overline{13}$ $\overline{25}$ $\overline{7}$ $\overline{42}$ $\overline{1}$ $\overline{19}$ $\overline{11}$

A joint in the finger

$\overline{12}$ $\overline{39}$ $\overline{20}$ $\overline{26}$ $\overline{46}$ $\overline{6}$ $\overline{44}$

Excessive, beyond reason

$\overline{18}$ $\overline{10}$ $\overline{45}$ $\overline{29}$ $\overline{49}$ $\overline{24}$ $\overline{47}$ $\overline{5}$ $\overline{40}$ $\overline{17}$ $\overline{34}$

Evoking a question

$\overline{9}$ $\overline{33}$ $\overline{2}$ $\overline{43}$ $\overline{21}$ $\overline{35}$ $\overline{51}$ $\overline{14}$ $\overline{31}$ $\overline{3}$ $\overline{52}$ $\overline{48}$

Articles such as tools, utensils, and nails

$\overline{36}$ $\overline{38}$ $\overline{15}$ $\overline{27}$ $\overline{22}$ $\overline{55}$ $\overline{4}$ $\overline{54}$

A person sent to a foreign country for ministry

$\overline{30}$ $\overline{8}$ $\overline{53}$ $\overline{37}$ $\overline{32}$ $\overline{50}$ $\overline{16}$ $\overline{28}$ $\overline{41}$ $\overline{23}$

3-44   11-40-4-2-1-20-6   1-50-15

16-50-21-36-32-14-5;   3-20-21   42-17

18-24-44-29-23   34-36-8-17-5   3-23   13-29-38-23-48-41

49-39-27   53-33-13-13-6-19-26-25-21-35-51-16

22-8-21-36   21-36-28-16-46-37-5-32-24-35-16-5

52-18-34   23-51-20-29   15-44-9-20-2-37-45-43   3-48

30-31-27-54   12-39-50-22-16   33-14-21-51   5-50-27.

PHILIPPIANS 2:3

Any day except Saturday and Sunday

— — — — — — —
29 14 1 6 27 41 37

To steal money from an employer

— — — — — — — —
20 36 13 44 5 28 22 12

Flawless

— — — — — — —
15 38 30 19 43 31 4

The area in which a baseball team waits between innings

— — — — — —
16 34 7 23 3 21

To dissolve into the air

— — — — — — — — —
24 8 33 2 32 17 40 11 26

The current style of dress

— — — — — — —
10 35 25 18 42 39 9

22-20-4   9-39-11-18-42-9-7   13-44   16-39-9-26

11-18-17-39-3-7-18   25-4-30-42-19-38   23-30

8-41-42-9-7-22-39-30-37;   13-34-4   42-9

22-23-29-22-42-9-43-25-25   32-10   36-42-9-27

22-38-4   24-33-31-18   38-25-4-20-14-36

32-4-18-43-30   13-12-4-21-43-30   11-18-35-9

21-18-43-36-25-1-22-8-24-25.

PSALM 19:1

A large tank used for storing liquids

$\overline{11}$ $\overline{36}$ $\overline{12}$

The arrangement of a dance

$\overline{7}$ $\overline{35}$ $\overline{19}$ $\overline{42}$ $\overline{27}$ $\overline{39}$ $\overline{1}$ $\overline{43}$ $\overline{20}$ $\overline{45}$ $\overline{28}$ $\overline{8}$

Lack of hope

$\overline{2}$ $\overline{38}$ $\overline{9}$ $\overline{34}$ $\overline{26}$ $\overline{17}$ $\overline{21}$

Laboring

$\overline{18}$ $\overline{41}$ $\overline{25}$ $\overline{33}$ $\overline{10}$ $\overline{6}$ $\overline{16}$

Erroneous thinking

$\overline{4}$ $\overline{22}$ $\overline{40}$ $\overline{13}$ $\overline{46}$ $\overline{37}$ $\overline{29}$ $\overline{23}$ $\overline{15}$

The art of folding paper

$\overline{14}$ $\overline{32}$ $\overline{31}$ $\overline{44}$ $\overline{24}$ $\overline{30}$ $\overline{5}$

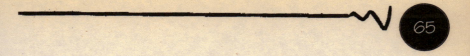

12-35-27   35-46-36-11-23-6-9   2-46-7-37-20-32-46

12-28-27   44-37-19-21-8   14-15   1-39-2;

20-6-2   12-35-46   15-5-21-4-24-30-23-6-12

40-35-14-18-38-12-28   35-22-9

28-26-6-2-17-18-41-25-33.

ROMANS 12:9

An opening in a building for letting in light or air

—— —— —— —— —— ——
16 22   5 28 32 20

An understanding after an event of what should have been done

—— —— —— —— —— —— —— —— ——
14 36   6 21   1 42 37 26   9

Usable

—— —— —— —— —— ——
 3 15 41   8 27 33

The month after February

—— —— —— —— ——
19 39 13 10 31

Innocent

—— —— —— —— —— —— —— —— ——
38 11 35 23 43 17 25   4 30

Migraine

—— —— —— —— —— —— —— ——
 2 34   7 24 29 18 12 40

27-33-9   23-32-3-25   8-40   16-35-9-31-32-11-43

21-15-1-30-15-19-11-27-7-9-22-32-5.   39-8-14-32-13

43-2-7-43   20-12-35-18-31   36-1   25-3-42-17;

10-27-34-41-3-25   43-32   43-2-29-43

16-26-22-18-2   42-4   37-32-32-24.

ROMANS 12:21

Getting back at someone

$$\overline{20}\ \overline{29}\ \overline{5}\ \overline{16}\ \overline{11}\ \overline{2}\ \overline{22}$$

A piece of furniture to sit on

$$\overline{4}\ \overline{18}\ \overline{7}\ \overline{10}\ \overline{32}$$

To remove an arm or leg, usually in surgery

$$\overline{28}\ \overline{12}\ \overline{35}\ \overline{17}\ \overline{25}\ \overline{3}\ \overline{21}\ \overline{34}$$

Made from a tree

$$\overline{15}\ \overline{23}\ \overline{19}\ \overline{1}\ \overline{26}\ \overline{8}$$

Costing nothing

$$\overline{13}\ \overline{31}\ \overline{9}\ \overline{24}$$

To assess fault

$$\overline{27}\ \overline{33}\ \overline{6}\ \overline{14}\ \overline{30}$$

27-34   11-19-25   23-5-29-20-4-23-12-16   19-13

26-5-10-33,   27-17-25   23-5-22-31-4-19-14-30

9-5-10-33   15-10-21-18   2-23-19-1.

1 Corinthians 10:31

To make someone laugh by a touch

$$\overline{10}\ \overline{36}\ \overline{32}\ \overline{3}\ \overline{26}\ \overline{43}$$

A creature said to have breathed fire

$$\overline{39}\ \overline{9}\ \overline{30}\ \overline{14}\ \overline{19}\ \overline{2}$$

Foolishness

$$\overline{31}\ \overline{11}\ \overline{15}\ \overline{6}\ \overline{23}$$

A forked breastbone in most birds

$$\overline{16}\ \overline{42}\ \overline{24}\ \overline{1}\ \overline{12}\ \overline{28}\ \overline{4}\ \overline{33}$$

The science of farming

$$\overline{35}\ \overline{5}\ \overline{25}\ \overline{45}\ \overline{40}\ \overline{27}\ \overline{22}\ \overline{13}\ \overline{38}\ \overline{29}\ \overline{20}$$

Able to shield from injury

$$\overline{18}\ \overline{8}\ \overline{41}\ \overline{34}\ \overline{21}\ \overline{7}\ \overline{37}\ \overline{46}\ \overline{17}\ \overline{44}$$

16-1-43-13-1-21-29   37-1-33-25-43-31-41-29-33

23-21   20-35-10,   19-8   39-25-36-2-3,   11-8

16-1-30-13-24-41-44-17-21-9   23-20   39-28,   39-19

35-22-15   13-41   34-1-43   14-26-28-25-23

41-31   5-28-39.

1 Corinthians 12:13

A man's suit worn for a semi-formal or formal occasion

$\overline{11}$ $\overline{39}$ $\overline{20}$ $\overline{2}$ $\overline{26}$ $\overline{35}$

A collection of rings, bracelets, or necklaces

$\overline{30}$ $\overline{5}$ $\overline{25}$ $\overline{12}$ $\overline{16}$ $\overline{19}$ $\overline{8}$

The branch of biology that studies animals

$\overline{29}$ $\overline{36}$ $\overline{4}$ $\overline{24}$ $\overline{33}$ $\overline{15}$ $\overline{38}$

Material

$\overline{32}$ $\overline{3}$ $\overline{21}$ $\overline{13}$ $\overline{7}$ $\overline{6}$

A trail

$\overline{17}$ $\overline{22}$ $\overline{1}$ $\overline{27}$

A ship that can operate underwater

$\overline{14}$ $\overline{34}$ $\overline{9}$ $\overline{28}$ $\overline{18}$ $\overline{37}$ $\overline{31}$ $\overline{10}$ $\overline{23}$

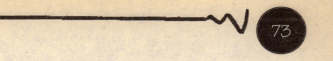

32-35-13   9-38   35-10-23   14-17-7-37-31-1

22-13-12   25-2   18-16-24

9-3-17-11-7-29-2-26   31-10-11-35   4-10-12

9-35-26-8,   25-27-5-1-27-23-13   25-12   21-2

30-12-25-14   35-13   15-2-10-11-7-16-12-14,

25-27-23-1-27-23-37   25-12   9-23   21-4-10-26

33-19   32-19-23-12.

1 CORINTHIANS 10:33

A violent tropical storm with winds over 74 mph

$\overline{23}\ \overline{38}\ \overline{9}\ \overline{20}\ \overline{40}\ \overline{30}\ \overline{34}\ \overline{13}\ \overline{28}$

General good health and strength

$\overline{36}\ \overline{10}\ \overline{33}\ \overline{21}\ \overline{4}\ \overline{27}\ \overline{14}$

The use of charms or spells, supposedly to control events

$\overline{15}\ \overline{31}\ \overline{5}\ \overline{41}\ \overline{22}$

A light, purplish blue

$\overline{37}\ \overline{42}\ \overline{8}\ \overline{7}\ \overline{25}\ \overline{46}\ \overline{3}\ \overline{39}\ \overline{18}\ \overline{47}$

Open to criticism

$\overline{32}\ \overline{6}\ \overline{24}\ \overline{2}\ \overline{35}\ \overline{16}\ \overline{26}\ \overline{45}\ \overline{29}\ \overline{19}$

At a distance

$\overline{44}\ \overline{17}\ \overline{11}\ \overline{43}\ \overline{1}\ \overline{12}$

4-32-35-21   31-27   46   37-24-35-26-14-35

26-18-29   15-4-13   40-11   34-24-18

33-23-10-2-5-14,   3-17-33   27-4-28-39-41-21-5

15-41-21-47   17-25-13   37-20-17-36-10-33,   45-6-33

33-23-42   37-12-17-36-41-33   17-36   15-34-21-44,

33-23-31-33   33-23-19-44   15-26-44   45-28

27-31-32-4-43.

1 CORINTHIANS 6:12

One's natural disposition

$\overline{39}$ $\overline{16}$ $\overline{37}$ $\overline{11}$ $\overline{25}$ $\overline{28}$ $\overline{1}$ $\overline{19}$ $\overline{33}$ $\overline{24}$ $\overline{45}$

More than accounted for

$\overline{43}$ $\overline{6}$ $\overline{15}$ $\overline{2}$ $\overline{38}$

Wailed, as wolves

$\overline{34}$ $\overline{29}$ $\overline{10}$ $\overline{20}$ $\overline{44}$ $\overline{5}$

Protective gear for a rainy day

$\overline{12}$ $\overline{27}$ $\overline{3}$ $\overline{31}$ $\overline{21}$ $\overline{40}$ $\overline{17}$ $\overline{8}$

Relating to an overall plan

$\overline{41}$ $\overline{13}$ $\overline{30}$ $\overline{4}$ $\overline{22}$ $\overline{18}$ $\overline{7}$ $\overline{36}$ $\overline{26}$

A second-person singular pronoun

$\overline{32}$ $\overline{46}$ $\overline{14}$ $\overline{47}$ $\overline{9}$ $\overline{35}$ $\overline{23}$ $\overline{42}$

4-40-20   39-34-36-24-7-4I   38-47-25

20-38-10-42-12-23   12-24-15-29   19-21,   3-12-45

1-40-20   15-34-36-24-7-41   8-2-35   24-29-22

43-6-11-18-5-36-18-24-45;   1-20-23   15-34-36-24-7-9

4-30-35   17-38-10-42-14-23   42-29-31   27-33,

3-12-22   36   10-36-17-40   24-29-13   3-43

3-2-29-12-7-34-15   12-24-5-21-47   13-34-16

11-46-10-44-28   29-42   38-24-32.

1 CORINTHIANS 4:10

Appropriate for the occasion

$\overline{42}$ $\overline{11}$ $\overline{27}$ $\overline{5}$ $\overline{21}$ $\overline{35}$ $\overline{15}$ $\overline{29}$

Polite

$\overline{17}$ $\overline{30}$ $\overline{9}$ $\overline{26}$ $\overline{34}$ $\overline{3}$ $\overline{36}$ $\overline{14}$ $\overline{20}$

To grow in number (adverb)

$\overline{44}$ $\overline{10}$ $\overline{37}$ $\overline{4}$ $\overline{41}$ $\overline{16}$ $\overline{31}$ $\overline{8}$ $\overline{39}$ $\overline{13}$ $\overline{25}$ $\overline{33}$

Having much depth

$\overline{22}$ $\overline{18}$ $\overline{28}$ $\overline{2}$

A crisp batter cake with small, square hollows

$\overline{40}$ $\overline{1}$ $\overline{12}$ $\overline{23}$ $\overline{6}$ $\overline{32}$

An almond color used to describe pants

$\overline{24}$ $\overline{38}$ $\overline{7}$ $\overline{19}$ $\overline{43}$

40-29   21-26-41   12-30-36-25-20   23-30-26

37-38-26-43-20-34-'20   20-7-19-32,   35-11-34

33-3   21-26-41   40-8-31-3   27-10

17-38-26-44-31-34;   40-32   21-26-41   40-3-21-24,

35-14-34   33-3   16-4-41   20-34-26-36-10-13;

33-18   1-4-28   38-30-39-36-9-4-16-35-15-3,

35-14-5   40-29   16-4-29   22-28-31-2-43-20-29-22.

ROMANS 14:11

Appropriate

$\overline{11}$ $\overline{33}$ $\overline{6}$ $\overline{29}$ $\overline{23}$

One who follows Jesus

$\overline{22}$ $\overline{28}$ $\overline{10}$ $\overline{43}$ $\overline{38}$ $\overline{15}$ $\overline{34}$ $\overline{1}$ $\overline{21}$

A sport played with clubs and tees

$\overline{16}$ $\overline{7}$ $\overline{27}$ $\overline{37}$

Generous welcome

$\overline{44}$ $\overline{2}$ $\overline{5}$ $\overline{12}$ $\overline{14}$ $\overline{30}$ $\overline{41}$ $\overline{8}$ $\overline{24}$ $\overline{35}$ $\overline{18}$

The exercise with routine

$\overline{17}$ $\overline{42}$ $\overline{25}$ $\overline{3}$ $\overline{39}$ $\overline{31}$ $\overline{20}$

An instrument used for measuring atmospheric pressure

$\overline{26}$ $\overline{13}$ $\overline{45}$ $\overline{36}$ $\overline{4}$ $\overline{19}$ $\overline{9}$ $\overline{40}$ $\overline{32}$

37-2-32   14-15   34-38   17-10-34-15-9-19-21,

33-5   29   27-34-11-19,   38-41-43-9-28   15-28-19

27-7-10-23   19-11-40-45-18   3-21-40-19

38-28-33-6-27   26-2-17   20-36   4-40,   1-21-23

40-11-19-25-18   15-36-21-16-31-19   38-44-13-6-27

22-39-21-37-19-5-38   15-42   16-36-23.

1 Corinthians 6:15

Cold and unfeeling

— — — — — — — — — —
30 14 43   7 31 25 18 38   2 48

Relating to the sense of smell

— — — — — — — — —
21 29   8 35 13   1 42 26 16

Cookout

— — — — — — — —
39 19 46   6 34 28 44 12

When the sun rises

— — — —
24   9   3 37

Plural for a male ruler of a monarchy

— — — — —
41   4 33 10 23

Based on an assumption

— — — — — — — — — — — —
17 36 40   5 45 20 11 32 27 15 22 47

41-37-18-3   16-12   33-21-1   45-17-2-32

36-5-44-31   39-21-24-27-11-23   19-31-34   1-17-34

14-7-14-39-11-31-25   21-8   13-20-31-30-25-45?

25-20-22-48-47   4   45-17-34-37   1-35-41-12

45-20-12   14-34-14-6-7-31-25   21-8

15-17-31-27-25-45,   9-37-24   14-19-41-7   1-17-7-14

45-20-7   14-12-14-39-34-46-25   5-8   2-33

17-22-31-29-21-1?   10-42-24   8-21-26-6-30-24.

1 CORINTHIANS 5:8

A purposeful exaggeration

$\overline{33}$ $\overline{21}$ $\overline{8}$ $\overline{39}$ $\overline{15}$ $\overline{10}$ $\overline{31}$ $\overline{1}$ $\overline{26}$

Something regarded with a special liking

$\overline{20}$ $\overline{44}$ $\overline{7}$ $\overline{34}$ $\overline{25}$ $\overline{16}$ $\overline{12}$ $\overline{40}$

Bright red

$\overline{49}$ $\overline{17}$ $\overline{41}$ $\overline{32}$ $\overline{24}$ $\overline{6}$ $\overline{46}$

Exchanging information or talk

$\overline{38}$ $\overline{22}$ $\overline{47}$ $\overline{3}$ $\overline{43}$ $\overline{9}$ $\overline{35}$ $\overline{27}$ $\overline{13}$ $\overline{5}$ $\overline{30}$ $\overline{45}$ $\overline{18}$

To move on foot

$\overline{29}$ $\overline{36}$ $\overline{2}$ $\overline{14}$

Bought

$\overline{48}$ $\overline{19}$ $\overline{23}$ $\overline{4}$ $\overline{37}$ $\overline{28}$ $\overline{11}$ $\overline{42}$ $\overline{50}$

12-33-40-32-6-20-34-32-6   24-26-5   43-49

14-42-6-8   12-37-42   20-6-44-11-46,   9-45-12

29-16-12-33   31-1-50   2-42-28-7-6-9,

18-40-16-46-33-40-32   29-35-5-37   5-37-42

2-40-44-7-39-9   45-20   47-28-2-35-38-42   44-18-50

29-16-17-14-6-50-18-39-49-11;   10-43-46   29-35-12-33

5-37-42   43-9-24-40-41-7-26-9-39-50   10-25-39-44-50

22-20   49-16-18-27-39-15-30-5-21   36-9-50

46-23-19-5-37.

ROMANS 15:4

To go after

$$\overline{}\ \overline{}\ \overline{}\ \overline{}\ \overline{}\ \overline{}$$
17 4 31 16 10 3

Predilection

$$\overline{}\ \overline{}\ \overline{}\ \overline{}\ \overline{}\ \overline{}\ \overline{}\ \overline{}\ \overline{}\ \overline{}$$
45 5 32 14 23 1 40 34 9 42

Unnamed

$$\overline{}\ \overline{}\ \overline{}\ \overline{}\ \overline{}\ \overline{}\ \overline{}\ \overline{}\ \overline{}$$
36 15 48 24 44 39 35 41 25

A chief angel

$$\overline{}\ \overline{}\ \overline{}\ \overline{}\ \overline{}\ \overline{}\ \overline{}\ \overline{}\ \overline{}$$
47 18 43 6 26 13 22 7 30

An unbranded animal

$$\overline{}\ \overline{}\ \overline{}\ \overline{}\ \overline{}\ \overline{}\ \overline{}\ \overline{}$$
33 8 27 19 46 12 37 50

Concerning the home or family

$$\overline{}\ \overline{}\ \overline{}\ \overline{}\ \overline{}\ \overline{}\ \overline{}\ \overline{}$$
28 49 11 20 38 2 29 21

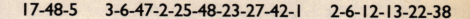

17-48-5   3-6-47-2-25-48-23-27-42-1   2-6-12-13-22-38

3-19-46-7   3-5-29-2-2-42-34   36-14-48-1-32-2-12-33-19

3-7-18-20   3-46-29-2-2-20-13   17-4-18   35-41-1

31-42-26-5-34-12-24-22,   2-6-8-2   3-19

2-6-5-4-41-22-6   45-36-2-29-32-15-43-19   8-13-28

21-49-39-14-4-1-2   10-17   2-6-32

25-37-18-12-45-2-41-5-23-38   11-29-22-6-2

6-36-27-42   6-10-45-32.

1 Corinthians 2:9

A warning to be careful

$$\overline{46}\ \overline{25}\ \overline{12}\ \overline{39}\ \overline{19}\ \overline{3}$$

Pardon

$$\overline{24}\ \overline{48}\ \overline{6}\ \overline{40}\ \overline{51}\ \overline{4}\ \overline{33}\ \overline{45}\ \overline{18}\ \overline{41}\ \overline{11}$$

A record of the past

$$\overline{52}\ \overline{26}\ \overline{5}\ \overline{20}\ \overline{13}\ \overline{47}\ \overline{34}$$

Something made better

$$\overline{38}\ \overline{21}\ \overline{32}\ \overline{2}\ \overline{29}\ \overline{43}\ \overline{9}\ \overline{15}\ \overline{8}\ \overline{36}\ \overline{27}$$

Apt to lie or cheat

$$\overline{14}\ \overline{42}\ \overline{22}\ \overline{1}\ \overline{35}\ \overline{50}\ \overline{7}\ \overline{28}\ \overline{16}$$

To keep up

$$\overline{37}\ \overline{23}\ \overline{44}\ \overline{10}\ \overline{49}\ \overline{30}\ \overline{17}\ \overline{31}$$

46-28-20   39-5   26-27   44-41   12-2-26-20-27-1-10,

42-34-8   52-23-49-52   45-13-20   5-33-3-36,

31-29-47   42-23-19   52-33-23-2-14,

31-1-35-50-52-3-47   52-39-43-3   42-45-20-33-6-9-14

35-10-49-29   27-52-42   52-25-39-47-20   48-24

37-30-31,   27-52-18   20-52-51-45-40-11

12-52-38-22-52   40-29-14   52-39-49-52

32-47-3-32-23-2-18-14   7-29-2   20-52-9-21

50-52-30-49   16-13-4-1   52-17-15.

ROMANS 14:9

A person from another country

$\overline{26}$ $\overline{42}$ $\overline{33}$ $\overline{5}$ $\overline{35}$ $\overline{12}$ $\overline{4}$ $\overline{23}$ $\overline{18}$

The month after September

$\overline{32}$ $\overline{40}$ $\overline{6}$ $\overline{47}$ $\overline{43}$ $\overline{13}$ $\overline{36}$

A daytime performance

$\overline{44}$ $\overline{20}$ $\overline{14}$ $\overline{41}$ $\overline{1}$ $\overline{37}$ $\overline{31}$

Vindictive

$\overline{34}$ $\overline{39}$ $\overline{3}$ $\overline{27}$ $\overline{22}$ $\overline{17}$ $\overline{7}$ $\overline{28}$

Not seen

$\overline{2}$ $\overline{21}$ $\overline{11}$ $\overline{29}$ $\overline{24}$ $\overline{16}$

Incapable of occurring

$\overline{25}$ $\overline{45}$ $\overline{10}$ $\overline{19}$ $\overline{15}$ $\overline{8}$ $\overline{9}$ $\overline{46}$ $\overline{38}$ $\overline{30}$

26-32-36   6-19   14-2-35-15   13-1-11

40-2-18-21-15-6   43-32-14-2   11-25-23-11,

20-1-11   36-47-8-30,   20-4-11   18-24-34-9-34-22-11,

6-2-20-6   2-5   44-35-27-2-6   43-37   28-19-33-11

46-32-6-2   42-17   14-2-39   11-31-20-11

20-3-29   38-25-34-41-16-12.

WORD SEARCH PUZZLES

by John Hudson Tiner

Find and circle the search words in the puzzle grid. Spell out the hidden phrase with the leftover letters.

BREAD OF
THE PHARISEES

MATTHEW 16:6–12

AMONG	FOUR	SADDUCEES
BADE	HEED	SAYING
BASKETS	LEAVEN	SEVEN
BECAUSE	LITTLE	SPAKE
BEWARE	LOAVES	TAKEN
BREAD	MANY	THEMSELVES
BROUGHT	NEITHER	THEY
CONCERNING	PERCEIVED	THOUSAND
DOCTRINE	PHARISEES	TOOK
FAITH	REASONED	UNDERSTAND
FIVE	REMEMBER	

```
C H R U O F M S T T A K E N
O B R E A D A P E H O S S A
N I D I L Y N A T O E E U O
C B T U I T Y K T U E Y A T
E H E N N S T E K S A B C P
R N G W H D R I I A E M E R
N R I O A E E R L N Y R B E
I E E R H R A R A D C E D A
N B V T T H E M S E L V E S
G M I A P C O O I T F L E O
I E F T E N O V T B A V H N
N M L E G L E D F A A N I E
S E E C U D D A S O T D D D
B R O U G H T H L N E V E S
```

Hidden Phrase: HE SAID TO THEM, O YE OF LITTLE FAITH

JESUS PAYS TAXES

MATTHEW 17:24–27; 22:15–22

CAESAR

CAPERNAUM

CAST

CHILDREN

COUNSEL

CUSTOM

EARTH

ENTANGLE

FISH

FREE

HOOK

HOUSE

HYPOCRITES

IMAGE

JESUS

KINGS

MASTER

MONEY

MOUTH

OFFEND

OPENED

PENNY

PERCEIVED

PETER

PHARISEES

PREVENTED

RECEIVED

RENDER

SIMON

STRANGERS

SUPERSCRIPTION

TEMPT

THINKEST

TRIBUTE

WICKEDNESS

```
R H E S N D E S U S E J R T E O
C S Y U A F E S A R T G H E T T
H T S P R E V E N T E D A I U N
G R E E O F F E N D S T H M B A
T A E R N C H I L D R E N L I A
R N S S E D R D E V I E C E R P
C G I C M A E I E S A A D S T E
R E R R O A E K T S P E C N A T
N R A I N D S A C E V U T U E E
H S H P E T E T R I S S H O O R
S T P T Y S O N E T W G I C O R
I P U I U P A C O R H D N M A T
F M H O E U R M S G N I K S O C
E E H N M E L G N A T N E O A N
T T E H P E N N Y I N A S S O G
S D T H A T A R E G C O T D S H
```

Hidden Phrase: __ __ __ __ __ __   __ __

__ __ __ __ __ __   __ __ __   __ __ __ __ __ __

__ __ __ __   __ __ __   __ __ __ __ __ __ __ ' __ ,

__ __ __   __ __   __ __ __   __ __ __

__ __ __ __ __ __   __ __ __ __   __ __ __

__ __ __ ' __

BEING PREPARED

MATTHEW 25:1–13

AFTERWARD	KINGDOM	SAYING
ANSWERED	KNOW	SELL
AROSE	LAMPS	SHUT
BEHOLD	LIKENED	SLEPT
BRIDEGROOM	LORD	SLUMBERED
DOOR	MARRIAGE	TARRIED
ENOUGH	MEET	TOOK
FIVE	MIDNIGHT	TRIMMED
FOOLISH	NEITHER	VESSELS
GIVE	OPEN	VIRGINS
GONE	RATHER	WATCH
HEAVEN	READY	WISE
HOUR		

```
W A T C L O R D M M H Y T E
T A R R I E D T O A S S H H
T A F N H L N O O R H L G E
R E H T A R M O R R C E I A
B D I M E O O K G I T S N V
N E P O D R E O E A A S D E
N S H G U E W V D G W E I N
F V N O N A R A I E S V M S
A I H O L S T E R F T E E M
K R U W A D Y E B D I V L N
T G O Y I H D E M M I R T L
H I I S E S A F A G U I U T
K N O W E D E N E K I L H H
G S L E P T R F O O L I S H
```

Hidden Phrase: _ _ _ _ _ _ _,

_ _ _ _ _ _ _ _ _ _ _ _ _ _ _

_ _ _ _ _ _

The Talents

Matthew 25:14–30

ABILITY	GAINED	RULER
ACCORDING	GATHERING	SAYING
AFRAID	GOODS	SERVANTS
ANSWERED	HARD	SEVERAL
AWAY	JOURNEY	SLOTHFUL
CALLED	KINGDOM	SOWED
CAST	LIKEWISE	STRAIGHTWAY
COMING	LORD	TALENTS
COUNTRY	MADE	THINGS
DARKNESS	MONEY	TRADED
EARTH	OUTER	UNPROFITABLE
ENTER	REAPING	WEEPING
FAITHFUL	RECEIVED	WICKED
FIVE		

```
M T H R H E S D L I K E W I S E
L A O U T D E K C I W T D R O L
C A D L R D H A B I L I T Y A B
O A F E A K I N G D O M F R U A
M S L R E S L S M N G A E N C T
I D T L A S S W S N I V A C I I
N O A U E I T E I T E P O Y T F
G O L F C D D R N S E R E H H O
G G E H A A E E A K D N I E L R
N C N T S H V D I I R N T O W P
I O T I T N I I N U G A S E I N
Y U S A P N E G O S T H D H R U
A N G F E A C J L U F H T O L S
S T N A V R E S S I A D E W O S
T R O U T E R R R V R D E N I A G
R Y A W A E E E D T S M O N E Y
```

Hidden Phrase: __ __ __ __ __ __ __ __ __ __ __

__ __ __ __ __ __ __ __ ... __ __ __ __ __

__ __ __ __ __ __ __ __ __ __ __ __ __

Apostles Sent Out

Mark 6:7–13

ABIDE	FORTH	PURSE
ANOINTED	GAVE	RECEIVE
BEGAN	HEALED	REPENT
BREAD	HEAR	SANDALS
CALLED	HOUSE	SCRIP
CAST	JOURNEY	SEND
COATS	JUDGMENT	SHAKE
COMMANDED	MONEY	SICK
DEPART	NOTHING	SPIRITS
DEVILS	OVER	STAFF
DUST	PLACE	TAKE
ENTER	POWER	TESTIMONY
FEET	PREACHED	TWELVE

```
H  P  L  A  C  E  K  E  C  A  L  L  E  D
T  R  E  W  O  P  B  C  S  M  O  N  E  Y
W  E  B  E  S  T  I  R  I  P  S  D  V  N
E  A  S  E  T  T  N  H  E  S  N  S  A  T
L  C  L  T  G  H  E  E  E  A  T  Y  G  S
V  H  I  M  I  A  T  E  M  A  D  E  E  C
E  E  V  O  L  M  N  M  F  G  S  N  K  R
D  D  E  E  P  S  O  F  A  L  D  R  A  I
O  U  D  E  T  C  R  N  A  E  A  U  T  P
V  C  S  A  D  H  O  D  Y  T  F  O  J  T
E  N  O  T  H  I  N  G  R  N  O  J  S  H
R  C  S  O  N  A  B  A  E  E  R  K  H  I
N  A  U  T  S  G  P  A  D  P  T  O  A  M
C  S  E  V  I  E  C  E  R  E  H  N  K  O
E  D  F  H  D  G  O  E  S  R  U  P  E  D
```

Hidden Phrase: __ __ __ __ __ __ __ __ __ __
__ __ __ __ __ __ __ __ __ __ __
__ __ __ __ __ __ __ __ __ __ __ __

NONE GREATER THAN JESUS

MARK 9:2–9

AFRAID	HIGH	ROUND
ANSWERED	JAMES	SAYING
APART	JESUS	SHINING
APPEARED	JOHN	SNOW
BELOVED	LEADETH	SORE
CHARGED	LOOKED	SUDDENLY
CLOUD	MASTER	TABERNACLES
DEAD	MOSES	TAKETH
EARTH	MOUNTAIN	TALKING
ELIAS	OVERSHADOWED	THEMSELVES
EXCEEDING	PETER	TRANSFIGURED
FULLER	RAIMENT	VOICE
GOOD	RISEN	WHITE

```
M T H T S I S H I L O O K E D
S O H U R M S Y T B V O I C E R
E S S G F A Y L N E D D U S R O
L E E E I U N O R V K E D H O S
J S A L S H L S S E T A O I S W
N N E R C I H L F N T N T N W A
M O U N T A I N E I H E D I A F
O W M T D H N M T R G E P N F R
I A M O R W I R H D A U E G R A
E D W C H A R G E D L X R W A I
L E G R R P P R M B C L H E I D
D R N I E A E A S E A I T N D
N A I S S W S A E E T T E H D
U E K E S T Y D L E H E D O A
O P L N E I I R V S E M A J Y
R P A R N N E D E V O L E B H
I A T G G O O D S D U O L C M
```

Hidden Phrase: __ ___ ___ __ __ __

_____ ___, __ _____

_ __ ____ _____;

____ __ ___

Jesus Heals a Beggar's Eyes

Mark 10:46–52

ANSWERED

BARTIMAEUS

BEGGING

BLIND

CALLED

CASTING

CHARGED

COMFORT

COMMANDED

DAVID

DISCIPLES

FAITH

FOLLOWED

GARMENT

HIGHWAY

HOLD

IMMEDIATELY

JERICHO

JESUS

MERCY

MIGHT

NAZARETH

NUMBER

PEACE

PEOPLE

RECEIVED

SAYING

SIGHT

STILL

STOOD

WHOLE

```
Y T E S U S E J L L J O H
C L C H A R G E D B N H O
R M E Y S N A Z A R E T H
E C I T I H W R T H R N P
M N O G A A T D L O H E T
G O G M H I T I F H O M E
D E C O M T D M A P B R L
B S D A H A O E L F I A N
A N E N L C N E M D S G E
N U W L I L I D S M H E T
S M O H P L E R E I I E L
W B L L A I B D E D G W L
E E L P E A C E M J H H I
R R O G N I T S A C W O T
E E F W A D A V I D A L S
D E V I E C E R L D Y E K
```

Hidden Phrase: ___ ___ ___ ___   ___ ___ ___ ___ ... ___ ___ ___

___ ___ ___ ___ ___ ___ ___ ___ ___ ___ ___ ___ ___ ___ ___ ,

___ ___ ___ ___ ___ ___ ___ ___ ___ ___ ___

A Beloved Son
Is Sent

Mark 12:1–12

ANOTHER	GIVE	REJECTED
BEAT	HANDLED	REVERENCE
BELOVED	HEAD	SENT
BUILDERS	HEIR	SERVANT
CAST	HUSBANDMEN	SHAMEFULLY
CAUGHT	INHERITANCE	STONE
CORNER	KILL	TOWER
COUNTRY	LORD	VINEYARD
DESTROY	OTHERS	WELL
DIGGED	PLANTED	WINEFAT
EMPTY	RECEIVE	WOUNDED
FRUIT		

```
W R E H T O N A R H A T S H
A L C O U N T R Y E M P T Y
D L W D E S T R O Y N L S L
D E V O L E B I D O E R S W
R W T T H G U A C C E R O S
I S W N I I L L N H E U H C
D R E V A D S A T D N A E N
D E E R A L T O L D M D W D
R V T E V I P I E E H E I R
A E H C R A U D F L D G N O
Y R T E E B N U M D T G E L
E E H I Y J L T C N N I F T
N N B V U L E L E A E D A L
I C O E Y R V R I H S E T E
V E N O T S F D S K B T O N
```

Hidden Phrase: __ __ __ __   __ __ __ __ __ __   __

__ __?   __   __ __ __ __   __ __ __ __   __ __

__ __ __ __ __ __ __   __ __ __

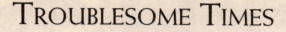

Troublesome Times

Mark 13:1–13

ANOTHER	GOSPEL	PUBLISHED
ANSWERED	HATED	RULERS
BEGINNINGS	HEED	SAVED
BUILDINGS	JESUS	SHALL
CHRIST	KINGDOM	SORROWS
COME	KINGS	STONE
DECEIVE	LEFT	TAKE
DISCIPLES	MANNER	TEMPLE
DOWN	MANY	TESTIMONY
EARTHQUAKES	MASTER	THROWN
ENDURE	NAME	TROUBLES
FAMINES	NATION	WARS

```
H E A R V E V I E C E D E N M
A N D E U T R O U B L E S A O
S R T B S L T H S W A R S T D
G J H A E G E S T O N E C E G
N A E P K G N R L L R W H S N
I W S S A E I I S U P S R T I
K O O H U A S N D Y I N I I K
G S E R Q S N N N L D A S M A
D E T A H A E A B I I W T O A
D Y B U T T M U S T N U M N Y
M W O I R M P C R W N G B Y D
A S O F A M I N E S O A S S L
S N H N E P A L L M D R M N L
T O N E L P M E T T O P R E A
E E R E H T O N A A W C F O H
R S S A V E D S A W N T A Y S
```

Hidden Phrase: __ __ __ __ __ __ __ __ __
__ __ __ __ __ __ __ __ __ __ __ __ __ __
__ __ __ __ __, __ __ __ __ __ __ __ __ __ __
__ __ __ __ __ __ __ __ __ __ __ __ __ __ __ __

Joseph of Arimathaea

Mark 15:42–46; John 19:38–42

ALOES	DOWN	MIXTURE
ALREADY	EVEN	MYRRH
ARIMATHAEA	FEAR	NICODEMUS
AWAY	GAVE	POUND
BEFORE	HEWN	PREPARATION
BODY	HONOURABLE	ROCK
BROUGHT	HUNDRED	ROLLED
CALLED	JESUS	SABBATH
CENTURION	JEWS	SECRETLY
COME	JOSEPH	SEPULCHRE
COUNSELLOR	LAID	STONE
DEAD	LINEN	TOOK
DISCIPLE	MARVELLED	WRAPPED
DOOR		

W H O A B E F O R E N W E H
M H P E S O J B R O U G H T
A W K L L E S U I O N H R O
R R H C W B T T I O T J R O
V A I S O X A M I A E A Y K
E P G M I R S R B S E E M C
L P A M A L U B U F H F O D
L E V P P T A S B O U U E O
E D E O N S H A W O N A E O
D R U E A U I A L S D O R R
P N C T D M N Y E O R Y H E
D E Y D A E R L A A E D C F
O N R T V D L O E W D S L H
E I K E M O C L L N A I U N
Y L T E R C E S A L O G P D
O D I S C I P L E C E T E M
O F D O W N G O L A I D S D

Hidden Phrase: __ __ __   __ __ __ __

__ __ __ __ __ __   __ __ __ __ __

__ __ __   __ __ __   __ __ __ __ __ __ __

__ __   __ __ __

Jesus in His Hometown

Luke 4:14–23

ANOINTED

BLIND

BOOK

BROKENHEARTED

BRUISED

CAPERNAUM

CAPTIVES

COUNTRY

DELIVERED

ESAIAS

FAME

GALILEE

GLORIFIED

GOSPEL

GRACIOUS

HEAL

JESUS

LIBERTY

LORD

MINISTER

NAZARETH

OPENED

PHYSICIAN

POOR

POWER

PREACH

PROPHET

READ

SABBATH

SCRIPTURE

SIGHT

SPIRIT

STOOD

SYNAGOGUES

TAUGHT

WRITTEN

```
T H G I S Y E S E E K J B R
B I E S S C R I P T U R E E
M O R Y T R E B I L O T U W
S U O I C A R G L K S J S O
A O A K P U F N E I E A Z P
B S A N I S T N N S N M R E
B T Y S R H H I U D L D A H
A W E N G E M S E E G O W F
T D H U A I P T A L C L R H
H H A R P G N A O I N E I D
H T T W O I O R C V A P T A
R E A D O S I G P E I S T C
D R A N R F A R U R C O E R
E A A L I L E D U E I G N C
N Z I E I A O F I D S E D H
E A D L C O U N T R Y E I S
P N E H T R P R O P H E T I
O E S S E S E V I T P A C N
```

Hidden Phrase: __ __   __ __ __ __   __ __ __ __ __
__ __   __ __ __ __ __ __ __ __ ,   __ __ __ __ __
__ __ __   __ __ __ __ __ __ __ __ :   __ __
__ __   __ __ __ __ __

Jesus Teaches in Galilee

Luke 4:42–44; 5:1–11

ALL	HEAR	PRESSED
CITIES	KINGDOM	SAID
DEEP	LAKE	SHIPS
ENTERED	LAND	SIMON
FISHERMEN	LAUGH	SOUGHT
FISHES	MASTER	SYNAGOGUES
FOLLOWED	MIGHT	TAKEN
FORSOOK	MULTITUDE	TAUGHT
FROM	NETS	THRUST
GENNESARET	NOTHING	TOILED
GONE	OTHER	WASHING
GREAT	PEOPLE	WORD
HAVE	PREACH	

```
W N O T H I N G F G R O F N
O S E H S I F M E K E N O G
R H E M T Y W N L O N M L A
D A O A R A N C A O I E L O
P R E S S E D A U S F L O T
F R A H S E H O G R R T W H
G I I A E S L S H O H T E E
D N R T I P H P I F G N D R
G E O H T I T T O F T U U M
T E S G I H H H O E T A E A
D L V U C S P M R I P T K S
N E K A T C I E T U L A A T
A T E T H G D L E C S E L E
L R H T H G U O S D M T D R
P N E T S M O D G N I K E N
```

Hidden Phrase: __ __ __ __

__ __ __ __ __ __ __ __ __ __ __ __ __

__ __ __ __ __ __ __ __ __ __ __ __

The Good News Goes Out

Luke 10:1–17

APPOINTED

ASHES

BEHOLD

BETHSAIDA

CARRY

CHORAZIN

CITY

COME

DRINKING

EATING

ENTER

EVERY

GREAT

HARVEST

HEAL

HIMSELF

HIRE

HOUSE

KINGDOM

LABOURERS

LAMBS

LORD

MIGHTY

PEACE

PURSE

REMAIN

REPENTED

SACKCLOTH

SALUTE

SCRIP

SEND

SEVENTY

SHOES

SICK

TRULY

WOLVES

WORKS

WORTHY

```
A T H E H T S E H Y S A P R V
W P M I R K G E T S T E S T K
T O P U R E T N E A A H O R C
C U L O E E E H I C P L G H I
L Y W V I V L E E K Y I U I S
I Y E L N T A S C N N R T M E
P R O S S T L B L I E C E S S
Y R E P E N T E D O N Z R T S
D A E V N H T O D T U A U D R
S C R B D H S U T H G R R W U
T A H E S B M A L L N O E O P
H A B A O F L E S M I H M R Y
U K I N G D O M R E T C A T S
R D L O H E B G R E A T I H S
A A R E F E H O U S E C N Y W
```

Hidden Phrase: __ __ __   __ __ __ __ __ __ __ __

__ __ __ __ __   __ __   __ __ __ __ __ __ __ __ __,

__ __ __   __ __ __   __ __ __ __ __ __ __ __

__ __ __   __ __ __

A Lost Son

Luke 15:11–24

ALIVE

BELLY

BREAD

CALF

CITIZEN

COMPASSION

COUNTRY

DIVIDED

FAMINE

FATHER

FATTED

FEED

FIELDS

FILLED

GATHERED

GOODS

HEAVEN

HIRED

HUNGER

HUSKS

JOURNEY

KISSED

LIVING

LOST

MERRY

MIGHTY

PERISH

PORTION

RING

RIOTOUS

ROBE

SERVANTS

SHOES

SINNED

SONS

SPARE

SPENT

SUBSTANCE

SWINE

WASTED

YOUNGER

```
S E S   D O N O F K C H   M A   N   I
O B S   E S U O T O I R I   S B   Y
N O I T R O P M C O S M R R   E
S R T S N O P H U S K S R R E S
E U E A F A M I N E D E E A D
K S B W S A V N D T M L R D O
C D R S J O U R N E Y S E M A
O O I D T Y L L E B F V G I E F
U O N E T A G H F S A A N G F
N G G D A N N I T W T H U H L
T T I I I E L C C H H D O T A
R S H V Z L S S E U E E Y Y C
Y O I I E P H R N T R A W F A
S L T D E O E G T A L I V E L
S I N N E D E A P H S I R E P
C O T S S R F S W I N E T D N
```

Hidden Phrase: __ __ __ __ __ __ __ __ __ __

__ __ __ __ __ __ __ __ __ __ __ __ __

__ __ __ __ __ __ __ __ __ __ __ __ __ __ __

__ __ __ __ __ __ __

THE RICH MAN AND LAZARUS

LUKE 16:19–31

ABRAHAM	EYES	LINEN
ANGELS	FARED	MERCY
BEGGAR	FINGER	PASS
BOSOM	FIXED	PURPLE
BURIED	FLAME	REMEMBER
CARRIED	GATE	RICH
CLOTHED	GULF	SUMPTUOUSLY
COMFORTED	LAID	TABLE
COOL	LAZARUS	TONGUE
CRUMBS	LIFETIME	TORMENTS
DIED	LIFTED	WATER

```
H I F T H L E Y H E E A R N
O C T M O Y O G S T E S A N
D T I O C S U R A Z A L R H
F E C R S L E G N A Y L E P
R A E O F B E O E L B A T P
M M R D M Y H E S T C I A S
A E O E E F N U P T A D W T
H E M S D T O I O U R T E O
A E H I O U F R F E R R M N
R S W I T B M I T L I P A G
B B L P N E N I L E E A L U
A M M T N G F I X E D S F E
H U E T E G D I E D Y S B E
S R S R P A E C L O T H E D
R C S B U R I E D U A D E D
```

Hidden Phrase: __ __   __ __ __ __   __ __ __ __

__ __ __   __ __ __ __ __   __ __ __   __ __ __

__ __ __ __ __ __ __ __ ,   __ __ __ __ __ __ __

__ __ __ __   __ __ __ __   __ __

__ __ __ __ __ __ __ __ __ __

Zacchaeus Climbs a Tree to See Jesus

Luke 19:1–10

ABIDE	HALF	POOR
ABRAHAM	HASTE	PUBLICANS
ACCUSATION	HOUSE	RECEIVED
BEHOLD	JERICHO	RESTORE
CLIMBED	JOYFULLY	SALVATION
COME	LITTLE	SAVE
DOWN	LOOKED	SEEK
ENTERED	LOST	SINNER
FALSE	MAKE	STATURE
FOURFOLD	MURMURED	SYCAMORE
GIVE	PASSED	THROUGH
GOODS	PLACE	ZACCHAEUS

```
N F I E N T E R E D C A E M E
N O O J O Y F U L L Y V V T B
T U I O I S D O O G I M A K E
C R L T T H R O U G H A S R H
L F L O A T E H W Z E J U R O
I O D P S V G L A N E T D D L
H L E L U T L C T R A D E T D
E D R O C B C A I T E V B O U
S E U O C H L C S S I D M S B
U R M K A O H I S E T L I S I
N O R E R O M A C Y S N L B H
N T U D C E P E R A N S C O A
T S M A H A R B A E N O U R L
E E T S A H L P R E E S L A F
N R O O P T A P S E E K N C E
```

Hidden Phrase: __ ____ ___ __ ____ ___ _____, ___ _____ __ _____

BREAD OF LIFE

JOHN 6:26–59

ANSWERED	FLESH	MURMURED
BELIEVE	GIVETH	NEVER
BLOOD	HUNGER	PERISHETH
BREAD	JESUS	RAISE
COMETH	JEWS	SEALED
DESERT	LABOUR	SENT
DRINK	LIFE	SHALL
ENDURETH	LOAVES	SIGN
ETERNAL	MANNA	THIRST
EVERLASTING	MEAT	VERILY
FATHER	MIGHT	WORK
FILLED	MIRACLES	

```
M S E A L E D B T J H I K
H I A N N A M L N E V E R
T U G S P I B O S S M F O
D N N H T E M O C U U I W
T A E G T H R D U S R L A
T R E S E D T I E R M G B
K N I R D R E L S T U I R
E A D W B H C R S H R V H
G N I T S A L R E V E E I
D Y C E R H I N V W D T C
E A L I M H D E E D S H H
L F M I T U R A I S E N S
L E T E R N A L L J V H A
I T A E M E O W E N A F R
F A T H E R V W B L O O M
H H E N G I S A L V L E N
```

Hidden Phrase: __ __ __ __ __ __ __ __ __ __ __ __ __ __

__ __ __ __ __ __ __ __ __ __ __ __ __ __

__ __ __ __ __ __ __ __ __ __ __ __ __ __

THE PRINCE OF LIFE

ACTS 3:12–26

BLESSED	HEAVEN	POWER
CHILDREN	HOLY	PREACHED
CHRIST	IGNORANCE	PRINCE
COVENANT	INIQUITIES	PROPHETS
DELIVERED	ISRAEL	RAISED
DESIRED	JESUS	REFRESHING
DESTROYED	LIFE	REPENT
FAITH	MARVEL	RULERS
FATHERS	MOSES	SEED
FORETOLD	NAME	SOUNDNESS
FULFILLED	PEOPLE	STRONG
GLORIFIED	PERFECT	SUFFER
GRANTED	PETER	TURNING
HEAR	PILATE	

```
J E E C N I R P D R E F F U S D S
U S P E O P L E S O U N D N E S S
F O R E T O L D F H C H R L I E T
N E R D L I H C O R H L L I T C R
S T O F V P I L A T E I D N I N O
A T Z E A P Y E I A F S E R U A N
D N R E T R H A R L G F H H Q R G
W E H O G O F S U M A R C I I O Y
D P Y E L P I F R T D C A C N N R
U E C O O H I F H U H E E N I G L
P R E W R E I E D R L E R D T I W
H E E S I T R E I N L E P I F E O
R R R M F S S S G I E M R E S J D
E O D F I S T E R N V V O S A E I
T N A N E V O C D G R S A S E S D
E D F L D C D E S I A R R E E U O
P M B T H E T D N A M E E A H S D
```

Hidden Phrase: __ __ __ __ __ __ __ __ __ __ __

__ __ __ __ __ __ __ __ __ __ __, __ __ __ __ __ __

__ __ __ __ __ __ __ __ __ __, __ __ __ __ __ __ __

__ __ __ __ __ __ __ __ __ __ __ __ __

__ __ __ __

BOLD BELIEVERS

ACTS 4:1–31

BEHOLD	JESUS	REPORTED
BOLDNESS	LIFTED	SADDUCEES
CAPTAIN	LORD	SALVATION
CORNER	MADE	SERVANTS
DEAD	NAME	SPEAK
EARTH	NONE	STOKE
GRANT	OTHER	THREATENINGS
GRIEVED	POWER	VOICE
HEAD	PRIESTS	WONDERS
HEAVEN	RAISED	WORD

```
W S T O K E B E W E S D D M
N R E H B O L O D A E A A I
A E N D R O L O L T E D U R
M G V O E E D V F D E E R K
E T C A P T A I N J N V A A
O C R D E T L T E S S E I E
P T I L I H D S E E A I S P
H P N O N E U E D N K R E S
U O N H V S C R T O I G D N
T W O E Y U O V G R T N O U
T E H B D W E A G R O H G O
S R E D N O W N S P A P E S
E D A E H L O T C O R N E R
F S G O D S T S E I R P T R
```

Hidden Phrase: __ __ __ __ __ __ __ __ __ __

__ __ __ __ __ __ __ __ __ __ __ __ __ __ __ __ __ __

__ __ __ __ __ __ __ __ __ __ __ __ __ __ __ __ __ __

__ __ __ __ __

Who Should Believers Obey?

Acts 5:17–40

AGREED

ANGEL

ANSWERED

APOSTLES

BEATEN

CALLED

CANNOT

COMMAND

COUNSEL

DOCTOR

DOCTRINE

DOORS

FEARED

FILLED

HIGH

INDIGNATION

JERUSALEM

MORNING

NAME

NOUGHT

OFFICERS

OPENED

OVERTHROW

PETER

PHARISEE

PRIEST

PRISON

REFRAIN

SLAY

TEACHING

TEMPLE

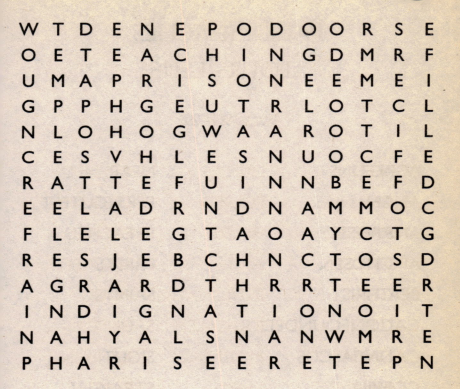

```
W T D E N E P O D O O R S E
O E T E A C H I N G D M R F
U M A P R I S O N E E M E I
G P P H G E U T R L O T C L
N L O H O G W A A R O T I L
C E S V H L E S N U O C F E
R A T T E F U I N N B E F D
E E L A D R N D N A M M O C
F L E L E G T A O A Y C T G
R E S J E B C H N C T O S D
A G R A R D T H R R T E E R
I N D I G N A T I O N O I T
N A H Y A L S N A N W M R E
P H A R I S E E R E T E P N
```

Hidden Phrase: __ __   __ __ __ __ __   __ __

__ __ __ __   __ __ __   __ __ __ __ __ __

__ __ __ __   __ __ __

Paul Preaches about Jesus

Acts 9:1–22

AGAINST

ANANIAS

AROSE

CHOSEN

CHRIST

CONFOUNDED

DAMASCUS

EVIL

GENTILES

HARD

HEAVEN

ISRAEL

KICK

LIGHT

NEAR

PERSECUTEST

PREACHED

PRICKS

SAINTS

SAUL

SIGHT

STRAIGHT

STREET

TARSUS

TREMBLING

VESSEL

VOICE

WITHOUT

I A M T V D H S E A P P A
O S T P R E A C H E D R L
D E V A T I S G R O O F S
A E H O N R E S U S R A T
M V D T I N E P E T U H H
A I S N T C R M U L T E G
S L T I U I E O B S H A I
C N L T C O H T N L G V L
U E E K H T F I E E I E T
S S S A I N A N A E A N H
T O E W G G E N O T R R G
I H L E A R S I L C T T I
K C I K E S C H R I S T S

Hidden Phrase: __ __ __ __ __ __

__ __ __ __ __ __ __ __ __ __ __ __ __

__ __ __ __ __ __ __ __ __

SERVE THE TRUE GOD

ACTS 14:8–20

ANTIOCH	HEALED	PAUL
BARNABAS	HEARTS	PEOPLE
CHIEF	HEAVEN	PRIEST
DEPARTED	ICONIUM	RESTRAINED
DISCIPLES	JUPITER	SACRIFICE
EARTH	LEAPED	SEASONS
FAITH	LIFTED	SPEAKER
FEET	LIKENESS	STONED
FILLING	LOUD	SUFFERED
FOOD	LYSTRA	VOICE
FRUITFUL	MERCURIUS	WALKED
GARLANDS	NATIONS	WITNESS
GLADNESS	OXEN	

```
D Y M E T U R N E D S T O N E D
L E L E A P E D T O N S G H A E
E I N F R U I T F U L E O T R K
V C F I H C O I T N A I V I T L
G O I T A L U A P W D R F A H A
R N I F E R O R S D I P M F E W
I I I C I D T N I D S T R A E H
O U L L E R O S S U D D N P T S
O M S S L I C B E E S J O E E N
R V S T T I S A T R D U C O S O
E T E A P P F R S H N P H P F S
H E N L E E A N E L A I I L I A
F V E A O P I A N N L T E E G E
A S K N E U L B D E R E F F U S
D E I D T E D A R X A R T S Y L
R G L A D N E S S O G U E G O D
```

Hidden Phrase: __ __ __ __ __ __ __ __ __ __

__ __ __ __ __ __ __ __ __ __ __

__ __ __ __ __ __ __ __ __ __ __ __ __ __

__ __ __ __ __ __ __ __ __ __ __

CHRISTIANS UNDER ATTACK

ACTS 17:4–9

ANOTHER

BOND

BRING

BROTHERS

CAESARS

CAUSED

CHARACTERS

CITY

CROWD

DECREES

DEFYING

DRAGGED

FORMED

GREEKS

HOUSE

JASON

JEALOUS

JESUS

JEWS

JOINED

KING

LARGE

MARKETPLACE

NUMBER

OFFICIALS

PAUL

PERSUADED

POST

PROMINENT

RIOT

ROUNDED

SEARCH

SHOUTING

SILAS

STARTED

THROWN

TROUBLE

TURMOIL

WELCOMED

WOMEN

WORLD

```
W R B K I N G L P E M S S E D A
O O O R S R A S E A C D T B P E
R E M U E S E E R C E D R R Y D
L E S E N W H K S S G I O I N E
D U K U N D E R U N N M U O O M
E S A N O T E A A G I S B H C T
C A S P P H C D D N Y N L L R L
H H F L T O E L E I F W E I O R
E C A O A T S N D T E O V O W I
L C R R R I T T E U D R J M D Y
E B O A A M C A N O T H E R L U
C I T Y E C E I A H N T A U A D
S S A L I S T D F S P G L T R E
R W E L C O M E D F F G S O E G C
U T E N U M B E R E O S U S E J
E Y O J O I N E D S N O S A J U
```

Hidden Phrase: _ _ _ _ _ _ _ _ _ _ _ _ _ ,

_ _ _ _ _ _ _ _ _ _ _ _ _ _ _ _ _ _ , _ _ _

_ _ _ _ _ _ _ _ _ _ _ _

PAUL SPEAKS AT ATHENS

ACTS 17:16–34

ALTAR	INSCRIPTION
AREOPAGUS	JESUS
ATHENS	LIVE
BABBLER	MARS
BEING	MOVE
DECLARE	PAUL
DEVOTIONS	PERCEIVE
DOCTRINE	PHILOSOPHER
EPICUREAN	PREACH
GIVEN	STOICKS
HEAR	TELL
HILL	UNKNOWN
IDOLATRY	WHOLLY
IGNORANTLY	WORSHIP

```
G O D S N W O N K N U D
W J E S U S M O V E U R L
E N E V U G L I H E L R I
T I S R A M A T H T E R D
B H G L N O O P O N A I O
W A T N I O T R D E I N L
O E B E O R N C E M R T A
R S N B L P A S V P T C T
S S S L L E N V O Y C O R
H H I T A R R I T L O D Y
I H C U I U E E I I L Y A
P L L A S C M L O D Y I T
E V I L I K O O N Y H I A
D E C N G P N H W I D H T
B E I N G H P H S W H A S
D N P E R C E I V E D S
```

Hidden Phrase: ___ ___ ... _____

___ __ _____ _____

____ _____

Paul Arrested

Acts 21:26–22:29

AGAINST

AUDIENCE

BROUGHT

CAPTAIN

CASTLE

CENTURIONS

COMMANDED

CRIED

CRYING

ENTERED

EXAMINED

FREEBORN

HEED

HOLY

JEWS

PAUL

PEOPLE

PLACE

POLLUTED

ROMAN

SCOURGING

SPAKE

STAIRS

STIRRED

STOOD

TAKE

TEMPLE

```
S A G A I N S T E K A P S
E B E N I A T P A C O N E
C R X E I C M N A M O R L
N O A L U G R S S I T T P
E U M P H O R I R O E U O
I G I M B B E U E I K A E
D H N E A E T C O D A N P
U T E T C N A R W C T T G
A R D A E S D H I E S N S
F H L C T L D E R R I T S
T P O L L U T E D Y O W N
E S E L S A D D R O E A L
S O A T Y P R C D J O M E
```

Hidden Phrase: __ __ __ __ __ __ __ __ __ __ __

__ __ __ __ __ __ __ __ __ __ __ __ __ __ __

__ __ __ __ __ __

Paul on Trial

Acts 24:10–27; 25:1–12

AGAINST

ANSWERED

ANYTHING

APPEAL

BROUGHT

CAESAR

CHEERFULLY

CHRIST

COMMANDED

CONVENIENT

DRUSILLA

FAITH

FELIX

FESTUS

JUDGMENT

NEITHER

OFFENDED

PAUL

REASONED

RIGHTEOUS

SEASON

SEAT

TEMPERANCE

TEMPLE

TREMBLED

WIFE

```
T H G I D T R E M B L E D T
S A N S W E R E D C C R S E
M G I A A N D D O N S I U M
O A H R P E T N A E R G T P
H I T E N P V R A H O H S L
T N Y H H E E S C M S T E E
I S N T N P O A C N M E F G
W T A I M N E L L A L O A O
C H E E R F U L L Y E U C T
R N T N I H T I A F T S A H
T Y O W R E A S O N E D A P
F T N E M G D U J D E L A R
T H T H G U O R B O R O I F
B O N D S D E D N E F F O X
```

Hidden Phrase: __ __ __ __ __   __ __ __   __ __ __ __ __ __

__ __ __ __ __ __ __ __   __ __ __ __ __ __   __ __

__ __ __ __ __ __ __   __ __   __ __ __ __ __ __

STORM WARNING

ACTS 27:1–12

ADVISED

ALEXANDRIA

ATTAIN

AUGUSTUS

BAND

BELIEVED

CENTURION

CONTRARY

CRETE

DAMAGE

DEPART

FAIR

FOUND

HAVEN

HURT

ITALY

JULIUS

LIVES

MASTER

OWNER

PERCEIVE

PRISONERS

SAILING

SHIP

VOYAGE

WINDS

```
N I A T T A S A I L I N G
F O U N D U E I P O N C S
J E I W A G S R N E V A H
I U S R A U I D T V O N I
E C L Y U S D N T I D H P
R I O I O T C A E E E I S
S V U N U U N X V C S H D
M C E F T S R E F R I U N
A R E G O R I L C E V R I
S E R W A L A A I P D T W
T T N E E M F R D V A S H
E E I B D N A B Y L E P W
R R T R A P E D Y E C S K
```

Hidden Phrase: __ __ __ __   __ __ __   __

__ __ __ __ __ __ __,   __ __ __ __ __ __   __

__ __ __ __ __ __ __ __   __ __ __ __ __ __ __

PAUL IN ROME

ACTS 28:11–31

CASTOR

COURAGE

DELIVERED

DEPARTED

DULL

DWELL

DWELT

EARS

EXPOUNDED

GROSS

HANDS

HEART

HIMSELF

HIRED

HOUSE

JERUSALEM

KEPT

PAUL

POLLUX

PRISONER

ROMANS

ROME

SHIP

SIGN

SOLDIER

SYRACUSE

THANKED

WAXED

WINTERED

```
P H A L D E K N A H T L T H
W I N T E R E D E S A C I N
A M H T R X R E I D L O S E
X S S S E R P P O L L U X S
E E M S V O A O R A L R N U
D L U E I T U N U O E A T O
S F L S L S L G E N M G D H
Y D O U E A U I O O D E D C
H I N C D C S S R W P E E F
G L Y A T H I U E A R D D E
Y R T R H R H L R I W A T A
R E O Y P O L T H E A R T F
C A E S R A E S L A J R S H
O U S E S D H T P E K O L D
```

Hidden Phrase: ___ ___ _____

_____ ___, _____

____ ____ ___ __

_____'_ _____

Pressing Ahead

Philippians 3:7–14

ALREADY

APPREHEND

ATTAIN

BEHIND

BRETHREN

CALLING

CHRIST

CONFORMABLE

COUNT

DEAD

DOUBTLESS

EXCELLENCY

FAITH

FELLOWSHIP

FOLLOW

FORGETTING

GAIN

HIGH

KNOWLEDGE

LOSS

MARK

MEANS

MINE

MYSELF

PERFECT

POWER

PRESS

PRIZE

REACHING

RESURRECTION

RIGHTEOUSNESS

SUFFERED

THINGS

TOWARD

```
T T H A T I M B A Y K S S N O
S N A E M F E L L O W S H I P
N U C W C H R I S T E E I H R
I O M O I A P S N G L G C R E
N C I N N E D R S D T T H A S
G I D T R F E U E O H B H L S
N E A F C A O L P I L U E L O
I W E T C E W R N F H O X I D
T C D H T O R G M T O D C N E
T R I H N A S R I A O L E G F
E N G K H K I A U S B H L T R
G I D E R E F F U S E L L O E
R A R A B R E T H R E N E W W
O G M I N E E S P U R R N A O
F L E S Y M R P R I Z E C R P
Y D A E R L A E C T I O Y D N
```

Hidden Phrase: __ __ __ __   __   __ __ __

__ __ __ __   __ __ __,   __ __ __   __ __ __

__ __ __ __ __   __ __   __ __ __

__ __ __ __ __ __ __ __ __ __ __ __

John's Vision

Revelation 1:9–19

ALPHA

ASIA

BOOK

BRASS

BURNED

CANDLESTICKS

CHRIST

CHURCHES

CLOTHED

COUNTENANCE

EPHESUS

FIRE

FIRST

FLAME

FURNACE

GARMENT

GOLDEN

GREAT

JESUS

JOHN

KINGDOM

LAODICEA

LAST

OMEGA

PATIENCE

PATMOS

PERGAMOS

PHILADELPHIA

SARDIS

SEEN

SEVEN

SMYRNA

SNOW

SPIRIT

STRENGTH

SWORD

TESTIMONY

THYATIRA

TRIBULATION

TRUMPET

TWOEDGED

VOICE

WHITE

WOOL

WRITE

```
W O T T H Y A T I R A H C C T E
O M C S O N O S U S E J H F E M
O E S O M A G R E P C R U A P N S
L G T S U H S A R D I S R A M S
P A T I E N C E Y S D J C P U L
L S S A R B T N T S O I H S R T
N W K T I W O E N H A I E T T H
E O C A H M T T N H L H S R K T S
O R I I I T F S A A P A T M O S
D D T T G S N U D E N N W E O R
E E S O A O A E R M R C O F B I
H E E S W L L N M N O G E B S F
T M L E M P U D E R A D D U P H
O A D C H Y S B E V A C G R I I
L L N I F I R E I N E G E N R S
C F A O H T G N E R T S D E I G
L O C V A H P L A N T R Y D T K
```

Hidden Phrase: ___ ___ __ ___

___ ___ __ ___

___ __ ___ ___

SCRAMBLED CIRCLE PUZZLES

by Ken Save

Unscramble the letters from the list provided, placing the corrected words in the numbered blanks. Then use the circled letters to answer the question following.

1. POCSMAS

5. VGLRAE

2. AEITCVP

6. NNSDEPA

3. TSLEDAOE

7. TTRSIA

4. OBBYANL

8. DHMAESA

Jewish men would meet here to talk and do business.

1. C O M P A S S

2. C A P T I V E

3. D E S O L A T E

4. B A B Y L O N

5. G R A V E L

6. S P A N N E D

7. S T R A I T

8. A S H A M E D

Answer: CITY GATE

SL DOE
ATE

SEDOLATE

1. AEHJERMI
2. BUEDLO
3. RBNO
4. SHRUENT

5. VIERDN
6. CUEJSIT
7. EASCSRCAS
8. OARBH

Another son of David who wanted to be king.

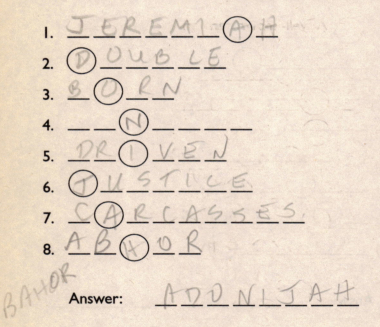

1. J E R E M I (A) H
2. (D) O U B L E
3. B (O) R N
4. _ _ (N) _ _ _ _
5. D R (I) V E N
6. (J) U S T I C E
7. C (A) R C A S S E S
8. A B (H) O R

BAHOR

Answer: A D D N I J A H

1. NMEAIF
2. VOEFGRI
3. AUDHJ
4. ONTNEDC
5. YANIVT
6. KRNOEFAS
7. LFLDEI
8. INTIBHA
9. OAVAINTLS
10. MEERJLUSA
11. SPRTEIS

A well-known sermon was given here.

1. FAMINE
2. FORGIVE
3. JUDAH
4. CONTEND
5. VANITY
6. FORSAKEN
7. FILLED
8. INHABIT
9. SALVATION
10. JERUSALEM
11. PRIESTS

Answer: The MOUNT of OLIVES

1. HNSCAEADL

2. NLISA

3. MRUOR

4. CIEVONEL

5. DUMEULTTI

6. EUSMLARJE

Camels

These acted as trucks in the ancient times.

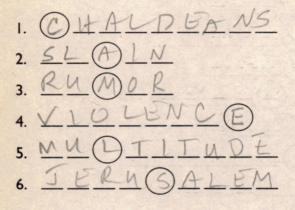

1. (C)HALDEANS
2. SL(A)IN
3. RU(M)OR
4. VIOLENC(E)
5. MU(L)TITUDE
6. JERU(S)ALEM

Answer: __ __ __ __ __ __

1. ISEMT
2. NOURD
3. DUNRE
4. NINOJSTCURT
5. CHKTI

6. HSTIG
7. MOCEUNS *CON* *MUSE*
8. ARSOVI *VIASOR*
9. NERTAMN
10. UERBEK *BURK*

NISTCUR

URBEEK

Another name for Mount Sinai.

1. S(M)ILE
2. R(O)UND
3. (U)NDER
4. I(N)STRUCTION
5. (T)HICK
6. SIG(H)T
7. C(O)NSUME
8. SAVIO(R)
9. R(E)MNANT
10. RE(B)UKE

Answer: MOUNT HOREB

1. EELZIEK ✓
2. DKMOIGN ✓
3. IEATPHOI
4. CELARCNBU ✓
5. HPOHAAR
6. ELDITF

7. ILASN ✓
8. BETLERIR
9. DEJGU ✓
10. APECHROR
11. HHNEAET

FILT

These two men went to heaven without dying.

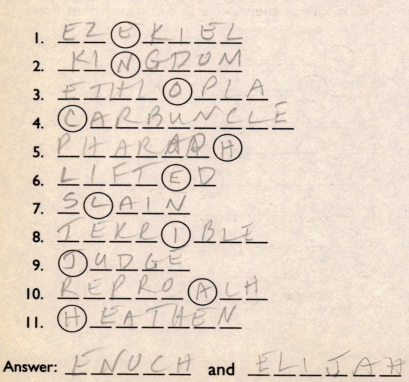

1. EZ(E)KIEL
2. KI(N)GDOM
3. ETHI(O)PIA
4. (C)ARBUNCLE
5. PHARAO(H)
6. LIFT(E)D
7. S(L)AIN
8. TERR(I)BLE
9. (J)UDGE
10. REPRO(A)CH
11. (H)EATHEN

Answer: ENUCH **and** ELIJAH

1. NRUGBIN
2. OENSSA
3. TMTARE
4. AODHTNUS
5. NPESARIS   _TH_
6. NSITEG
7. AYREL

This town was known as Jesus' home away from home.

1. (B) U R N I N G
2. S (E) A S O N
3. M A T (T) E R
4. I T (H) O U S A N D
5. P E R S I (A) N S
6. S I G (N) E T
7. E A R L (Y)

Answer: _B E T H A N Y_

1. WDEPOL
2. TEHELB
3. DVDIDEI
4. SCNEINE
5. GMIEAS
6. RENTUR
7. HRBESACN
8. RPDAET
9. NDEOIRIS

BASN
CHER

The great devourer as described in Job.

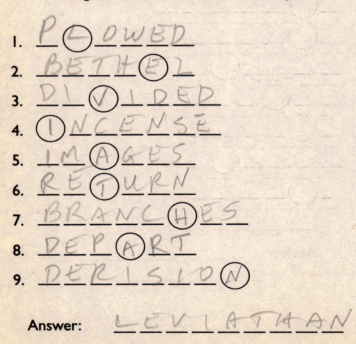

1. P L O W E D
2. B E T H E L
3. D I V I D E D
4. I N C E N S E
5. I M A G E S
6. R E T U R N
7. B R A N C H E S
8. D E P A R T
9. D E R I S I O N

Answer: L E V I A T H A N

1. NUTJDEMG

2. CHEKOML

3. NREGVA

4. URSUPE

5. ESIFIMHC

6. OFWLAL

7. LTUTUM

8. RAEDEP

9. RMERDU

Well known as the city of David.

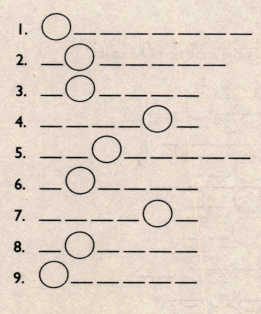

1. ◯ __ __ __ __ __ __

2. __ ◯ __ __ __ __

3. __ ◯ __ __ __ __

4. __ __ __ __ ◯ __

5. __ __ ◯ __ __ __ __ __

6. __ ◯ __ __ __ __

7. __ __ __ __ ◯ __

8. __ ◯ __ __ __ __

9. ◯ __ __ __ __ __

Answer: __ __ __ __ __ __ __ __ __

1. AOHBIAD

2. ETLSUBB

3. YIMTHG

4. IRNEMA

5. DISFLE

6. STHTRI

7. LPRIAEV

8. ERBSEHCA

She was the mother of Ahaziah.

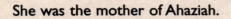

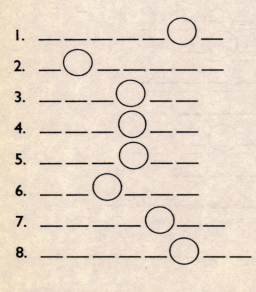

1. _ _ _ _ _ ◯ _

2. _ ◯ _ _ _ _ _

3. _ _ ◯ _ _ _

4. _ _ _ ◯ _ _

5. _ _ _ ◯ _ _

6. _ _ ◯ _ _ _

7. _ _ _ ◯ _ _

8. _ _ _ _ ◯ _ _

Answer: _ _ _ _ _ _ _ _

1. TEDEADCI

2. ETNWIRT

3. OGORNVRE

4. NESTARV

5. VREIR

6. GBNUIDLI

7. OPUN

8. OSENIDTI

This Roman coin was equivalent in weight to the Hebrew shekel.

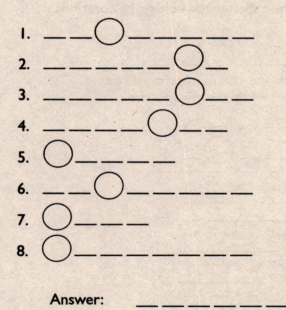

1. _ _ ◯ _ _ _ _ _

2. _ _ _ _ _ _ ◯ _

3. _ _ _ _ _ _ ◯ _ _

4. _ _ _ _ ◯ _ _ _

5. ◯ _ _ _ _

6. _ _ ◯ _ _ _ _ _

7. ◯ _ _ _

8. ◯ _ _ _ _ _ _ _

Answer: _ _ _ _ _ _ _ _

1. ELSETIV

2. EPRAVSOS

3. BALSM

4. ETRIBM

5. SRMA

6. URENBM

7. ASUDIR

8. CEERED

9. LIDKEL

10. VNESE

An outdoor shelter for holding celebrations.

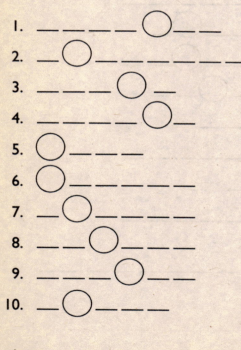

1. _ _ _ _ ◯ _ _

2. _ ◯ _ _ _ _ _ _

3. _ _ _ ◯ _

4. _ _ _ _ ◯ _

5. ◯ _ _ _

6. ◯ _ _ _ _

7. _ ◯ _ _ _ _

8. _ _ ◯ _ _ _

9. _ _ _ ◯ _

10. _ ◯ _ _ _

Answer: _ _ _ _ _ _ _ _ _

1. ICTUB
2. SPHUBIL
3. NPEI
4. GBRTHOU
5. DIIVDE

6. RASWET
7. NPSOROIT
8. PEYTG
9. ERDEVIG

The job of a high government official.

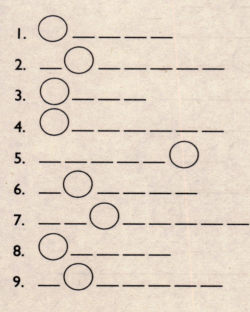

1. ◯ __ __ __ __
2. __ ◯ __ __ __ __ __
3. ◯ __ __ __
4. ◯ __ __ __ __ __ __
5. __ __ __ __ __ ◯
6. __ ◯ __ __ __ __
7. __ __ ◯ __ __ __ __ __
8. ◯ __ __ __ __
9. __ ◯ __ __ __ __ __

Answer: __ __ __ __ __ __ __ __ __

1. SOPORT

2. VEANEH

3. HASVIN

4. REEDVLI

5. NETVEID

6. TMIMOC

7. SOSESPS

8. NDEIRCS

A letter was written to this believer, the master of a runaway slave.

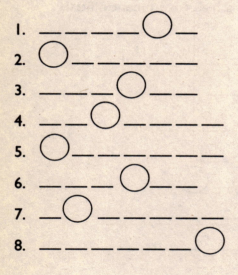

1. _ _ _ _ O _

2. O _ _ _ _ _

3. _ _ _ O _ _

4. _ _ O _ _ _ _

5. O _ _ _ _ _

6. _ _ _ O _ _

7. _ O _ _ _ _ _

8. _ _ _ _ _ _ O

Answer: _ _ _ _ _ _ _ _

1. TOTNNEC

2. WASROR

3. GSONIST

4. ELOMOASTH

5. HODLCET

6. MOROCTF

7. NREUTR

8. DESRRWA

A method that ancient pagans used to determine the future.

1. ◯ _ _ _ _ _ _

2. ◯ _ _ _ _ _

3. _ _ _ ◯ _ _ _

4. _ _ _ ◯ _ _ _ _

5. _ ◯ _ _ _ _

6. _ _ _ _ ◯ _ _

7. _ _ ◯ _ _ _

8. _ _ _ _ _ ◯

Answer: _ _ _ _   _ _ _ _

1. EPRESREV

2. NGIHIERL

3. UOETNG

4. NIMEGIA

5. OSNEKT

6. WHTRA

7. ACEREDL

8. EISNCAER

9. LWNBO

10. RAENG

Pressed into clay to seal important documents.

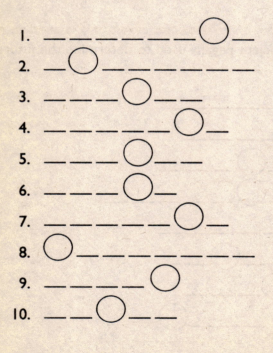

1. _ _ _ _ _ _ ◯ _

2. _ ◯ _ _ _ _ _ _

3. _ _ _ ◯ _ _

4. _ _ _ _ _ ◯ _

5. _ _ _ ◯ _ _ _

6. _ _ _ ◯ _

7. _ _ _ _ _ ◯ _

8. ◯ _ _ _ _ _ _ _

9. _ _ _ _ ◯ _

10. _ _ ◯ _ _

Answer: _ _ _ _ _ _   _ _ _ _ _

1. YPUTIR

2. ANEHTS

3. CYTAIPVTI

4. YNDEE

5. TRSTU

6. TOHMU

7. HESPIR

A tall plant that grows in swamps and rivers and is used to make heavy paper.

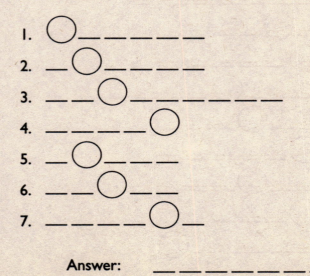

1. ◯ _ _ _ _ _

2. _ ◯ _ _ _ _

3. _ _ ◯ _ _ _ _ _ _

4. _ _ _ _ ◯

5. _ ◯ _ _ _

6. _ _ ◯ _ _

7. _ _ _ _ ◯ _

Answer: _ _ _ _ _ _ _

1. NUEBDR

2. EMSROHTO

3. WRNDA

4. DATENT

5. FACECIISR

6. YEDOSRT

7. RUETTB

8. RANDEW

9. TECIED

10. SEENIEM

Special words from Jesus on the Mount of Olives.

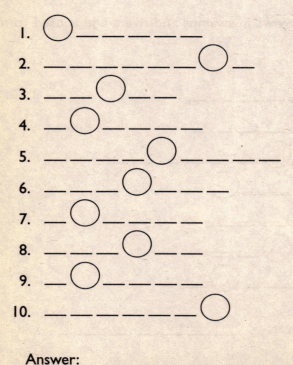

1. ◯ — — — — —

2. — — — — — — ◯ —

3. — — ◯ — — —

4. — ◯ — — — —

5. — — — — ◯ — — — — —

6. — — — ◯ — — —

7. — ◯ — — — —

8. — — — ◯ — — —

9. — ◯ — — — —

10. — — — — — ◯

Answer: — — — — — — — — — —

1. BAML
2. DLBESES
3. REROCTC
4. WOLFOL
5. INOZ

6. TEYBAU
7. NBRU
8. DJUEG
9. EBVEILE

Another name for Satan.

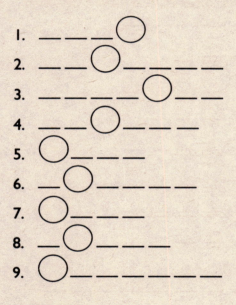

1. ___ ___ ___ ◯
2. ___ ___ ◯ ___ ___ ___ ___
3. ___ ___ ___ ___ ◯ ___ ___
4. ___ ___ ◯ ___ ___ ___
5. ◯ ___ ___ ___
6. ___ ◯ ___ ___ ___ ___
7. ◯ ___ ___ ___
8. ___ ◯ ___ ___ ___
9. ◯ ___ ___ ___ ___ ___ ___

Answer: ___ ___ ___ ___ ___ ___ ___ ___ ___

1. EATTIMED

2. SAVEW

3. HRTIG

4. ETLRBEM

5. DHIAANMD

6. NIEM

7. TTTSESAU

8. SURCED

Chosen to replace Judas as one of the twelve apostles.

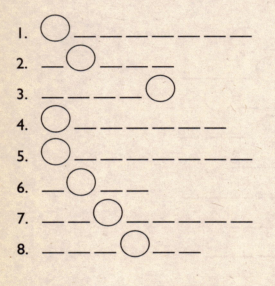

1. ◯ __ __ __ __ __ __

2. __ ◯ __ __ __ __

3. __ __ __ __ __ ◯

4. ◯ __ __ __ __ __ __

5. ◯ __ __ __ __ __ __

6. __ ◯ __ __ __

7. __ __ ◯ __ __ __ __

8. __ __ __ ◯ __ __

Answer: __ __ __ __ __ __ __

1. PPROREOSS
2. ROHEDSLU
3. NOREHT
4. DRIPE

5. THREA
6. SIMESND
7. TUCEISJ
8. ASRYI

It's not about reading the future, but about speaking the Word of God.

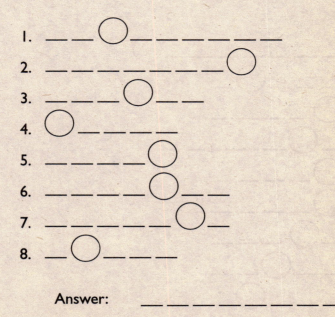

1. __ __ ◯ __ __ __ __ __ __
2. __ __ __ __ __ __ ◯
3. __ __ __ ◯ __ __
4. ◯ __ __ __ __
5. __ __ __ __ ◯
6. __ __ __ __ ◯ __ __
7. __ __ __ __ ◯ __
8. __ ◯ __ __ __

Answer: __ __ __ __ __ __ __

1. SSSEITDR

2. MEADR

3. NESIO

4. RTEHDUN

5. YETPM

6. EBTEAD

7. KDNRI

8. LIDHC

9. RUNT

The governing council of the Jews.

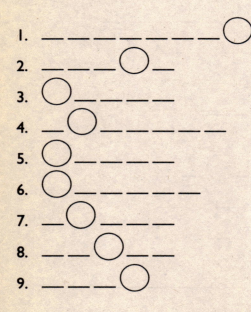

1. __ __ __ __ __ __ __ ⃝

2. __ __ __ __ ⃝ __

3. ⃝ __ __ __ __

4. __ ⃝ __ __ __ __ __

5. ⃝ __ __ __ __

6. ⃝ __ __ __ __ __

7. __ ⃝ __ __ __

8. __ __ ⃝ __ __

9. __ __ __ ⃝

Answer: __ __ __ __ __ __ __ __ __

1. TSNERAV

2. NETURR

3. DARBACKW

4. RSDHEPEH

5. YANITV

6. THSUO

7. TULIB

8. HOSOIFL

9. ONWD

10. GPNSRI

Rules made by people that may not have anything to do with God's requirements.

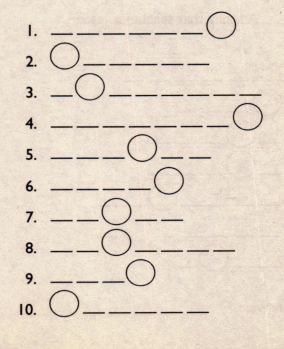

1. _ _ _ _ _ _ ◯

2. ◯ _ _ _ _ _

3. _ ◯ _ _ _ _ _ _

4. _ _ _ _ _ _ _ ◯

5. _ _ _ ◯ _ _

6. _ _ _ _ ◯

7. _ _ ◯ _ _

8. _ _ ◯ _ _ _ _

9. _ _ _ ◯

10. ◯ _ _ _ _ _

Answer: _ _ _ _ _ _ _ _ _ _

180

1. NTPROOI

2. YAMRR

3. EGRTOF

4. UBTEAY

5. EREMREMB

6. LPSERKNI

7. FRIEG

A story that teaches a lesson.

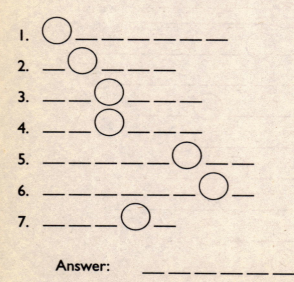

1. ◯ __ __ __ __ __ __

2. __ ◯ __ __ __

3. __ __ ◯ __ __ __

4. __ __ ◯ __ __ __

5. __ __ __ __ ◯ __ __

6. __ __ __ __ __ ◯ __

7. __ __ __ ◯ __

Answer: __ __ __ __ __ __ __

1. SHTTRI   6. RJECET

2. WSSRHEO   7. EORPRSP

3. IEASR   8. NAGHEC

4. NPLTA   9. NGKIS

5. WYAA

It was because of this that Paul ended up on the island of Melita.

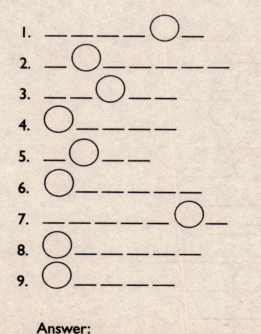

Answer: _ _ _ _ _ _ _ _ _

1. DLOBO
2. ODWIW
3. REWAS
4. SDTU
5. SYFLALE
6. NSDTA

7. SACEU
8. YGPLNIA
9. LEPEPO
10. EECEUTX
11. URODN

A celebration to help us remember all that the Lord has done for us.

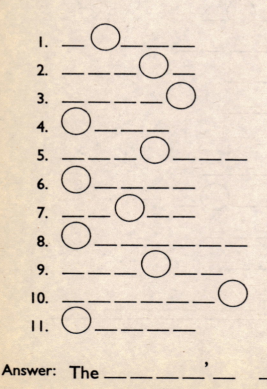

1. __ ◯ __ __ __
2. __ __ __ __ ◯ __
3. __ __ __ __ ◯
4. ◯ __ __ __ __
5. __ __ __ __ ◯ __ __ __
6. ◯ __ __ __ __
7. __ __ ◯ __ __
8. ◯ __ __ __ __ __ __
9. __ __ __ ◯ __ __
10. __ __ __ __ __ __ ◯
11. ◯ __ __ __ __

Answer: The __ __ __ __' __ __ __ __ __ __ __ __

1. EISNNCE
2. DANME
3. NGLAE
4. RTLEVO
5. DUBENR

6. TPRAUER
7. IANTON
8. OWYLHL
9. DFNREI

An important Roman army officer.

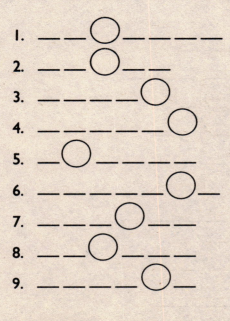

1. _ _ ◯ _ _ _ _
2. _ _ ◯ _ _ _
3. _ _ _ _ ◯
4. _ _ _ _ _ ◯
5. _ ◯ _ _ _ _
6. _ _ _ _ ◯ _
7. _ _ _ ◯ _ _
8. _ _ ◯ _ _ _
9. _ _ _ _ ◯ _

Answer: _ _ _ _ _ _ _ _

1. DGIAEL

2. EVCINOEL

3. EKLIDN

4. POWIRHS

5. ETNER

6. SOFOR

7. TFREAHR

8. EFRI

9. FILE

10. ANLEONB

11. BADIE

Flowers that grow wild all over Galilee.

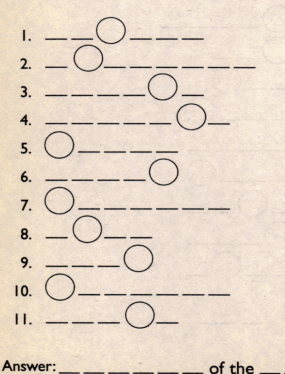

1. _ _ ◯ _ _ _

2. _ ◯ _ _ _ _ _

3. _ _ _ _ ◯ _

4. _ _ _ _ _ ◯ _

5. ◯ _ _ _ _

6. _ _ _ _ ◯

7. ◯ _ _ _ _ _

8. _ ◯ _ _

9. _ _ _ ◯ _

10. ◯ _ _ _ _ _

11. _ _ _ ◯ _

Answer: _ _ _ _ _ of the _ _ _ _ _

1. DEBOLH

2. HATWC

3. SALZEUO

4. CEPESA

5. KROBO

6. FRUY

7. SHESA

He smelled bad, but he did live again.

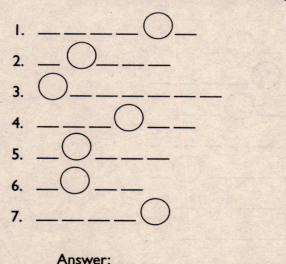

1. __ __ __ __ ◯ __

2. __ ◯ __ __ __

3. ◯ __ __ __ __ __ __

4. __ __ __ ◯ __ __

5. __ ◯ __ __ __

6. __ ◯ __ __

7. __ __ __ __ ◯

Answer: __ __ __ __ __ __ __

1. HASGN

2. TOPEHRP

3. TRECSE

4. DOREVEC

5. RENDUKN

6. YMRIES

7. YDOERST

A kind of magic.

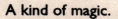

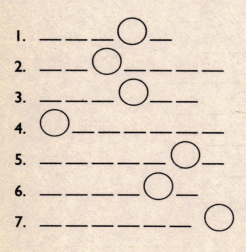

1. ___ ___ ___ ___ ◯ ___

2. ___ ___ ◯ ___ ___ ___ ___

3. ___ ___ ___ ◯ ___ ___

4. ◯ ___ ___ ___ ___ ___ ___

5. ___ ___ ___ ___ ___ ◯ ___

6. ___ ___ ___ ___ ◯ ___

7. ___ ___ ___ ___ ___ ___ ◯

Answer: ___ ___ ___ ___ ___ ___ ___

1. NOTES
2. MEYEN
3. GONUY
4. RAWOR
5. TAINSAG

6. TOHUS
7. VALREG
8. GOSUHT
9. RIVEUQ

A place where Jewish people gathered to worship each Sabbath day.

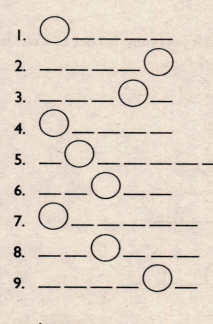

1. ◯ _ _ _ _
2. _ _ _ _ _ ◯
3. _ _ _ ◯ _
4. ◯ _ _ _ _
5. _ ◯ _ _ _ _ _
6. _ _ ◯ _ _
7. ◯ _ _ _ _
8. _ _ ◯ _ _ _
9. _ _ _ _ ◯ _

Answer: _ _ _ _ _ _ _ _ _

1. NAMEIF
2. DRUNE
3. NATUT
4. TINYNE
5. ROUNYCT
6. HGIH
7. STETTUSA
8. GISEE

Paul's long preaching caused this person to fall out of a window.

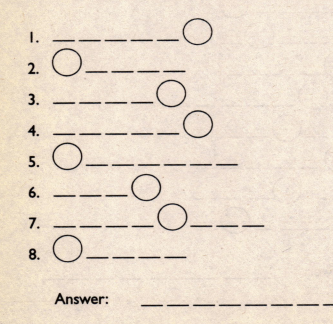

1. _ _ _ _ _ ◯
2. ◯ _ _ _ _
3. _ _ _ _ ◯
4. _ _ _ _ _ ◯
5. ◯ _ _ _ _ _ _
6. _ _ _ ◯
7. _ _ _ _ ◯ _ _ _
8. ◯ _ _ _ _

Answer: _ _ _ _ _ _ _ _

1. BETODR

2. TEBGE

3. CRABNH

4. SITDM

5. NITENEM

6. ROWADT

7. KANET

8. KREBON

9. OPOR

This trade was learned by every Jewish boy.

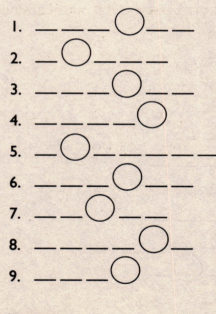

1. _ _ _ ◯ _ _

2. _ ◯ _ _ _ _

3. _ _ _ ◯ _ _

4. _ _ _ _ ◯

5. _ ◯ _ _ _ _ _

6. _ _ _ ◯ _ _

7. _ _ ◯ _ _

8. _ _ _ _ ◯ _

9. _ _ _ ◯

Answer: _ _ _ _ _ _ _ _ _ _

1. SHLEF
2. NARENM
3. LETAD
4. HISERP
5. TECUXEE
6. NALELF
7. CHRETST
8. RIDEES
9. TIDEESP
10. RUNOM
11. DASHEW

Paul was kept under arrest for two years by these two Roman governors.

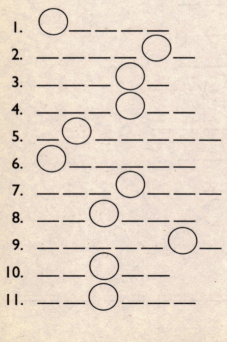

1. ⦿ _ _ _ _
2. _ _ _ _ ⦿ _
3. _ _ _ ⦿ _ _
4. _ _ _ ⦿ _ _
5. _ ⦿ _ _ _ _ _
6. ⦿ _ _ _ _ _
7. _ _ _ ⦿ _ _ _
8. _ _ ⦿ _ _ _ _
9. _ _ _ _ ⦿ _
10. _ _ ⦿ _ _ _
11. _ _ ⦿ _ _ _

Answer: _ _ _ _ _ and _ _ _ _ _ _

1. NAROFEP

2. TORNERISF

3. YLROG

4. HEAHNET

5. LATESTY

6. SONEB

7. CIVEO

8. MUBD

9. PORPHYSE

A person is made this way because of Christ's sacrifice on the cross.

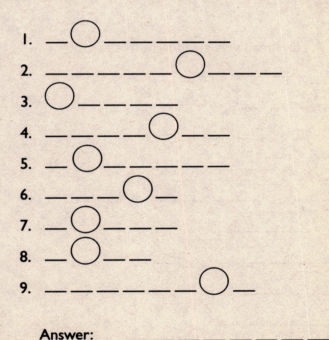

1. _ O _ _ _ _ _

2. _ _ _ _ _ _ O _ _ _

3. O _ _ _ _

4. _ _ _ _ _ O _ _

5. _ O _ _ _ _ _

6. _ _ _ O _

7. _ O _ _ _

8. _ O _ _

9. _ _ _ _ _ _ O _

Answer: _ _ _ _ _ _ _ _ _

1. DORSW

2. LATEX

3. GONAM

4. RATTESC

5. SAPKE

6. THERSTC

7. NIRU

8. SIRERV

A blind man was given sight in this city.

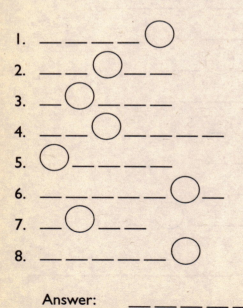

1. ___ ___ ___ ___ ⊙

2. ___ ___ ⊙ ___ ___

3. ___ ⊙ ___ ___ ___

4. ___ ___ ⊙ ___ ___ ___ ___

5. ⊙ ___ ___ ___ ___

6. ___ ___ ___ ___ ⊙ ___

7. ___ ⊙ ___ ___

8. ___ ___ ___ ___ ⊙

Answer: ___ ___ ___ ___ ___ ___ ___ ___

1. NORAG

2. NESTUCHT

3. TENLAM

4. DREAPS

5. NADH

6. LINAS

7. NADERG

8. NODUB

9. WAHSOD

Well-to-do Greek children were accompanied everywhere by these.

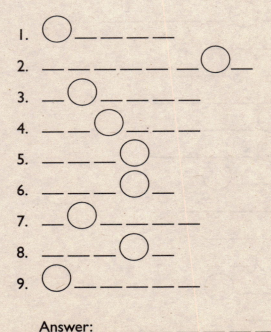

1. ◯ _ _ _ _

2. _ _ _ _ _ _ ◯ _

3. _ ◯ _ _ _ _

4. _ _ ◯ _ _ _

5. _ _ _ ◯ _

6. _ _ _ ◯ _

7. _ ◯ _ _ _ _

8. _ _ _ ◯ _

9. ◯ _ _ _ _ _

Answer: _ _ _ _ _ _ _ _ _

1. SGAEILRLE
2. SOSTP
3. NAELEV
4. NEBEETW
5. ROTSIES
6. DRENDUH
7. EHERT

8. RARONW
9. TORHN
10. RADOB
11. TUCIB
12. DAEH
13. RAMBEHC
14. SAERHC

A new commandment to live by.

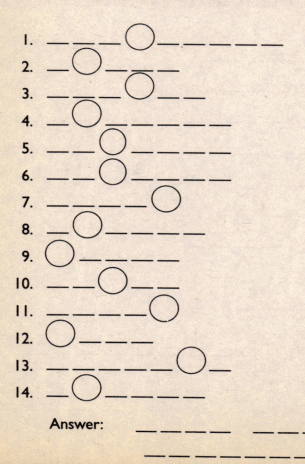

1. _ _ _ ◯ _ _ _ _ _
2. _ ◯ _ _ _ _
3. _ _ ◯ _ _ _
4. _ _ ◯ _ _ _ _
5. _ _ _ ◯ _ _ _ _ _
6. _ _ ◯ _ _ _ _ _
7. _ _ _ _ _ ◯
8. _ ◯ _ _ _ _ _
9. ◯ _ _ _ _ _
10. _ _ ◯ _ _ _
11. _ _ _ _ ◯
12. ◯ _ _ _ _
13. _ _ _ _ _ ◯ _
14. _ ◯ _ _ _ _ _

Answer: _ _ _ _   _ _ _

_ _ _ _ _ _

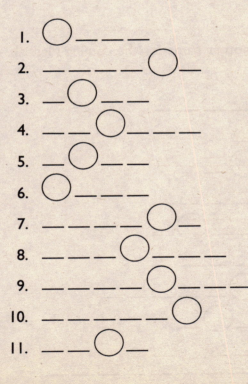

1. LPAM
2. RATESM
3. IFRA
4. DORACC
5. WEHN
6. RUNB
7. TORNEC
8. BULEROT
9. NOMDINIO
10. TEHIGH
11. OHMW

Jesus was fond of saying this in greeting.

1. O _ _ _
2. _ _ _ _ O _
3. _ O _ _ _
4. _ _ O _ _ _
5. _ O _ _
6. O _ _ _
7. _ _ _ _ O _
8. _ _ _ O _ _ _
9. _ _ _ _ O _ _ _
10. _ _ _ _ _ O
11. _ _ O _

Answer: _ _ _ _ _   _ _   _ _ _ _ _ you

1. REVIDSE

2. EIMT

3. MAELF

4. TNNIECA

5. REMNATG

6. DUCKELP

7. DENIEGECX

8. LESEHW

"God is with us." Another name for the coming Messiah.

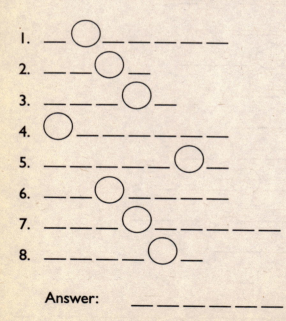

1. __ ◯ __ __ __ __ __

2. __ __ ◯ __

3. __ __ __ ◯ __

4. ◯ __ __ __ __ __ __

5. __ __ __ __ ◯ __

6. __ __ ◯ __ __ __

7. __ __ __ ◯ __ __ __ __

8. __ __ __ __ ◯ __

Answer: __ __ __ __ __ __ __

1. SOPORT
2. TESVARH
3. KICEDW
4. SILE
5. NIEW
6. BERBORS

7. TONSENC
8. TISDM
9. WNOK
10. REROMF
11. ROSU

Enemies of Israel who lived in Palestine.

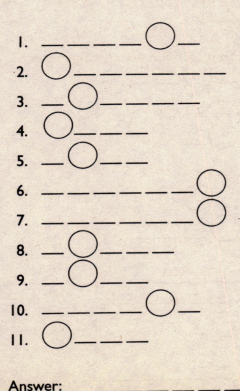

1. __ __ __ __ O __
2. O __ __ __ __ __ __
3. __ O __ __ __ __ __
4. O __ __ __ __
5. __ O __ __ __
6. __ __ __ __ __ __ O
7. __ __ __ __ __ __ O
8. __ O __ __ __
9. __ O __ __ __
10. __ __ __ __ O __
11. O __ __ __ __

Answer: __ __ __ __ __ __ __ __ __ __ __ __ __

1. NELAC

2. HISLPBU

3. DITHOLHW

4. RANEDW

5. SETORF

6. KDNRI

7. CALAEP

8. SONELISH

A dark and scary place for this prophet.

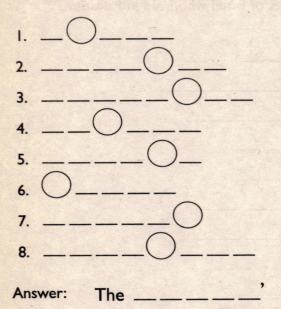

1. __ ⃝ __ __ __

2. __ __ __ __ ⃝ __ __

3. __ __ __ __ __ ⃝ __ __

4. __ __ ⃝ __ __ __ __

5. __ __ __ __ ⃝ __

6. ⃝ __ __ __ __

7. __ __ __ __ __ ⃝

8. __ __ __ __ ⃝ __ __ __

Answer: The __ __ __ __ __ ' __ __ __

1. REDAC
2. DESOILP
3. DOLTHEA
4. NROKEB
5. KFCLO
6. YOGODL

7. ROECNR
8. IGNK
9. EVIGATN
10. TAPERD
11. TIMES

They believe our lives are controlled by something other than God.

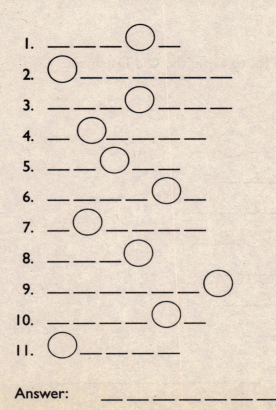

1. __ __ __ ◯ __
2. ◯ __ __ __ __ __ __
3. __ __ __ ◯ __ __ __
4. __ ◯ __ __ __ __
5. __ __ ◯ __ __
6. __ __ __ __ ◯ __
7. __ ◯ __ __ __ __
8. __ __ __ ◯
9. __ __ __ __ __ __ ◯
10. __ __ __ __ ◯ __
11. ◯ __ __ __ __

Answer: __ __ __ __ __ __ __ __ __ __

1. PYRA

2. DERWAR

3. ROTEH

4. LONEYP

5. RATGHE

6. EBETRT

7. RALTA

8. NISP

They had a lot to say in the Old Testament.

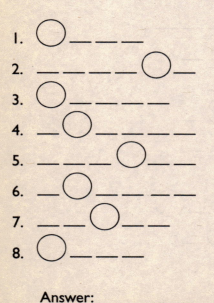

1. ◯ _ _ _

2. _ _ _ _ ◯ _

3. ◯ _ _ _ _

4. _ ◯ _ _ _ _

5. _ _ _ ◯ _ _

6. _ ◯ _ _ _ _

7. _ _ ◯ _ _

8. ◯ _ _ _

Answer: _ _ _ _ _ _ _

1. NONERCC

2. RODENW

3. VOSELA

4. DEBRA

5. GOINRMN

6. WEREAB

7. NSOOLMO

8. THAFI

Old or new, it's almost the same thing.

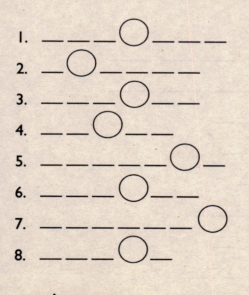

1. _ _ _ ◯ _ _ _ _

2. _ ◯ _ _ _ _ _

3. _ _ _ ◯ _ _ _

4. _ _ ◯ _ _ _

5. _ _ _ _ _ ◯ _

6. _ _ _ ◯ _ _

7. _ _ _ _ _ _ ◯

8. _ _ _ ◯ _

Answer: _ _ _ _ _ _ _ _

1. DEPEVRICE

2. SISELIDPC

3. VNESE

4. TEPARD

5. TEMA

6. DOTERO

7. TANIF

8. HIFESS

Jerusalem had thirty-seven of these cut into the rock under the city.

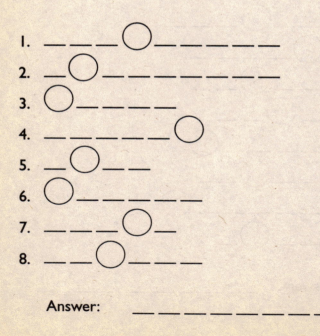

1. _ _ _ _ ◯ _ _ _ _ _

2. _ ◯ _ _ _ _ _ _ _

3. ◯ _ _ _ _

4. _ _ _ _ _ _ ◯

5. _ ◯ _ _

6. ◯ _ _ _ _ _

7. _ _ _ ◯ _

8. _ _ ◯ _ _ _

Answer: _ _ _ _ _ _ _ _

1. WASEV

2. YSASGIN

3. YUSTBLET

4. SCAAHIAP

5. UREHGN

6. RSLEUBM

7. SCESRBI

8. LANEG

An ancient early warning system.

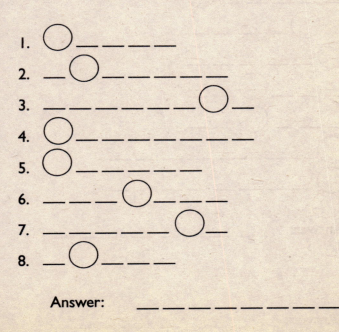

1. ○ __ __ __ __

2. __ ○ __ __ __ __ __

3. __ __ __ __ __ __ ○ __

4. ○ __ __ __ __ __ __

5. ○ __ __ __ __ __

6. __ __ __ ○ __ __ __

7. __ __ __ __ __ ○ __

8. __ ○ __ __ __

Answer: __ __ __ __ __ __ __ __ __

1. NAMEIF
2. LIVERE
3. ROVEDU
4. LNDEKI

5. DONEPE
6. NASERV
7. NSATMAIRA
8. RESEHPCUL

To the world, something to be avoided—but to God, a valuable character trait.

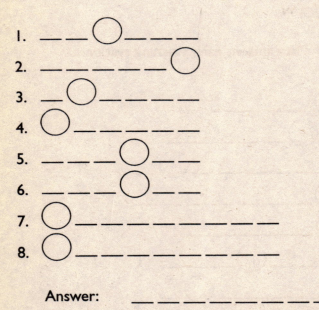

1. _ _ ◯ _ _ _
2. _ _ _ _ _ _ ◯
3. _ ◯ _ _ _ _
4. ◯ _ _ _ _ _
5. _ _ _ ◯ _ _
6. _ _ _ ◯ _ _
7. ◯ _ _ _ _ _ _ _
8. ◯ _ _ _ _ _ _ _

Answer: _ _ _ _ _ _ _ _

1. FREEOB

2. NATIPCA

3. SONEDSLB

4. YEARL

5. LINUOCC

6. ROWEP

7. TACNON

Place known for its beauty and riches.

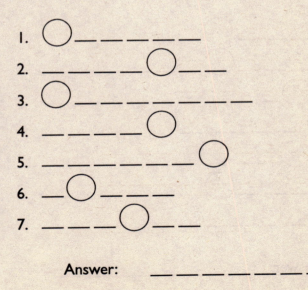

1. ◯ _ _ _ _ _

2. _ _ _ _ ◯ _ _

3. ◯ _ _ _ _ _ _ _

4. _ _ _ ◯ _

5. _ _ _ _ _ _ ◯

6. _ ◯ _ _ _

7. _ _ _ ◯ _ _

Answer: _ _ _ _ _ _ _

1. YSATFE

2. EIGCNNOAR

3. UHORM

4. YMTIHG

5. RUROPA

6. LAMESD

7. CETAH

An ancient method to communicate a call to worship or war.

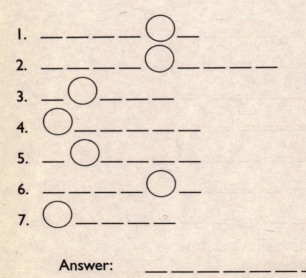

1. _ _ _ _ ⃝ _

2. _ _ _ _ ⃝ _ _ _

3. _ ⃝ _ _ _

4. ⃝ _ _ _ _ _

5. _ ⃝ _ _ _ _

6. _ _ _ _ ⃝ _

7. ⃝ _ _ _ _

Answer: _ _ _ _ _ _ _

1. LPUA	7. PSENHAIES
2. NAREVG	8. ACIAHA
3. DIERC	9. ENTERVF
4. ADLEDN	10. LARVET
5. DAROCC	11. HEETR
6. EADRUJ	

A title given by Jesus to this evil one.

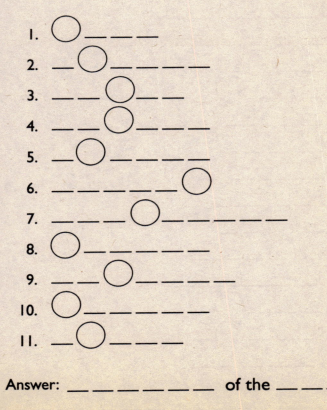

1. ◯ _ _ _
2. _ ◯ _ _ _ _
3. _ _ ◯ _ _
4. _ _ ◯ _ _
5. _ ◯ _ _ _
6. _ _ _ _ _ ◯
7. _ _ _ ◯ _ _ _ _ _
8. ◯ _ _ _ _ _ _
9. _ _ ◯ _ _ _
10. ◯ _ _ _ _ _
11. _ ◯ _ _ _

Answer: _ _ _ _ _ _ of the _ _ _ _ _

1. GFNEIAR
2. NCEONITRU
3. CSECRA
4. TREEC
5. ITANGCLK
6. LODGY
7. NITEEFF

8. REHEC
9. ROLOC
10. DOLUHS
11. YTFEIST
12. HOTRF
13. RIBETS
14. DESLIA

The Jewish people were not allowed to wear this.

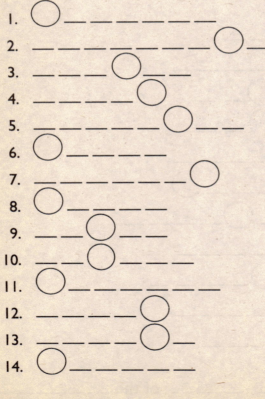

1.
2.
3.
4.
5.
6.
7.
8.
9.
10.
11.
12.
13.
14.

Answer: ___ ___ ___ ___ ___ ___   ___ ___ ___ ___ ___

1. DARMERI   6. TRPNESE

2. DESVA   7. ENRATU

3. RANEG   8. DIEBA

4. YCTHIAR   9. HUTTR

5. NHEAVS   10. TAPIEZB

A person of authority then, and still today.

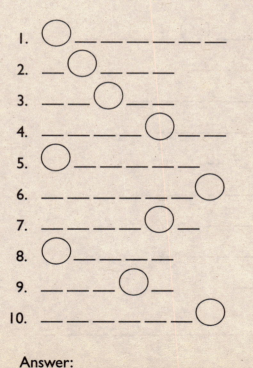

1. ◯ __ __ __ __ __

2. __ ◯ __ __ __

3. __ __ ◯ __ __

4. __ __ __ ◯ __ __

5. ◯ __ __ __ __ __

6. __ __ __ __ __ ◯

7. __ __ __ ◯ __

8. ◯ __ __ __ __

9. __ __ __ ◯ __

10. __ __ __ __ __ ◯

Answer: __ __ __ __ __ __ __ __ __ __

1. EHTHNROCFE
2. MCMNOO
3. TANBUADN
4. ODCNRCO
5. HETDA

6. ASDSERKN
7. NFTAI
8. DENERWE
9. EORS

Springs of water bubbling from the earth.

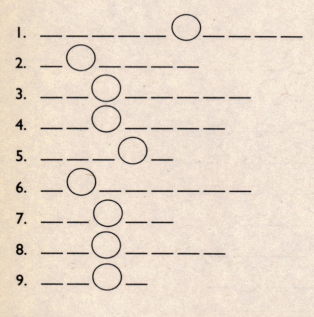

1. __ __ __ __ __ ◯ __ __ __ __
2. __ ◯ __ __ __ __ __
3. __ __ ◯ __ __ __ __ __
4. __ __ ◯ __ __ __ __ __
5. __ __ __ ◯ __ __
6. __ ◯ __ __ __ __ __ __
7. __ __ ◯ __ __ __
8. __ __ ◯ __ __ __ __
9. __ __ ◯ __

Answer: __ __ __ __ __ __ __ __ __

1. DCEONNTIA

2. PDEHT

3. VLEO

4. TRCSIH

5. SAECU

6. YMLAIF

7. YELHNAEV

8. ROWPE

9. SEGELNTI

10. RIMTISEN

A word on everyone's lips at the end.

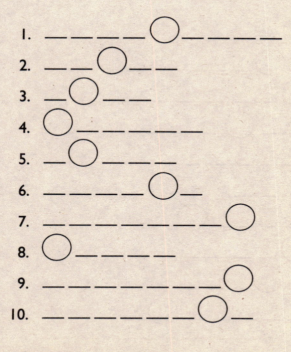

1. _ _ _ _ ◯ _ _ _ _

2. _ _ ◯ _ _ _

3. _ ◯ _ _ _

4. ◯ _ _ _ _ _

5. _ ◯ _ _ _ _

6. _ _ _ _ ◯ _

7. _ _ _ _ _ _ ◯

8. ◯ _ _ _ _ _

9. _ _ _ _ _ _ ◯

10. _ _ _ _ _ _ ◯ _

Answer: _ _ _ _ _ _ _ _ _

1. ALKW

2. SMATENFI

3. VRNTSIIG

4. CAEPTNEI

5. TOINSCS

6. OEPH

7. YMYRTSE

8. DINDEM

9. LOGPES

10. TREQUESS

He stands opposed to Jesus Christ.

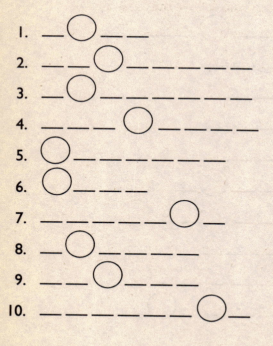

1. __ ◯ __ __ __

2. __ __ ◯ __ __ __ __ __

3. __ ◯ __ __ __ __ __ __

4. __ __ __ ◯ __ __ __ __

5. ◯ __ __ __ __ __ __

6. ◯ __ __ __

7. __ __ __ __ __ ◯ __

8. __ ◯ __ __ __ __ __

9. __ __ ◯ __ __ __ __

10. __ __ __ __ __ __ ◯ __

Answer: __ __ __ __ __ __ __ __ __ __

1. CNSYHTAI

2. LARREQU

3. NERTHERB

4. TORFMOC

5. EPLETIS

6. ETDUNR

To obey and follow the One above.

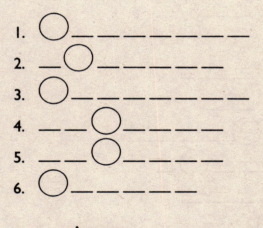

1. ◯ __ __ __ __ __ __ __

2. __ ◯ __ __ __ __ __ __

3. ◯ __ __ __ __ __ __ __

4. __ __ ◯ __ __ __ __

5. __ __ ◯ __ __ __ __

6. ◯ __ __ __ __ __

Answer: __ __ __ __ __ __

1. HERISHC

6. KOVTEREA

2. TRIEW

7. NATISBA

3. GONMA

8. TEEESM

4. TORHEX

9. HEBCESE

5. VREOP

10. TUEIQ

This man was the people's only way to be forgiven, before Jesus.

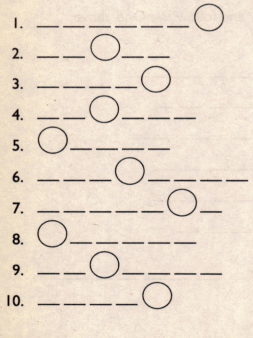

1. _ _ _ _ _ _ ⃝

2. _ _ ⃝ _ _

3. _ _ _ _ ⃝

4. _ _ ⃝ _ _ _

5. ⃝ _ _ _ _

6. _ _ _ ⃝ _ _ _ _

7. _ _ _ _ _ ⃝ _

8. ⃝ _ _ _ _ _

9. _ _ ⃝ _ _ _ _

10. _ _ _ _ ⃝

Answer: _ _ _ _ _   _ _ _ _ _ _

1. KEBEUR
2. SWRALREB
3. REHIS
4. EBSLILE

5. SBSLAELME
6. PISHOB
7. TUREBSV
8. YCTHAIR

Another "monster" from the book of Job.

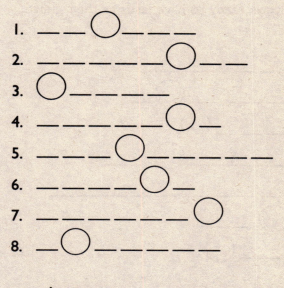

1. _ _ O _ _ _

2. _ _ _ _ _ O _ _

3. O _ _ _ _

4. _ _ _ _ _ O _

5. _ _ _ O _ _ _ _ _

6. _ _ _ _ O _

7. _ _ _ _ _ _ O

8. _ O _ _ _ _ _

Answer: _ _ _ _ _ _ _ _

1. SEEKEMNS
2. RPEACILU
3. ROSIAV
4. RAINSGAYE
5. SAMETSITARG

6. CREGA
7. ROVEL
8. ROETHX
9. NADH
10. READPEAP

They were always ready to have Jesus as their guest.

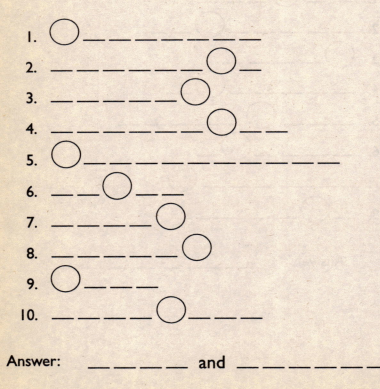

1. ◯ _ _ _ _ _ _
2. _ _ _ _ _ _ ◯ _
3. _ _ _ _ _ ◯
4. _ _ _ _ _ _ ◯ _ _
5. ◯ _ _ _ _ _ _ _ _ _
6. _ _ ◯ _ _
7. _ _ _ _ ◯
8. _ _ _ _ _ _ ◯
9. ◯ _ _ _
10. _ _ _ _ ◯ _ _ _

Answer: _ _ _ _ and _ _ _ _ _ _

CROSSWORD PUZZLES

by Evelyn Boyington

Place answers from numbered clues in the appropriately numbered puzzle grid spaces, making sure to match the clues "across" or "down." When completed correctly, all answers should interlock in the puzzle grid.

ACROSS

1 "Melchizedek, king of _____, priest of the most high God." Heb. 7:1
6 "When the _____ was sprung up." Matt. 13:26
11 "The Jews therefore _____ among themselves." John 6:52
12 "Concerning therefore the _____ of those things. . .sacrifice." 1 Cor. 8:4
14 "Sir, come down _____ my child die." John 4:49
15 "_____ and Medad do prophesy in the camp." Num. 11:27
17 "Neither did Manasseh drive out. . . the inhabitants of _____." Judg. 1:27
18 Prefix meaning "earliest."
19 "I heard, as it were the _____ of thunder." Rev. 6:1
20 Diphthong.
21 "He maketh them also to _____ like a calf." Ps. 29:6
24 "At thy word I will let down the _____." Luke 5:5
25 Drags.
27 "One board had two _____." Exod. 36:22
29 "The carpenters and the _____ were departed from Jerusalem." Jer. 29:2
31 Oshea (or Joshua) was the son of _____. Num. 13:8
32 "Rabbi, thou _____ the Son of God." John 1:49
33 "The angel of the Lord by night _____ the prison doors." Acts 5:19
36 "His throne. . .and his _____ as burning fire." Dan. 7:9
39 "The _____ of the Lord endureth for ever." 1 Pet. 1:25
40 Three vowels.
42 "There cometh a woman of Samaria to _____ water." John 4:7
43 "There is none righteous, _____, not one." Rom. 3:10
44 "Offering. . .thou wouldst not, neither _____ pleasure therein." Heb. 10:8
46 European river.
47 "Do ye not therefore _____, because ye know not?" Mark 12:24
49 "Ezion-geber, which is beside _____, on the shore of the Red sea." 1 Kings 9:26
50 Fourth month of the year: abbr.
51 "_____, stay not; for I will bring evil." Jer. 4:6
53 "The young lions roared upon him, and _____." Jer. 2:15
55 Allude.
56 "Ought not Christ. . ._____ into his glory?" Luke 24:26

DOWN

1 "Remove thy _____ away from me." Ps. 39:10
2 "What _____ we, that ye murmur against us?" Exod. 16:7
3 "_____ I come. . .to do thy will." Heb. 10:7
4 "He. . .became obedient unto. . . _____ the death of the cross." Phil. 2:8
5 "We remember. . .the cucumbers, and the _____." Num. 11:5
6 "He. . .was with the wild _____." Mark 1:13
7 "Ye _____ men with burdens grievous." Luke 11:46
8 "Ahimelech was afraid _____ the meeting of David." 1 Sam. 21:1
9 "Which thing I also _____ in Jerusalem." Acts 26:10
10 "When they had eaten _____." Acts 27:38
11 "What thou _____, write in a book." Rev. 1:11
13 Immediately obvious.

16 "Ye. . .shall _____ in your sins."
John 8:21

22 "Strengthened with might. . .in the
_____ man." Eph. 3:16

23 "Then took Mary a _____ of oint-
ment." John 12:3

25 "She. . ._____ her head."
2 Kings 9:30

26 "Unspeakable words. . .not lawful
for a man to _____."
2 Cor. 12:4

28 Compass point.

30 Angel: Persian.

33 "The centurion believed the master and the _____ of the ship."
Acts 27:11

34 "He be _____ than thy estima-
tion." Lev. 27:8

35 "The treacherous _____ dealeth
treacherously." Isa. 21:2

36 "_____ _____ not that I must be
about my Father's business?"
Luke 2:49

37 A person who laps the water
would be called a _____.
Judg. 7:5

38 "The _____ of the Spirit, which is
the Word of God." Eph. 6:17

41 "Why make ye this _____ and
weep?" Mark 5:39

44 "_____ is the patience and the
faith of the saints." Rev. 13:10

45 "_____ said Jesus unto them, Yet a
little while." John 7:33

48 Highway: abbr.

50 Lager.

52 "_____ they shall enter into my
rest." Heb. 4:3

54 Army officer: abbr.

ACROSS

1 "Every _____ of the field before it was in the earth." Gen. 2:5
6 "_____ him mercy in the sight of this man." Neh. 1:11
11 "The rain is _____ and gone." Song of Sol. 2:11
12 "Even I have seen it, saith the _____." Jer. 7:11
14 "_____ Lord GOD! Behold, thou hast made the heaven." Jer. 32:17
16 "I took the little book...and _____ it up." Rev. 10:10
17 "His master shall bore his _____ through." Exod. 21:6
18 Nashville is the capital of this state: abbr.
19 Henpeck.
21 Bible order: Ruth, 1 & 2 _____ (abbr.), 1 & 2 Kings.
22 "The ark rested...upon the mountains of _____." Gen. 8:4
24 "Put off thy _____ from thy foot." Isa. 20:2
26 "Thy God, O _____, liveth." Amos 8:14
28 "In the _____ that king Uzziah died." Isa. 6:1
29 "Thou preparest a _____ before me." Ps. 23:5
31 "In the seventh year thou shalt _____ him go free." Deut. 15:12
33 "I will _____ up her sea." Jer. 51:36
34 "I have trusted also in the LORD; therefore I shall not _____." Ps. 26:1
36 Aurora.
39 "_____ them about thy neck." Prov. 6:21
40 "_____ and Abihu died before the LORD." Num. 3:4
45 "I will fasten him as a _____ in a sure place." Isa. 22:23
47 "He that shall endure unto the _____." Mark 13:13
49 "Thou art the _____ and thy years shall not fail." Heb. 1:12
50 "Enter ye in at the _____ gate." Matt. 7:13
52 "Judgment must begin _____ the house of God." 1 Pet. 4:17
54 "_____, and all that will live godly in Christ." 2 Tim. 3:12
55 "These men which have companied with _____." Acts 1:21
56 Adjective suffix.
57 "Sons of Zilpah, Leah's handmaid; _____ and Asher." Gen. 35:26
59 Canadian province: abbr.
60 Nahum's father. Luke 3:25
61 "...of the Midianites, _____ and Zeeb." Judg. 7:25
63 Pale.
64 "Jeroboam the son of _____, who made Israel to sin." 2 Kings 10:29

DOWN

2 "And, _____, I am with you alway." Matt. 28:20
3 "The king of Assyria brought men from Babylon...and from _____." 2 Kings 17:24
4 "They forsook their _____ and followed him." Mark 1:18
5 "Thou shalt _____ upon the lion and adder." Ps. 91:13
6 "She..._____ in the field after the reapers." Ruth 2:3
7 "We _____ all like bears." Isa. 59:11
8 "The terrors of God do set themselves in _____ against me." Job 6:4
9 Northwestern state: abbr.
10 "If thou _____ do anything." Mark 9:22
13 "Being over the host of the Lord, were keepers of the _____." 1 Chron. 9:19
15 "He saith among the trumpets, _____, _____." Job 39:25

18 Arabian tambourine.
20 "There was again a battle. . .at
_____." 2 Sam. 21:18
23 "A man riding upon a _____
horse." Zech. 1:8
25 "He built there an altar and called
the place _____Bethel." Gen. 35:7
27 "I have been an _____ in a strange
land." Exod. 18:3
30 Superlative ending.
32 "David sent out _____ young
men." 1 Sam. 25:5
35 "As much as _____ _____ you."
Rom. 12:18
36 "Let him seek peace and _____ it."
1 Pet. 3:11
37 Cereal.
38 "_____, give me this water."
John 4:15

41 "The glory _____ of the only
begotten of the Father." John 1:14
42 "On thee do I wait all the _____."
Ps. 25:5
43 "The promises of God in him are
yea, and in him _____." 2 Cor. 1:20
44 "I have made the earth, the man
and the _____." Jer. 27:5
46 "Five men that went to spy out
the country of _____." Judg. 18:14
48 "Philistines. . .offer a great sacrifice
unto _____ their god." Judg. 16:23
51 "The inhabitant of this _____ shall
say. . .Behold." Isa. 20:6
53 "The king arose and _____ his garments." 2 Sam. 13:31
58 Woman's nickname.
60 Plural suffix.
62 College degree.

ACROSS

1 "Their heart is _____ from me." Mark 7:6
4 "Every man that eateth the sour _____ his teeth. . .set on edge." Jer. 31:30
9 "Come and _____ thy hand upon her." Matt. 9:18
12 "_____ no man anything." Rom. 13:8
13 "The men of Shechem which _____ him in the killing." Judg. 9:24
14 Summer: French.
15 "O LORD, _____ thy work in the midst of the years." Hab. 3:2
17 "I will make thy windows of _____." Isa. 54:12
19 Bullfighter's cry.
20 "His taste remained. . .and his _____ is not changed." Jer. 48:11
21 "I turned, . . .and behold a flying _____." Zech. 5:1
23 "Little one" suffix.
24 "They have taken up their lodging at _____." Isa. 10:29
27 "Have chosen you _____ of the world." John 15:19
28 Compass point.
29 "The Amorites would dwell in Mount _____." Judg. 1:35
30 "The two kings. . .Sihon and _____." Josh. 2:10
31 "_____ also than honey and the honeycomb." Ps. 19:10
33 Opp. of wrong side.
34 "Where two or _____ are gathered together in my name." Matt. 18:20
36 "The LORD that delivered me out of the _____ of the lion." 1 Sam. 17:37
37 "Them that are afar off upon the _____." Ps. 65:5
38 A dish of food such as pottage in Gen. 25:29
39 "I cannot dig, to _____ I am ashamed." Luke 16:3

40 "Let him trust in the name of the LORD and _____ upon his God." Isa. 50:10
41 "The angels shall. . ._____ the wicked from among the just." Matt. 13:49
43 "I will break also the _____ of Damascus." Amos 1:5
44 The LORD _____ not, nor keeps his anger forever. Ps. 103:9
46 "Whosoever _____ his brother is a murderer." 1 John 3:15
49 Legal suit.
50 The Israelite was a _____ in the desert.
52 "How long will it be _____ they attain to innocency?" Hosea 8:5
53 "_____ not I, but Christ liveth in me." Gal. 2:20
54 "Insomuch that they _____ one upon another." Luke 12:1
55 "With silver, iron, _____, and lead they traded in thy fairs." Ezek. 27:12

DOWN

1 "Looking _____ and hastening unto the coming." 2 Pet. 3:12
2 "My heart standeth in _____ of thy word." Ps. 119:161
3 "Ye will _____ more and more." Isa. 1:5
4 "To them _____ he power to become the sons of God." John 1:12
5 "But the wheat and the _____ were not smitten." Exod. 9:32
6 Paid notice.
7 "_____ be on them and mercy." Gal. 6:16
8 "They shall fall by the _____ of the sword." Luke 21:24
9 "I have written a _____ unto you in few words." Heb. 13:22
10 "I _____ no pleasant bread." Dan. 10:3
11 "She answered and said unto him, _____ Lord." Mark 7:28

16 "Love worketh no _____ to his neighbor." Rom. 13:10

18 "The LORD is slow to _____ and great in power." Nah. 1:3

20 "What meanest thou, O _____? arise." Jonah 1:6

21 "Trees. . .plucked up by the _____." Jude 12

22 "We therefore _____ to receive such." 3 John 8

23 "A vessel. . .meet for the master's _____." 2 Tim. 2:21

25 "The brethren. . .sent away Paul and Silas by night unto _____." Acts 17:10

26 "If we _____ to commune with thee." Job 4:2

28 "The poor man had nothing save one little _____ lamb." 2 Sam. 12:3

29 "_____ ye down trees." Jer. 6:6

31 "They _____ fig leaves together, and made. . .aprons." Gen. 3:7

32 Child's game.

35 "Whom _____ steadfast in the faith." 1 Pet. 5:9

37 "And passed on through one _____." Acts 12:10

39 "David. . .came to the brook _____." 1 Sam. 30:9

40 "I _____ daily with you teaching in the temple." Matt. 26:55

42 "Wine which hath no _____." Job 32:19

43 "The Spirit _____ me go with them." Acts 11:12

44 "The stones would immediately _____ out." Luke 19:40

45 _____ haw.

46 "The glory which I _____ with thee." John 17:5

47 Three: prefix.

48 "As a _____ doth gather her brood." Luke 13:34

51 Jackson is its capital: abbr.

ACROSS

1 "Extol him by his name _____." Ps. 68:4
4 "Stand in the _____ of the Lord's house." Jer. 7:2
8 "The sabbath was made for _____." Mark 2:27
11 Leaf angle.
13 "The sons of Simeon; Jemuel, and Jamin, and _____." Exod. 6:15
14 "Abraham set seven _____ lambs of the flock by themselves." Gen. 21:28
15 "Repent. . .or _____ I will come unto thee quickly." Rev. 2:5
16 "Fear not, _____ of Zion, behold thy King cometh." John 12:15
18 "Unto me, who am _____ than the least of all saints." Eph. 3:8
19 Golf tool.
20 "_____ said, He that smiteth Kirjath-sepher and taketh it." Josh. 15:16
24 "I awaked. . .and my sleep was _____ unto me." Jer. 31:26
28 "_____ cried unto the Lord his God." 2 Chron. 14:11
30 "The portion of the men which went with me, _____, Eshcol, and Mamre." Gen. 14:24
32 Compass point.
33 One of Paul's letters: abbr.
34 "They. . .fastened his head in the temple of _____." 1 Chron. 10:10
36 Weight.
37 Farm implement.
38 "That my _____ might be declared throughout all the earth." Rom. 9:17
39 Apochrypha abbr.
40 "Let him seek peace and _____ it." 1 Pet. 3:11
43 "I will _____ leave thee nor forsake thee." Heb. 13:5
45 "I _____ the Spirit descending from heaven." John 1:32

47 "They came to the threshing floor of _____." Gen. 50:10
50 "Gideon _____ wheat by the winepress." Judg. 6:11
55 "And rejoiceth as a strong man to run a _____." Ps. 19:5
56 "_____ unto the world because of offenses." Matt. 18:7
57 Weird.
58 Beget.
59 "The _____ number of them is to be redeemed." Num. 3:48
60 Dagger.
61 Boy's name.

DOWN

1 "And _____ went out to meet Sisera." Judg. 4:18
2 Part of the stands in Solomon's palace. 1 Kings 7:32
3 "_____ _____ are his pride." Job 41:15
4 "_____ shall wipe away all tears." Rev. 21:4
5 "_____, even the ancient high places are ours." Ezek. 36:2
6 Tight.
7 "Saith he which hath the sharp sword with two _____." Rev. 2:12
8 "Melchizedek. . .who _____ Abraham. . .blessed him." Heb. 7:1
9 "Stand in _____, and sin not." Ps. 4:4
10 Saul's grandfather. 1 Chron. 9:39
12 Girl's name.
17 "He cried aloud. . ._____ down the tree." Dan. 4:14
21 "A _____ saw them, and told Absalom." 2 Sam. 17:18
22 "Over the host of. . .Napthali was Ahira the son of _____." Num. 10:27
23 "Inquired he. . .the hour when he _____ to amend." John 4:52

25 "Be not forgetful to _____ strangers." Heb. 13:2

26 "And Seth. . .begat _____." Gen. 5:6

27 "The thoughts of the diligent _____ only to plenteousness." Prov. 21:5

28 Pain.

29 "So _____ as I shall see how it will go." Phil. 2:23

31 "Claudius had commanded all Jews to depart from _____." Acts 18:2

35 Reno's state: abbr.

41 "He shall be a vessel. . .meet for the master's _____." 2 Tim. 2:21

42 Job says that his couch _____ his complaint. Job 7:13

44 "They shall turn away their _____ from the truth." 2 Tim. 4:4

46 "_____ he shall appear, we may have confidence." I John 2:28

48 "A half _____ of land, which a yoke of oxen might plow." I Sam. 14:14

49 "What _____ is this that ye have done?" Gen. 44:15

50 "That by _____ immutable things, in which it was impossible." Heb. 6:18

51 Coal scuttle.

52 "It will be fair weather; for the sky is _____." Matt. 16:2

53 "How long will it be _____ thou be quiet?" Jer. 47:6

54 Lydia was a seller of purple coloring or _____. Acts 16:14

ACROSS

1 "_____ told Jezebel all that Elijah had done." 1 Kings 19:1
5 "The sons of Noah, that went forth. . .were Shem, and _____, and Japheth." Gen. 9:18
8 "Repent. . .or _____ I will come unto thee." Rev. 2:5
12 "It was a _____, and a stone lay upon it." John 11:38
13 "They would have repented long _____." Matt. 11:21
14 "Let the sea _____." 1 Chron. 16:32
15 "Doth he thank that servant?. . .I _____ not." Luke 17:9
16 "Ye have made it a _____ of thieves." Matt. 21:13
17 Cast.
18 Alaskan town.
20 "_____, one of the twelve, called Didymus, was not with them." John 20:24
22 French king.
23 "Aaron and _____ stayed up his hands." Exod. 17:12
24 "And be _____ in the spirit of your mind." Eph. 4:23
28 Azel's brother. 1 Chron. 8:38–39
32 Fury.
33 "Sir, come down ere my child _____." John 4:49
35 One of the dukes of Sihon. Josh. 13:21
36 She was to have a shaven head and _____ nails. Deut. 21:12
39 "She. . .beat out that she had _____." Ruth 2:17
42 "It was impossible for God to _____." Heb. 6:18
44 "I have meat to _____ that ye know not." John 4:32
45 "Consider the _____ how they grow." Luke 12:27
48 "They had on their heads _____ of gold." Rev. 4:4

52 "Seth. . .called his name _____." Gen. 4:26
53 Make lace.
55 Tidy.
56 "I _____ above all things that thou mayest prosper." 3 John 2
57 "What mean these seven _____ lambs?" Gen. 21:29
58 "Take thine _____, eat, drink, and be merry." Luke 12:19
59 Information.
60 "They passed through the _____ Sea as by dry land." Heb. 11:29
61 A sip.

DOWN

1 "Praise him for his mighty _____." Ps. 150:2
2 "The _____. . .is unclean unto you." Lev. 11:6
3 "For he had _____ _____." Acts 18:18
4 "Take heed, and _____ of covetousness." Luke 12:15
5 "Would to God we _____ _____." Exod. 16:3
6 "The eyes of Israel were dim for _____." Gen. 48:10
7 "The tree. . .yielded her fruit every _____." Rev. 22:2
8 "Who can understand his _____?" Ps. 19:12
9 Emerge.
10 Cainan's son. Luke 3:35–36
11 Poetic befores.
19 "A _____ of new timber." Ezra 6:4
21 Outcry.
24 "Wilt thou _____ up their women." 2 Kings 8:12
25 Epoch.
26 Kish's father. 1 Chron. 8:33
27 ". . .if a man shall _____ a pit." Exod. 21:33
29 "Even as a _____ gathereth her chickens." Matt. 23:37

30 "For Adam was first formed, then _____." I Tim. 2:13

31 "Thou never gavest me a _____." Luke 15:29

34 "The church. . ._____together with you." I Pet. 5:13

37 "Then spake _____ unto the woman." 2 Kings 8:1

38 "Though I should _____ with thee." Matt. 26:35

40 "Bow down thine _____ to me." Ps. 31:2

41 Christ's death _____ for our sins.

43 Ethyl acetate.

45 "The Jews. . .took unto them certain _____ fellows." Acts 17:5

46 Dolphin genus.

47 "To seek and to save that which was _____." Luke 19:10

49 "They that _____ soft clothing." Matt. 11:8

50 Aeronautics administration: abbr.

51 "There shall come forth. . .out of the _____ of Jesse." Isa. 11:1

54 "Stand in _____, and sin not." Ps. 4:4

ACROSS

1 "He was _____ of the chief priests and elders." Matt. 27:12

7 "Over the course of the second month was _____ an Ahohite." 1 Chron. 27:4

8 "Where _____ both Peter, and James." Acts 1:13

10 "Behold, this _____ cometh." Gen. 37:19

12 Quantity: abbr.

14 Achim's son. Matt. 1:14

15 "Let her be as the loving hind and pleasant _____." Prov. 5:19

17 To mend.

19 "How long will it be _____ they believe me?" Num. 14:11

20 "The ruler. . .from _____ to the wilderness." Isa. 16:1

21 "_____ _____ thy voice in the garden." Gen. 3:10

23 "_____ end is worse with them." 2 Pet. 2:20

25 Fifty-six: Roman.

26 "Ye shall. . ._____ every good piece of land with stones." 2 Kings 3:19

27 When I go to bed, this is what I do. _____ _____.

30 "I might _____ my course with joy." Acts 20:24

32 "Jael. . .smote the _____ into his temples." Judg. 4:21

33 Compass point.

35 Leading computer maker.

36 Publishers: abbr.

37 "The water. . .make thy belly to _____." Num. 5:22

39 "In the _____ of our Lord Jesus Christ." 1 Cor. 1:8

40 "They went down into _____." Acts 14:25

42 "Them which are of the house of _____." 1 Cor. 1:11

43 "Let him seek peace, and _____ it." 1 Pet. 3:11

44 Ceremonial marches.

DOWN

1 "Which. . .can _____ one cubit unto his stature?" Matt. 6:27

2 "He. . .took _____ of him." Luke 10:34

3 "It is _____ with cedar, and painted." Jer. 22:14

4 "The word of _____ came to all Israel." 1 Sam. 4:1

5 "_____ the son of Jonathan." Ezra 8:6

6 "The king of _____ in the coast." Josh. 12:23

7 "The burden of _____." Isa. 21:11

9 French school.

11 "To meet the Lord in the _____." 1 Thess. 4:17

12 "_____ _____ sentence is in the lips of the king." Prov. 16:10

13 Latticework.

15 To try again: past tense.

16 "If I have told you _____ things. . ." John 3:12

18 "It shall be health to thy _____." Prov. 3:8

20 "_____ fast, and hold the traditions." 2 Thess. 2:15

22 "The wheat and the _____ were not smitten." Exod. 9:32

24 Some of the porters were the children of _____. Ezra 2:57

28 In Christ's lineage: son of Azor. Matt. 1:14

29 Alloy of tin.

30 "They _____ all the good trees."
   2 Kings 3:25
31 "Is he a homeborn _____?"
   Jer. 2:14
34 "Raging waves of the _____."
   Jude 13

37 Portico.
38 A geometric form.
40 High mountain.
41 "A colt, the foal of an _____."
   Matt. 21:5

ACROSS

1 "Then _____ one of the seraphim unto me." Isa. 6:6
5 "A prophet of the Lord...whose name was _____." 2 Chron. 28:9
9 Demon.
12 One of Zibeon's sons. 1 Chron. 1:40
13 "Make _____ the leg, uncover the thigh." Isa. 47:2
14 "Fight neither with small _____ great." 1 Kings 22:31
15 Northwestern state in US.
16 "Ye shall see heaven _____, and the angels." John 1:51
18 "Andrew his brother, casting a net _____ the sea." Matt. 4:18
19 "They took counsel to _____ them." Acts 5:33
20 "What fruit _____ ye then in those things?" Rom. 6:21
22 "The children of Gad called the altar_____." Josh. 22:34
23 "For I am meek and _____ in heart." Matt. 11:29
25 "Next unto them repaired..._____ the Meronothite." Neh. 3:7
27 "If _____ but touch his garment." Matt. 9:21
28 "Jesus came into the world to _____ sinners." 1 Tim. 1:15
29 "Take...one _____ lamb of the first year." Lev. 14:10
32 Weight: India.
33 "Jesus was...in the house of Simon the _____." Matt. 26:6
34 Always: poetic.
35 "With a high _____ brought he them out." Acts 13:17
36 Son of Shuthelah. Num. 26:36
37 "Him that holdeth the scepter from the house of _____." Amos 1:5
38 "He took the _____ loaves and the fishes." Matt. 15:36
40 "Ye shall not eat...ospray and the _____." Deut. 14:12–13
41 "To be...keepers _____ home." Titus 2:5

43 "That he might _____ him out of their hands." Gen. 37:22
44 "These things _____ he." John 11:11
45 "There was _____ other boat there." John 6:22
47 "A compass of seven _____ journey." 2 Kings 3:9
48 "_____, Lord GOD! behold." Ezek. 4:14
50 "The villages in the plain of _____." Neh. 6:2
51 "The LORD is _____ to anger." Nahum 1:3
53 "Do good to them that _____ you." Matt. 5:44
55 "At thy word I will let down the _____." Luke 5:5
56 "He...hath raised up a _____ of salvation." Luke 1:68–69
57 "Unto the king...glory for ever and ever. _____." 1 Tim. 1:17

DOWN

1 "Whose _____ is in his hand." Matt. 3:12
2 "A chest and bored a hole in the _____." 2 Kings 12:9
3 Per.
4 "The city _____ given to idolatry." Acts 17:16
5 "Them that..._____ not the gospel." 2 Thess. 1:8
6 "_____ shall judge his people." Gen. 49:16
7 "_____ Judah's first-born was wicked." Gen. 38:7
8 Fifth book of the OT: abbr.
9 "There was no room for them in the _____." Luke 2:7
10 "Let me pull out the _____ out of thine eye." Matt. 7:4
11 Poke.
17 "Doth not your master _____ tribute?" Matt. 17:24
18 "What shall _____ _____ then with Jesus?" Matt. 27:22

19 "No _____ of flies shall be there." Exod. 8:22

20 "He shall be for a _____ of ships." Gen. 49:13

21 Son of Beriah. 1 Chron. 8:15–16

23 Girl's name.

24 "According to his eating, an _____ for every man." Exod. 16:16

25 Asian country.

26 "_____ not that any should testify." John 2:25

28 A son of Zebulun. Gen. 46:14

30 Jonah said he had _____ wrapped around his head. Jonah 2:5 (singular)

31 Sea eagle.

33 "They that are of the sons of _____." Heb. 7:5

37 "_____, the prophet that is in Israel." 2 Kings 6:12

39 "Come down _____ my child die." John 4:49

40 "Ye have respect to him that weareth the _____ clothing." James 2:3

41 "And _____ with joy receiveth it." Matt. 13:20

42 Pitch.

44 "They were stoned, they were _____ asunder." Heb. 11:37

46 "An inheritance...that fadeth _____ away." 1 Pet. 1:4

47 "In the borders of _____ on the west." Josh. 11:2

48 "I _____ no pleasant bread." Dan. 10:3

49 "As a _____ doth gather her brood." Luke 13:34

51 Quiet!

52 "_____, the star, which they saw in the east." Matt. 2:9

54 "Lord, I _____ not worthy." Matt. 8:8

ACROSS

1 "Ye _____ men with burdens grievous." Luke 11:46
5 "A sword is upon the liars; and they shall _____." Jer. 50:36
9 Pat.
12 "Forbidden. . .to preach the word in _____." Acts 16:6
13 "He put in the breastplate the _____ and the Thummim." Lev. 8:8
14 Self.
15 "I have not hastened from being a _____." Jer. 17:16
17 "Ye shall be _____ in the midst thereof." Ezek. 22:21
19 "Inhabitants. . .of _____ brought water." Isa. 21:14
20 "Strengthen the hand of the poor and _____." Ezek. 16:49
21 "Let your light so _____ before men." Matt. 5:16
23 "Let it be written among the laws of. . .the _____." Esther 1:19
25 Suffer.
26 "_____ hairs are here and there upon him." Hosea 7:9
28 "No man shall _____ me of this boasting." 2 Cor. 11:10
31 "I. . .brought thee out of _____ of the Chaldees." Gen. 15:7
32 Assistants.
34 Last book in the NT: abbr.
35 "Shall bear thee up, _____ at any time." Luke 4:11
38 "The prince. . .shall stand by the _____ of the gate." Ezek. 46:2
39 Items in succession (abbr.).
40 "They were _____ with great fear." Luke 8:37
42 One of Benjamin's cities. Josh. 18:24
44 "The shadow of death _____ it." Job 3:5
46 God's Word is _____ .
47 "The _____ and the princes of the

provinces." Esther 1:3
49 "Their coast was from _____." Josh. 19:33
52 "_____ ye, assemble yourselves." Isa. 48:14
53 "Woe to them that are at _____ in Zion." Amos 6:1
55 Portico.
56 Command to horse.
57 "Let no man _____ him." Prov. 28:17
58 "Stand by the way, and _____." Jer. 48:19

DOWN

1 "I shook my _____, and said, So God shake out." Neh. 5:13
2 "Berechiah the son of _____. . . dwelt in the villages." 1 Chron. 9:16
3 "Which the clouds do drop and _____." Job 36:28
4 "They that had _____ were about four thousand." Mark 8:9
5 "He set it up in the plain of _____ in. . .Babylon." Dan. 3:1
6 "Give me children, _____ else I die." Gen. 30:1
7 Books of the Bible order: 1 & 2 Thess., 1 & 2 _____ (abbr.), Titus.
8 Correct.
9 "Thou shalt utterly _____ it." Deut. 7:26
10 "Such a one as Paul the _____." Philem. 9
11 "Not that thy whole _____ should be cast into hell." Matt. 5:29
16 "I am Alpha and _____." Rev. 1:8
18 "He hath settled on his _____." Jer. 48:11
21 "Brother _____, receive thy sight." Acts 22:13
22 "The laborer is worthy of his

_____." Luke 10:7

23 "He sent to Jobab king of _____." Josh. 11:1

24 "The _____ of the Lord are over the righteous." 1 Pet. 3:12

27 "Her grapes are fully _____." Rev. 14:18

29 A son of Jerahmel. 1 Chron. 2:25

30 About: prefix.

33 "Laying up in _____ for themselves a good foundation." 1 Tim. 6:19

36 "I will make Rabbah a _____ for camels." Ezek. 25:5

37 "His _____ drew the third part of the stars." Rev. 12:4

39 "Then shall ye give me thirty _____." Judg. 14:13

41 "For this cause I bow my _____." Eph. 3:14

43 "Melzar took away. . .their meat. . . and gave them _____." Dan. 1:16

44 Hitch.

45 Tempt.

46 "_____ are the enemies of the cross of Christ." Phil. 3:18

48 "The people which _____ in darkness saw great light." Matt. 4:16

50 Explode.

51 "If any man build upon this foundation. . .wood, _____ stubble." 1 Cor. 3:12

54 South America: abbr.

ACROSS

1 "Among his own _____ and in his own house." Mark 6:4
4 "Joseph, thou _____ of David, fear not." Matt. 1:20
7 "He will not always _____." Ps. 103:9
8 "Frogs. . .into thine _____, and into thy kneading troughs." Exod. 8:3
10 "I therein _____ rejoice." Phil. 1:18
12 Son of Jose. Luke 3:28–29
13 "Blind, or broken. . .or having a _____." Lev. 22:22
15 "There came a _____ and worshiped him." Matt. 8:2
18 "The trees of the Lord are full of _____." Ps. 104:16
20 "Do good to them that _____ you." Matt. 5:44
22 "His body was _____ with the dew of heaven." Dan. 5:21
23 "There was no small _____ among the soldiers." Acts 12:18
24 "Whosoever shall call _____ the name of the Lord." Acts 2:21
25 Compass point.
27 "No man _____ serve two masters." Matt. 6:24
29 "_____, these many years do I serve thee." Luke 15:29
30 Greek letter.
31 "Rising up a great while before _____, he went out." Mark 1:35
32 "She was troubled _____ his saying." Luke 1:29
34 "In the twinkling of an _____." 1 Cor. 15:52
36 "The LORD spake unto Moses and Aaron in mount _____." Num. 20:23
37 Opposite of yes.
39 "Come, and let us go to the _____." 1 Sam. 9:9
41 "We have seen his star in the east,

and _____ come to worship." Matt. 2:2
43 "Of Naphtali; Ahira the son of _____." Num. 1:15
45 "Jesus began both to do _____ teach." Acts 1:1
46 "And ye shall eat old _____." Lev. 26:10
48 "And _____ conceived again, and bare a daughter." Hos. 1:6
49 "_____! and he smelleth. . ." Job 39:25
50 "_____ it is written in the prophets." Mark 1:2
52 "The _____ of Jehoshaphat was quiet." 2 Chron. 20:30
54 "David delivered first this _____ to thank." 1 Chron. 16:7
55 "Ye _____ the distress that we are in." Neh. 2:17
56 "_____ thee out of thy country." Gen. 12:1

DOWN

1 Baby goat.
2 "Asa destroyed her _____, and burnt it." 1 Kings 15:13
3 Compass point.
4 "The dry land appear: and it was _____." Gen. 1:9
5 "Elah. . .to reign _____ Israel in Tirzah." 1 Kings 16:8
6 "Abner, the son of _____, Saul's uncle." 1 Sam. 14:50
7 "Now ye are _____ through the word." John 15:3
9 "As a _____ which melteth." Ps. 58:8
11 Mimic.
13 "But God, _____ is rich in mercy." Eph. 2:4
14 Part of the Bible: abbr.
16 "The poor man had. . .one little _____ lamb." 2 Sam. 12:3
17 And so forth: abbr.

18 Holy person: abbr.
19 In favor of.
21 "Whatsoever house ye _____."
Luke 10:5
23 "They may recover. . .out of the
_____ of the devil." 2 Tim. 2:26
26 "_____, ye do wrong, and
defraud." 1 Cor. 6:8
28 "Why make ye this _____, and
weep?" Mark 5:39
32 Jehoshaphat's father. Matt. 1:8
33 "After the _____ of these words I
have made a covenant." Exod.
34:27
35 "Shall not. . ._____ those things
which are offered to idols."
1 Cor. 8:10
36 "Peter answered unto _____, Tell
me." Acts 5:8
37 "The vision of _____ the
Elkoshite." Nah. 1:1

38 "_____ woe is past; and, behold,
there come two." Rev. 9:12
40 "The children of Gad called the
altar _____." Josh. 22:34
42 "The name of the wicked shall
_____." Prov. 10:7
44 Canadian province: abbr.
46 "That which cometh of the _____
of his patrimony." Deut. 18:8
47 "Tremble, ye women that are at
_____." Isa. 32:11
49 "_____ God indeed said you shall
not?" Gen. 3:1 NKJV
51 "The multitude _____ about him."
Mark 3:32
53 "My reward is with _____."
Rev. 22:12
54 Leaf of a book: abbr.

ACROSS

1 "Of the Kohathites: _____ a singer." 1 Chron. 6:33

6 "Thou shalt call his name _____." Matt. 1:21

11 "Gather a certain _____ every day." Exod. 16:4

12 "A man, which told me all things that ____ I did." John 4:29

14 Army officer: abbr.

16 "I shall _____ praise him for the help." Ps. 42:5

17 "It is vain. . .to _____ up late." Ps. 127:2

18 Chemical symbol for selenium.

19 "It may give. . .bread to the _____." Isa. 55:10

21 South latitude: abbr.

22 "_____ ye down trees, and cast a mount." Jer. 6:6

23 "The navy of Tharshish, bringing gold,. . .and _____." 1 Kings 10:22

24 "Where _____ their gods, their rock?" Deut. 32:37

26 "Their ears are _____ of hearing." Matt. 13:15

27 "I _____ him fourfold." Luke 19:8

30 "Wait, I _____, on the LORD." Ps. 27:14

31 "It was determined that we should sail into _____." Acts 27:1

33 "Now the sons of _____ were sons of Belial." 1 Sam. 2:12

35 Opposite of windward.

39 "Thou makest it _____ with showers." Ps. 65:10

40 Quantity: abbr.

41 "The portion of the young men. . . _____, Eshcol and Mamre." Gen. 14:24

42 "The _____ is withered away, the grass faileth." Isa. 15:6

43 "He built there an altar and called the place _____-Bethel." Gen. 35:7

44 Country in southern Asia.

45 "The children of Gad called the altar _____." Josh. 22:34

46 They were cast into the furnace with coat, _____, and other garments. Dan. 3:21

47 "They _____ not the land in possession by their own sword." Ps. 44:3

48 Compass point.

49 "Fret not thyself in any _____ to do evil." Ps. 37:8

50 Article.

52 "She scorneth the horse and his _____." Job 39:18

53 "Then went up Moses, and Aaron, _____ and Abihu." Exod. 24:9

DOWN

2 "Judah took a wife for _____ his first-born." Gen. 38:6

3 "If thou believest with all thine heart, thou _____." Acts 8:37

4 Porters: Shallum, _____, Talmon, Akkub. Neh. 7:45

5 "Peter and Andrew. . .casting a _____ into the sea." Matt. 4:18

6 "I have found David, the son of _____." Acts 13:22

7 "He shall not be afraid of _____ tidings." Ps. 112:7

8 "O LORD. . .who hast _____ thy glory above the heavens." Ps. 8:1

9 "I am the LORD that brought thee out of _____ of the Chaldees." Gen. 15:7

10 "Be _____ when thou judgest." Ps. 51:4

13 "They had but _____ set the watch." Judg. 7:19

15 Seal up.

18 Actress Ward.

20 "I will _____ unto thee." Ps. 81:8

22 "A virtuous woman is a crown to her _____." Prov. 12:4

24 "_____ not thou he, O LORD our God?" Jer. 14:22
25 "He shall stir up all against the _____ of Grecia." Dan. 11:2
28 "Thou anointest my head with _____." Ps. 23:5
29 "And thine _____ shall not pity." Deut. 19:21
32 "O _____ me not wander from thy commandments." Ps. 119:10
33 Azel's brother. 1 Chron. 8:38–39
34 Ps. 68:19 says that the Lord does _____ us with daily benefits.
36 "We have _____ all things." Jer. 44:18
37 Restrain.

38 "The wicked have _____ out the sword." Ps. 37:14
40 "Will I not break, nor _____ the thing that is gone out of my lips." Ps. 89:34
43 "His soul shall dwell at _____." Ps. 25:13
44 Ten: Greek.
46 "Mine iniquity have I not _____." Ps. 32:5
47 "For a _____ and a snare to. . . Jerusalem." Isa. 8:14
49 Abbreviation for state whose capital is Madison.
51 Boston's state: abbr.

ACROSS

1 "Ye have made it a _____ of thieves." Matt. 21:13
4 "Let us lay _____ every weight and the sin." Heb. 12:1
8 "Let all the inhabitants of the world stand in _____ of him." Ps. 33:8
11 "_____, and Pharah, and Ophrah." Josh. 18:23
13 Fruit drink.
14 "The LORD was my _____." Ps. 18:18
15 "My lord taketh away from _____ the stewardship." Luke 16:3
16 "Seven men. . .whom we may _____ over this business." Acts 6:3
19 Florida is in _____(abbr.) United States.
20 "We will not _____ upon horses." Hos. 14:3
22 "Charity. . .toward _____ other aboundeth." 2 Thess. 1:3
25 "In the clouds, to _____ the Lord in the air." 1 Thess. 4:17
27 Greek goddess.
29 "The sucking child shall play on the hole of the _____." Isa. 11:8
31 "God resisteth the _____." James 4:6
33 Baseball stat.
35 "Because _____ sins are forgiven you." 1 John 2:12
36 _____ and outs.
37 Dilbert character.
38 "_____ sanctify the Lord God in your hearts." 1 Pet. 3:15
39 "Thou shalt observe the feast of _____." Exod. 34:22
41 "The serpent deceived me, and I _____." Gen. 3:13 NIV
42 "Saul _____ David from that day." 1 Sam. 18:9
44 "They will _____ . . .like eagles." Isa. 40:31 NIV
46 "The land that was desolate is become like the garden of _____." Ezek. 36:35

48 "There went up a _____ from the earth." Gen. 2:6
50 Pierre is the capital of this state: abbr.
51 Jer. 2:32 asks if a bride can forget how she is _____.
54 Apiece: abbr.
56 "The words of _____ the son of Jakeh." Prov. 30:1
58 "The villages in the plain of _____." Neh. 6:2
59 "At _____ when the sun did set." Mark 1:32
61 "Is he not also of the Gentiles? _____." Rom. 3:29
62 "Does a fountain send forth at the same place _____ water and bitter?" James 3:11
63 Conjunction.

DOWN

1 "Thou shalt not take the _____ with the young." Deut. 22:6
2 "To. . .our Saviour be glory. . .now and _____." Jude 25
3 Metallic element: abbr.
5 "The trees of the Lord are full of _____." Ps. 104:16
6 "They offered sacrifices unto the _____." Acts 7:41
7 The gods.
8 "They were astonished _____ his doctrine." Mark 1:22
9 "Be baptized and _____ away thy sins." Acts 22:16
10 "He cometh. . .and every _____ shall see him." Rev. 1:7
12 "And he _____ haste and came down." Luke 19:6
14 "When they saw the _____, they rejoiced." Matt. 2:10
17 "The wizards that _____ and that mutter." Isa. 8:19
18 "And they _____ no candle, neither light of the sun." Rev. 22:5
21 "To whom it shall be _____ if we believe on him." Rom. 4:24

23 "Thou art not _____ friend." John 19:12

24 "That ye _____ _____ perfect and entire." James 1:4

26 "Buy of me gold _____ in the fire." Rev. 3:18

27 "He would fain have filled his belly with the _____." Luke 15:16

28 "Shall a man be more pure than his _____?" Job 4:17

30 French coin.

32 "Ye have need that _____ teach you again." Heb. 5:12

34 The name of the wicked shall _____." Prov. 10:7

39 "He _____ and preached unto the spirits in prison." I Pet. 3:19

40 "There are _____ of you that believe not." John 6:64

43 "His parents went to Jerusalem every _____." Luke 2:41

45 "With Joshua his _____ ." Exod. 24:13 NIV

46 "They shall fall by the _____ of the sword." Luke 21:24

47 "But where are the _____?" Luke 17:17

49 Adolescent.

50 "The Spirit and the bride _____, Come." Rev. 22:17

52 "And the strong shall be as _____." Isa. 1:31

53 "Be thou like a _____ or a young hart." Song of Sol. 2:17

55 "A day of trouble, _____ of treading down." Isa. 22:5

57 "Lay hold upon the hope set before _____." Heb. 6:18

60 Abbreviation of the state in which Richmond is the capital.

ACROSS

1 "We _____ our bread with the peril of our lives." Lam. 5:9

4 "The kings. . .of the _____ shall bring presents." Ps. 72:10

9 Son of Jether. 1 Chron. 7:38

12 "One was brought unto him, which _____ him ten thousand talents." Matt. 18:24

13 "The devil threw him down, and _____ him." Luke 9:42

14 "They passed through the _____ Sea." Heb. 11:29

15 "They. . .cast him into the _____ of lions." Dan. 6:16

16 "They. . .have given a _____ for a harlot." Joel 3:3

17 "Far above. . .every name that is _____." Eph. 1:21

19 "Their table be made a snare, and a _____." Rom. 11:9

21 "If any of you lack wisdom, let him _____ of God." James 1:5

22 "From the east side unto the west side, a portion for _____." Ezek. 48:2

24 Sparkle.

27 "If the will of God _____ so." 1 Pet. 3:17

28 "Lest he fall into reproach and the _____ of the devil." 1 Tim. 3:7

30 Caleb's sons were Iru, Elah, and _____." 1 Chron. 4:15

32 "He will not have sodden flesh of thee, but _____." 1 Sam. 2:15

34 "He that is surety for a stranger shall _____ for it." Prov. 11:15

36 "How is the gold become _____!" Lam. 4:1

37 "Surely, I come quickly. _____. Even so, come, Lord Jesus." Rev. 22:20

39 "Let us labor therefore to _____ into that rest." Heb. 4:11

41 "Men and brethren, what shall we _____?" Acts 2:37

42 "It shall be a reproach and a _____." Ezek. 5:15

44 "Angels. . .clothed in pure and white _____." Rev. 15:6

47 Indianapolis is in this state: abbr.

48 "In the first year of Darius the _____." Dan. 11:1

49 "Love not the _____, and neither the things that are in." 1 John 2:15

51 "There stood before the river a _____." Dan. 8:3

52 "He _____ down and the twelve apostles with him." Luke 22:14

55 "Why make ye this _____, and weep?" Mark 5:39

56 "Thy _____ and thy she goats have not cast their young." Gen. 31:38

58 "There arose no small _____ about that way." Acts 19:23

59 Female deer.

60 "The Lord shall _____ him up." James 5:15

61 Crafty.

DOWN

1 "I will be his _____, and he shall be my son." Rev. 21:7

2 "My heart standeth in _____ of thy word." Ps. 119:161

3 "It was about the _____ hour." John 1:39

5 "No man shall _____ me of this boasting." 2 Cor. 11:10

6 "_____ up for yourselves treasures in heaven." Matt. 6:20

7 "_____ the first born of Judah, was evil." 1 Chron. 2:3

8 According to Hebrews 5:14 we can discern both good and evil by our _____.

9 "_____ yourselves. . .with the same mind." 1 Pet. 4:1

10 "He. . .had a golden _____ to measure the city." Rev. 21:15

11 "I will _____ to your yoke." 1 Kings 12:11

16 "So shall thy _____ be filled with plenty." Prov. 3:10

18 "Bilhan, and Zaavan, and _____."
Gen. 36:27

20 "In medias _____."

21 Aware.

22 "Fear not, _____: I am thy shield."
Gen. 15:1

23 "The coat was without _____,
woven." John 19:23

24 "God. . ._____ you to be like-
minded." Rom. 15:5

25 "Much learning doth make thee
_____." Acts 26:24

26 "The children of _____ as
Gomorrah." Zeph. 2:9

29 "_____ your ways and your
doings." Jer. 7:3

31 Adjutant.

33 "They are _____ with the showers of the mountains." Job 24:8

35 One of the porters. Ezra 10:24

38 "I will fasten him as a _____ in a
sure place." Isa. 22:23

40 "_____ them out of the hand of
the wicked." Ps. 82:4

43 "Our fathers were _____ the
cloud." I Cor. 10:1

45 "The birds of the air have _____."
Luke 9:58

46 Tola's grandfather. Judg. 10:1

48 Bulk.

49 Lump.

50 "Let her be as the loving hind and
the pleasant _____." Prov. 5:19

51 "Shimei, and _____, and the
mighty men." I Kings 1:8

53 Suffer.

54 "_____ the spirits whether they
are of God." I John 4:1

57 This state (abbr.) has as its capital
Olympia.

ACROSS

1 "I have not hastened from being a
    _____." Jer. 17:16
5 "Not of works, lest any man
    should _____." Eph. 2:9
9 "Unto _____ that loved us."
    Rev. 1:5
10 "Thou shalt _____ children."
    Deut. 4:25
12 "Being many are one body _____
    Christ." Rom. 12:5
14 "When I came from _____."
    Gen. 48:7
16 "Jesus died and _____ again."
    1 Thess. 4:14
18 The book of the Bible between
    Ezra and Esther: abbr.
20 Jeremiah 46:8 says Egypt _____ up
    like a flood.
22 Foot: combining form.
23 "_____, the family of the Eranites."
    Num. 26:36
25 "Offering of three tenth _____ of
    flour." Num. 15:9
27 Richmond's state: abbr.
28 "Eye hath _____ seen, nor ear
    heard." 1 Cor. 2:9
30 Many churches have _____ glass
    windows.
32 City of the tribe of Benjamin.
    Josh. 18:23
34 City of the Levites. 1 Chron. 6:58
35 "They who separate themselves,
    _____, having not the Spirit."
    Jude 19
37 Scold.
39 "There appeared unto him _____
    angel of the Lord." Luke 1:11
40 "A woman that hath a familiar
    spirit at _____." 1 Sam. 28:7
42 "The kings of Sheba and _____
    shall offer gifts." Ps. 72:10
44 "He casteth forth his _____ like
    morsels." Ps. 147:17
46 "A _____ goeth up into the hand."
    Prov. 26:9

48 Animal doctor.
49 "Let them _____ thee now."
    Isa. 19:12
51 Composition.
53 Abbreviation for the opposite of
    right hand.
54 "From the tower of _____ shall
    they fall." Ezek. 30:6
56 "Peace, good will toward _____."
    Luke 2:14
58 "That he _____ _____ unclean
    thing in thee." Deut. 23:14
59 "I will _____ again unto you."
    Acts 18:21

DOWN

1 "The people shall be much
    _____." Joel 2:6
2 Be quiet!
3 "That he may dip the _____ of his
    finger in water." Luke 16:24
4 Son of Eliphaz. Gen. 36:11
5 "Lift up your eyes to the heavens,
    and look upon the earth _____."
    Isa. 51:6
6 "In the country. . .of _____ king of
    Bashan." 1 Kings 4:19
7 Air: combining form.
8 "No man shall _____ me of this
    boasting." 2 Cor. 11:10
10 "The pillars. . .and the _____, and
    the brazen sea." 2 Kings 25:13
11 "Two of the men in the camp. . .
    one was Eldad. . .the other
    _____." Num. 11:26
13 Kish's father. 1 Chron. 8:33
15 "Gideon. . ._____ as the LORD had
    said unto him." Judg. 6:27
17 "Go and wash in Jordan _____
    times." 2 Kings 5:10
19 "I brought them into. . .the
    chamber of the sons of _____."
    Jer. 35:4

21 "The Son of man must...be _____, and be raised the third day." Luke 9:22

24 Scandinavian.

26 "At midnight Paul and _____ prayed." Acts 16:25

29 "I will deliver them...to be...a _____ and a curse." Jer. 24:9

31 "Abraham went up from Egypt to the _____." Gen. 13:1 NIV

32 "One...which owed him a hundred _____." Matt. 18:28

33 "Yet _____ _____ _____ wages, nor his army." Ezek. 29:18

35 "Nevertheless what _____ the scripture?" Gal. 4:30

36 "Who is worthy...to _____ the seals thereof?" Rev. 5:2

38 "So did _____ speak unto David." 2 Sam. 7:17

41 Railways: abbr.

43 Apochryphal book: _____ and the Dragon.

45 "Repent, or _____ I will come unto thee quickly." Rev. 2:16

47 "Have we not prophesied in thy _____?" Matt. 7:22

50 Alkaline solution.

52 "_____ have I not seen the righteous forsaken." Ps. 37:25

55 Printers' measure.

57 Greek letter.

ACROSS

1 "Abraham set seven ewe _____. . . by themselves." Gen. 21:28
6 "A brightness. . .as the colour of _____." Ezek. 1:4
11 "As he saith also in _____, I will call." Rom. 9:25
12 Beverage.
14 "I will _____ me of mine adversaries." Isa. 1:24
15 "The pit. . .was it which _____. . . had made." Jer. 41:9
16 "Cottages for shepherds, and _____ for flocks." Zeph. 2:6
18 The _____ commandments.
19 "I. . .will _____ all men unto me." John 12:32
21 "It shall be. . .thrust through with a _____." Heb. 12:20
23 "Let none of you suffer. . .as an evil-_____." 1 Pet. 4:15
25 "The elements shall _____ with fervent heat." 2 Pet. 3:10
27 "There were windows in three _____." 1 Kings 7:4
28 "Why is thy countenance _____?" Neh. 2:2
30 "Ye know that summer is _____." Mark 13:28
32 "Now _____ length I might have a prosperous journey." Rom. 1:10
33 "They might attain to _____, and there to winter." Acts 27:12
34 "If the will of God _____ so." 1 Pet. 3:17
35 "_____ by nature the children of wrath." Eph. 2:3
37 "I took the little. . .book and _____ it up." Rev. 10:10
38 "Behold, the Lord stood upon a _____." Amos 7:7
40 "They _____ it with silver and with gold." Jer. 10:4
42 "Lord, if thou hadst been _____." John 11:21
44 "_____ up the gift of God which is in thee." 2 Tim. 1:6
46 "On either _____ of the river." Rev. 22:2

48 "The _____ fell upon Matthias." Acts 1:26
50 "For my life laid down their own _____." Rom. 16:4
52 "That if _____ of you shall agree." Matt. 18:19
54 One of Issachar's cities. 1 Chron. 6:73
56 "He rose again the third _____." 1 Cor. 15:4
57 "Mary. . .wiped his feet with her _____." John 11:2
58 "Lot went out of _____." Luke 17:29
59 "And they came with _____, and found. . .the babe." Luke 2:16

DOWN

1 "Neither had they. . .more than one _____." Mark 8:14
2 "The dumb _____ speaking with man's voice." 2 Pet. 2:16
3 "And they fed in a _____." Gen. 41:2
4 "If the will of God _____ so." 1 Pet. 3:17
5 "I will punish _____ in Babylon." Jer. 51:44
7 "And my reward is with _____." Rev. 22:12
8 "The _____ of that great day of God." Rev. 16:14
9 Compass point.
10 "Let us not _____ it but cast lots." John 19:24
12 "They are quenched as _____." Isa. 43:17
13 "_____ to your faith virtue." 2 Pet. 1:5
16 "A _____ more exceeding and eternal weight." 2 Cor. 4:17
17 The books which come after Ruth in the Bible are 1 & 2 _____: abbr.
20 "His eyes shall have _____ to the Holy One. " Isa. 17:7
22 "The inward man is _____ day by day." 2 Cor. 4:16
23 "Aholah. . ._____ on her lovers, on

the Assyrians." Ezek. 23:5

24 "He that ministered to my _____."
Phil. 2:25

26 "Thou preparest a _____ before
me." Ps. 23:5

27 "When the _____ flesh appeareth
in him." Lev. 13:14

28 "He...rebuked the wind, and said
unto the _____, Peace, be still."
Mark 4:39

29 "For as in Adam all _____."
1 Cor. 15:22

31 Xianity, for example.

36 "He _____ on the seventh day
from all his work." Gen. 2:2

39 "The governor under _____ the
king." 2 Cor. 11:32

41 "The man is near of _____ unto
us." Ruth 2:20

42 "He...was baptized, he and all
_____." Acts 16:33

43 "_____! for that day is great."
Jer. 30:7

45 "They passed through the _____
sea." Heb. 11:29

46 "So many as the stars of the
_____." Heb. 11:12

47 Job 14:19 says that the waters
_____ the stones.

49 "_____, the valley of craftsmen."
Neh. 11:35

51 "The fourth part of a _____ of
dove's dung." 2 Kings 6:25

53 "We do you to _____ of the
grace of God." 2 Cor. 8:1

55 "Show Me" state: abbr.

57 "Ha, _____; and he smelleth the
battle afar off." Job 39:25

ACROSS

1 "Not reckoned of grace, but of
_____." Rom. 4:4
5 "Heart of Egypt shall _____ in the
midst." Isa. 19:1
9 Forbid.
12 "Tobiah. . .was the son in law of
Schechaniah the son of _____."
Neh. 6:17–18
13 "We have heard. . .that Christ
abideth for _____." John 12:34
14 "They rejoice and _____ glad."
Hab. 1:15
15 "Called together his kinsmen and
_____ friends." Acts 10:24
16 "Such as I _____ _____ in all the
land of Egypt for badness."
Gen. 41:19
18 "The latter _____ is worse with
them." 2 Pet. 2:20
20 French for "me."
21 "_____ is the way, that leadeth to
destruction." Matt. 7:13
24 "It was told _____ _____ the
third day." Gen. 31:22
28 "The Lamb. . .shall feed them, and
shall _____ them." Rev. 7:17
29 "Without God in the _____."
Eph. 2:12
30 Fee, _____, Fo, Fum.
31 "Incline thine _____ unto me."
Ps. 17:6
32 "Put him to an open _____."
Heb. 6:6
33 "Because Judas had the _____."
John 13:29
34 Columbia's state: abbr.
35 "Overthrew. . .the _____ of them
that sold doves." Mark 11:15
36 Another word for seer.
37 "His countenance was as the sun
_____." Rev. 1:16
39 "He hath reserved in everlasting
chains _____ darkness." Jude 6
40 Mother.

41 "Then _____ was wroth with the
seer." 2 Chron. 16:10
42 "_____ _____ _____ do nothing."
2 Cor. 13:8
46 "Your peace shall _____ upon it."
Luke 10:6
50 Age.
51 "The glory of Jacob shall be made
_____." Isa. 17:4
52 "Or _____ believe me for the
very works' sake." John 14:11
53 _____ humbug!
54 "Neither will I _____ my face."
Ezek. 39:29
55 "They were _____ asunder."
Heb. 11:37

DOWN

1 "_____ also and Javan. . .occupied
in thy fairs." Ezek. 27:19
2 "Sir, come down _____ my child
die." John 4:49
3 Sheep's bleat.
4 "Thy lips are like a _____ of scar-
let." Song of Sol. 4:3
5 "Wrought iron and brass to
_____ the house of the LORD."
2 Chron. 24:12
6 "As the serpent beguiled _____
through his subtilty." 2 Cor. 11:3
7 Third book of the Bible: abbr.
8 "The devils also believe, and
_____." James 2:19
9 "Dip it in the blood that is in the
_____." Exod. 12:22
10 Son of Jether. 1 Chron. 7:38
11 "I saw a _____ heaven." Rev. 21:1
17 "Whither have ye made a _____
today?" 1 Sam. 27:10
19 Northwestern state: abbr.
21 "God, . . .sent him to _____ you."
Acts 3:26
22 "A measure to _____ even unto
you." 2 Cor. 10:13

23 "All that handle the _____, the mariners." Ezek. 27:29
24 Reluctant.
25 "Then took he him up in his _____, and blessed God." Luke 2:28
26 "He is _____ _____, ask him." John 9:21
27 "Simeon that was called _____." Acts 13:1
29 "But _____ I do, that I will do." 2 Cor. 11:12
32 "Now no chastening for the present _____ to be joyous." Heb. 12:11
33 "He hath done, whether it be good or _____." 2 Cor. 5:10
35 "Whose garment was white as _____." Dan. 7:9

36 "They have digged. . .and hid _____ for my feet." Jer. 18:22
38 A son of Zophah. 1 Chron. 7:36
39 "Put no difference between _____." Acts 15:9
41 _____ Boleyn.
42 Second month of the year.
43 "Sounding brass, _____ _____ tinkling cymbal." 1 Cor. 13:1
44 Greek letter.
45 The men of Schechem gave Abimelech _____ in killing. Judg. 9:24
47 Guido's note.
48 Compass point.
49 "The kingdom of heaven be likened unto _____ virgins." Matt. 25:1

ACROSS

1 "Ye pay tithe of _____ and anise." Matt. 23:23
5 "Jesus, when he had found a young _____, sat thereon." John 12:14
8 "The snorting of his horses was heard from _____." Jer. 8:16
11 "An half _____ of land, which. . . oxen might plow." 1 Sam. 14:14
12 "A serpent _____ him." Amos 5:19
13 Unrefined metal.
14 "The high priest alone once every _____." Heb. 9:7
15 "Her Nazarites were purer than _____." Lam. 4:7
17 "Judah shall not _____ Ephraim." Isa. 11:13
18 "A tree that will not _____." Isa. 40:20
20 "Blood is brought into the sanctuary by the high _____ for sin." Heb. 13:11
22 A son of Merari. 1 Chron. 24:27
25 "Thou knowest not whether shall prosper, either this _____ that." Eccles. 11:6
26 The children of _____ were porters. Neh. 7:45
27 That is: abbr.
28 "Jezebel. . .painted her face, and _____ her head." 2 Kings 9:30
32 "Fowls like as the sand of the _____." Ps. 78:27
33 "As a _____ shall it come on all them." Luke 21:35
35 "_____ no man any thing." Rom. 13:8
36 Adam and Eve each made an _____ of fig leaves. Gen. 3:7
38 Greek letter.
39 "The promises of God in him are yea, and in him _____." 2 Cor. 1:20
40 "Take therefore _____ thought for the morrow." Matt. 6:34
41 Sleeping sounds.
43 "The LORD smelled a sweet _____." Gen. 8:21
47 Teachers' association: abbr.
48 "How long will it be _____ they believe me." Num. 14:11
49 "The devil threw him down, and _____ him. " Luke 9:42
51 "The chariots shall _____ in the streets." Nahum 2:4
55 Hawaiian garland.
56 We: Latin
57 "I will even appoint over you terror, . . .and the burning _____." Lev. 26:16
58 "Whose _____ is in his hand." Matt. 3:12
59 "Arise therefore, and _____ thee down, and go." Acts 10:20
60 "For he hath _____, and he will heal us." Hos. 6:1

DOWN

1 "If I _____ but touch his garment." Matt. 9:21
2 "Which are blackish by reason of the _____." Job 6:16
3 Depression era agency.
4 "Thou shalt not be afraid for the _____ by night." Ps. 91:5
5 "_____ from fleshly lusts." 1 Pet. 2:11
6 "Neither do I condemn thee: go, and _____ no more." John 8:11
7 "All iniquity shall _____ her mouth." Ps. 107:42
8 "The Spirit of God descending like a _____." Matt. 3:16
9 Greek god of war.
10 "Let us go into the _____ towns." Mark 1:38
16 "Jesus. . .with his finger _____ on the ground." John 8:6
19 Exclamation.
21 Son of Bela (1 Chron. 7:7).

Across / Down Clues

22 "If my _____ hath turned out of the way." Job 31:7

23 "Thou wilt _____ me, O God." Ps. 17:6

24 "Nothing shall by any _____ hurt you." Luke 10:19

26 "In the twenty and sixth year of _____." 1 Kings 16:8

29 "I am ready to preach the gospel to you that are at _____." Rom. 1:15

30 "From following the _____ great with young." Ps. 78:71

31 "Will a young lion cry out of his _____?" Amos 3:4

33 "As a jewel of gold in a swine's _____." Prov. 11:22

34 "When thou _____, thou shalt not stumble." Prov. 4:12

37 "The villages in the plain of _____." Neh. 6:2

39 "Call together against her the kingdoms of _____." Jer. 51:27

42 Digraph.

43 "Who his own _____ bare our sins." 1 Pet. 2:24

44 The temple court was an uncovered _____.

45 "There is a _____ for the silver." Job 28:1

46 "So that the earth _____ again." 1 Sam. 4:5

50 "Be thou like a _____ or a young hart." Song of Sol. 2:17

52 "Four days _____ I was fasting." Acts 10:30

53 "They did so at the going up to _____." 2 Kings 9:27

54 Even: poetic.

ACROSS

1 "He will not have sodden flesh. . . but _____." 1 Sam. 2:15

4 "I _____ in the way a light." Acts 26:13

7 Blemish.

11 "_____, the valley of craftsmen." Neh. 11:35

12 "She shall shave her head, and _____ her nails." Deut. 21:12

13 Air: combining form.

14 "A voice declareth from _____, and publisheth." Jer. 4:15

15 "The king of Assyria brought men from. . ._____." 2 Kings 17:24

16 "For he knoweth our _____." Ps. 103:14

17 "But the Lord shall _____ for ever." Ps. 9:7

19 "Take heed that ye do not your _____ before men." Matt. 6:1

20 Superlative ending.

21 "He delivered _____ from my strong enemy." Ps. 18:17

22 "More than _____ mighty men." Eccles. 7:19

25 "An half _____ of land, which a yoke of oxen might plow." 1 Sam. 14:14

27 "_____ not unto thine own understanding." Prov. 3:5

29 "I will not fear what flesh can _____ unto me." Ps. 56:4

30 "A bound that they may not _____ over." Ps. 104:9

31 "Thy _____ shall fall by the sword." Isa. 3:25

32 Assist.

34 "Judah took a wife for _____ his firstborn." Gen. 38:6

35 "But _____ which ye have already." Rev. 2:25

37 "A soft tongue breaketh the _____." Prov. 25:15

38 "The waters shall fail from the _____." Isa. 19:5

40 "The children of Gad called the altar _____." Josh. 22:34

41 "I will break also the _____ of Damascus." Amos 1:5

42 "Canst thou. . ._____ his jaw through with a thorn?" Job 41:2

44 "I have smitten you with blasting and _____." Amos 4:9

47 "Your manifold transgressions. . . take a _____." Amos 5:12

49 "I am like a green _____ tree." Hos. 14:8

50 "He spake concerning the house of _____ in Shiloh." 1 Kings 2:27

51 Assistant.

52 "Them that dwell before the _____." Isa. 23:18

53 "The ram. . ._____ unto him in the fury." Dan. 8:6

54 "Let us not love in word, . . .but in _____." 1 John 3:18

55 "Your sins _____ forgiven you." 1 John 2:12

56 "_____ shall be called Woman." Gen. 2:23

DOWN

1 "Absalom _____ upon a mule." 2 Sam. 18:9

2 One of those who sealed the covenant. Neh. 10:26

3 "Who alone doeth great _____." Ps. 136:4

4 "He will come and _____ you." Isa. 35:4

5 A son of Jether. 1 Chron. 7:38

6 "_____ are fools for Christ's sake." 1 Cor. 4:10

7 "They. . .went their ways, one to his _____." Matt. 22:5

8 "Which indeed is the _____ of all seeds." Matt. 13:32

9 "Thou hast a mighty _____." Ps. 89:13

10 "But _____ to him that is alone." Eccles. 4:10

12 "Mary hath chosen that good _____." Luke 10:42

16 "The king. . .is come out to seek a _____." I Sam. 26:20

18 "Be merciful unto me, as thou _____ to do." Ps. 119:132

19 "The power, and the glory, for ever. _____." Matt. 6:13

23 "The land is as the garden of _____." Joel 2:3

24 "Who are of _____ among the apostles." Rom. 16:7

25 "The navy. . .bringing gold, and silver, ivory, and _____." I Kings 10:22

26 "The _____ of this world and the deceitfulness." Matt. 13:22

27 "Lest. . .we should _____ them slip." Heb. 2:1

28 "_____ did shear his sheep." I Sam. 25:4

31 "He that _____ them will not have mercy." Isa. 27:11

33 "All thy _____ of pleasant stones." Isa. 54:12

36 "A greater than Solomon is _____." Luke 11:31

39 "_____ in me, and I in you." John 15:4

41 "Their glory shall fly away like a _____." Hos. 9:11

43 "_____: he is the father of Jesse." Ruth 4:17

44 "I sink in deep _____." Ps. 69:2

45 "Baasha. . .and _____ his son reigned in his stead." I Kings 16:6

46 "Not given to _____." I Tim. 3:3

47 "Cast the _____ away." Matt. 13:48

48 "The wheat and the _____ were not smitten." Exod. 9:32

49 "_____ God so loved the world." John 3:16

52 Mardi Gras state: abbr.

ACROSS

1 "Sweet _____ from a far country?" Jer. 6:20
5 "He said, _____, father Abraham." Luke 16:30
8 "He saith among the trumpets, _____, _____." Job 39:25
12 "The servants of _____ conspired against him." 2 Kings 21:23
13 Anger.
14 A person who put his seal on the covenant was _____. Neh. 10:26
15 "Jesus went not. . .into the _____." John 6:22
16 "I will let down the _____." Luke 5:5
17 "Women adorn themselves. . .not with. . ._____, or pearls." 1 Tim. 2:9
18 "I will give you thirty _____." Judg. 14:12
20 "He began to be in _____." Luke 15:14
21 Cheerleaders say this.
22 "Thou shalt not call _____ name Sarai." Gen. 17:15
23 "He, . . .taketh with himself seven _____ spirits." Matt. 12:45
26 "I will send those. . .unto. . .Pul, and _____." Isa. 66:19
27 "If any man love not _____ Lord Jesus." 1 Cor. 16:22
30 "Each one should carry his own _____." Gal. 6:5 NIV
31 "The birds of the _____ have nests." Matt. 8:20
32 Another spelling for Zion.
33 "He walketh through _____ places." Luke 11:24
34 Compass point.
35 Pitchers.
36 Crafty.
37 "He is of _____; ask him." John 9:21
38 Bind.

40 "Seeth two _____ in white." John 20:12
43 "The Spirit like a _____ descending." Mark 1:10
44 People who returned from captivity. Ezra 2:57
45 "Panacea" poet.
47 Geographical location.
48 Some: French.
49 John also was baptizing in _____: var. spelling. John 3:23
50 "John, whose surname was _____." Acts 12:12
51 "There is none righteous, no, not _____." Rom. 3:10
52 "He. . .stood up for to _____." Luke 4:16

DOWN

1 "The fourth part of a _____." 2 Kings 6:25
2 "Then answered _____, and said." Amos 7:14
3 "By faith _____, being warned of God." Heb. 11:7
4 "He _____ into a ship." Matt. 9:1
5 "The hour of prayer, being the _____ hour." Acts 3:1
6 Mars.
7 "The time of figs was not _____." Mark 11:13
8 "The angel of God called to _____." Gen. 21:17
9 "And _____ with joy receiveth it." Matt. 13:20
10 "For I am ready to _____." Ps. 38:17
11 "His kindred, threescore _____ fifteen souls." Acts 7:14
19 "Cut off his _____." Mark 14:47
20 What a couple did at Cana. John 2:1
22 "Aaron and _____ stayed up his hands." Exod. 17:12

23 "When he was twelve years
_____, they went." Luke 2:42

24 Peak.

25 "The _____ is withered away."
Isa. 15:6

26 "When Jesus saw him _____."
John 5:6

27 "_____ them about thy neck."
Prov. 6:21

28 "The children of Israel, . . .came
unto Mount _____." Num. 20:22

29 Being.

31 "Forgive, if ye have aught against
_____." Mark 11:25

32 "_____ also than honey." Ps. 19:10

34 Eel: old English.

35 "Is there any taste in the white of
an _____?" Job 6:6

36 "How or what ye shall _____."
Matt. 10:19

37 "Ye pay tithe of mint and _____."
Matt. 23:23

38 Japanese victory shout.

39 Affirm.

40 "Surely I come quickly. _____."
Rev. 22:20

41 The master in Luke 14:21 told the
servant to go out in street and
_____. (Singular)

42 Colonnade.

43 "Thou shalt not take the _____
with the young." Deut. 22:6

44 "Why make ye this _____, and
weep?" Mark 5:39

46 "He that. . .keepeth my works
unto the _____." Rev. 2:26

ACROSS

1 "What I do thou knowest not
_____." John 13:7

4 In Haggai 1:6 it speaks of those
who _____ wages.

8 Prohibit.

11 "_____ gave names to all cattle."
Gen. 2:20

13 "Being then made _____ from
sin." Rom. 6:18

14 Compass point.

15 "The same measure that ye
_____. . .it shall be measured."
Luke 6:38

16 "The man, that _____ all men."
Acts 21:28

18 "All the trees of _____."
Ezek. 31:16

19 Greek letter.

20 "Whosesoever sins ye _____, they
are remitted." John 20:23

24 "For _____ foundation can no
man lay." 1 Cor. 3:11

28 "Pay all that was _____ unto him."
Matt. 18:34

30 "The sons of Shuthelah: of _____."
Num. 26:36

32 "They. . .brought the child to
_____." 1 Sam. 1:25

33 "He that shall endure unto the
_____, . . .shall be saved."
Mark 13:13

34 Shimei's family dwelt at Bilhah,
Ezem, and _____. 1 Chron. 4:29

36 "Will a man _____ God?"
Mal. 3:8

37 Commercials.

38 "Thou are _____, O LORD."
Ps. 119:151

39 Those in office.

40 "She _____ on her lovers."
Ezek. 23:5

43 "He that is surety for a stranger
shall _____ for it." Prov. 11:15

45 "Thou _____ the Son of God."
John 1:49

47 "Take thine _____, eat, drink, and
be merry." Luke 12:19

50 "Then I _____ that which I took
not away." Ps. 69:4

55 "In the _____ to come he might
show." Eph. 2:7

56 "Why make you this _____, and
weep?" Mark 5:39

57 "The hair of his head like the
_____ wool." Dan. 7:9

58 "Then shall the lame man _____
as an hart." Isa. 35:6

59 "He. . .gave gifts unto _____."
Eph. 4:8

60 "Tell John what things ye have
_____ and heard." Luke 7:22

61 Pig pen.

DOWN

1 "He. . .wrote, saying, His _____ is
John." Luke 1:63

2 "A prophet. . .was there, whose
name was _____." 2 Chron. 28:9

3 "Thou sowedst thy seed, and
_____ it." Deut. 11:10

4 Small lizard.

5 "People of Israel. . .which _____
minded of their own free will."
Ezra 7:13

6 "The fowls. . .neither do they
_____." Matt. 6:26

7 "_____ king of Egypt came up to
fight." 2 Chron. 35:20

8 "The LORD shall hiss. . .for the
_____ that is in the land of
Assyria." Isa. 7:18

9 "Go to the _____, thou sluggard."
Prov. 6:6

10 Ezra, _____, Esther: abbr.

12 "The interpretation. . ._____; God
hath numbered thy kingdom."
Dan. 5:26

17 "Against Saul, and the archers
_____ him." 1 Sam. 31:3

21 "When they were come. . .much
people _____ him." Luke 9:37

22 "They came unto the _____ gate." Acts 12:10

23 "Their words seemed to them as idle _____." Luke 24:11

25 "Cause to inherit the desolate _____." Isa. 49:8

26 "The son of Dekar in Makaz, . . . and _____-beth-hanan." 1 Kings 4:9

27 "The LORD God. . .took one of his _____." Gen. 2:21

28 "Who did eat. . .with him after he rose from the _____." Acts 10:41

29 "Is not this the fast. . .to _____ the heavy burdens." Isa. 58:6

31 One of Caleb's sons. 1 Chron. 4:15

35 Libyan measure.

41 "Take _____; this is my body." Matt. 26:26

42 "He maketh small the _____ of water." Job 36:27

44 _____ estate.

46 "My Father giveth you the _____ bread from heaven." John 6:32

48 "Nor sitteth in the _____ of the scornful." Ps. 1:1

49 "Stand by the way, and _____." Jer. 48:19

50 "There stood before the river a _____." Dan. 8:3

51 Dutch commune.

52 "The Father may be glorified in the _____." John 14:13

53 "Hebrew women. . .are delivered _____ the midwives come." Exod. 1:19

54 "He shall be cast into the _____ of lions." Dan. 6:7

ACROSS

1 "Zebul thrust out _____ and his brethren." Judg. 9:41
5 "Communicated unto them that _____." Gal. 2:2
7 "I will send. . .them. . .to Tarshish, Pul, and _____." Isa. 66:19
8 "Whole creation groaneth and travaileth in _____." Rom. 8:22
10 "All that handle the _____, the mariners." Ezek. 27:29
11 Sopater was a _____. Acts 20:4
13 "He hath shown strength with his _____." Luke 1:51
14 "_____ not unto thine own understanding." Prov. 3:5
15 "The strong shall be as _____." Isa. 1:31
17 Favorite.
19 Son of Japheth. Gen. 10:2
21 Dad.
22 "Give _____ to my words." Ps. 5:1
23 "No more children, tossed to and _____." Eph. 4:14
24 Fourth book of the Bible: abbr.
25 "Nabal did _____ his sheep." 1 Sam. 25:4
27 "Burned incense unto Baal,. . .and to the _____." 2 Kings 23:5
29 Distress signal.
30 Ooze.
31 Hawaiian garland.
32 "He shall neither have son nor _____." Job 18:19
34 "What fruit _____ ye then in those things." Rom. 6:21
35 "The nations are as a _____ of a bucket." Isa. 40:15
36 "Thou shalt not take the _____ with the young." Deut. 22:6
37 "They took both _____ _____." Ezek. 23:13
39 "All the trees of _____, the choice and best." Ezek. 31:16

DOWN

1 "For _____ is my defence." Ps. 59:9
2 "Love thy neighbour _____ thyself." Matt. 19:19
3 "I was constrained to _____ unto Caesar." Acts 28:19
4 "Now _____ a parable of the fig tree." Matt. 24:32
5 "They did so at the going up to _____." 2 Kings 9:27
6 "They went to _____ in ambush." Josh. 8:9
7 "The _____ walk, the lepers are cleansed." Matt. 11:5
9 "Jesus should die for that _____." John 11:51
10 _____ sister-in-law was Ruth. Ruth 1:3–4
11 "Whosoever doth not _____ his cross." Luke 14:27
12 "Fight neither with small _____ great." 1 Kings 22:31
13 "The poison of _____ is under their lips." Rom. 3:13
14 "God be true, but every man a _____." Rom. 3:4
16 "When they _____ wine, the mother of Jesus." John 2:3
18 "The wind _____, and there was a great calm." Mark 4:39
19 "The snare is laid. . .and a _____ for him." Job 18:10
20 Father of one of the spies sent to Canaan. Num. 13:11
23 "Then _____ one of the seraphims unto me." Isa. 6:6
26 Geological time.
27 "There was none that. . .opened the mouth, or _____." Isa. 10:14
28 "There is _____ and all her multitude." Ezek. 32:24
30 "Moses wist not that the skin of his face _____." Exod. 34:29
33 For.

34 "The _____ appeareth, and the tender grass." Prov. 27:25

36 "Why did _____ remain in ships?" Judg. 5:17

38 "Ordained that _____ should walk in them." Eph. 2:10

ACROSS

1 "_____ them in pieces, as for the pot." Mic. 3:3
5 "The words of _____ the son of Jakeh." Prov. 30:1
9 "Of _____, the family of Arelites." Num. 26:17
10 "He went out...a _____ as white as snow." 2 Kings 5:27
12 The Lord God _____ upon the high places of the earth. Amos 4:13
13 A tuft of corn silk.
15 "The fourteenth day of the month _____ a day of gladness." Esther 9:19
16 A duke of the sons of Esau. Gen. 36:15
18 "_____ took all the silver and the gold." 1 Kings 15:18
19 "And _____ lifted up his eyes, and beheld all the plain." Gen. 13:10
20 "Out of the half tribe of Manasseh; _____ with her suburbs." 1 Chron. 6:70
21 "But Moses _____ from the face of Pharaoh." Exod. 2:15
22 "O come, let us..._____ before the LORD." Ps. 95:6
24 "Phenice,...which is an haven of _____." Acts 27:12
25 "He...did as it is written in the _____." 2 Chron. 25:4
26 "The great _____ of their right foot." Exod. 29:20
27 "When she had heard of Jesus, came in the _____ behind." Mark 5:27
31 Jesus is the only one who can _____ for our sins. Rom. 5:11
35 "Ye women that are at _____." Isa. 32:9
36 Actual.
38 "The _____ cannot leave his father." Gen. 44:22
39 "A bishop then must be..._____

to teach." 1 Tim. 3:2
40 "The Lord himself shall give you a _____." Isa. 7:14
41 "She shall rejoice in _____ to come." Prov. 31:25
42 "Neither repented they of their... _____." Rev. 9:21
44 "The writing of God, _____ upon the tables." Exod. 32:16
46 Eagle's nest.
47 "A rough valley, which is neither _____ nor sown." Deut. 21:4
48 He came into the temple early in the _____. John 8:2
49 "A feast of wines on the _____." Isa. 25:6

DOWN

1 "I _____ the fruit of the lips." Isa. 57:19
2 "_____, O LORD, when I cry." Ps. 27:7
3 "Thy counsels of _____ are faithfulness and truth." Isa. 25:1
4 "The name of the first is _____." Gen. 2:11
5 "And Noah builded an _____ unto the LORD." Gen. 8:20
6 Equipment.
7 _____ and downs.
8 The act of selling again.
9 One of Caleb's sons. 1 Chron. 2:18
11 Replant.
12 "Should a man full of _____ be justified?" Job 11:2
14 "Ye _____ men with burdens grievous." Luke 11:46
17 "Jesus _____ them, saying, All hail." Matt. 28:9
20 "_____! for that day is great." Jer. 30:7
21 "_____ not thyself because of evil men." Prov. 24:19
23 "This is nothing _____ but sorrow

of heart." Neh. 2:2

24 "One of the seraphims. . .having a live _____ in his hand." Isa. 6:6

27 Turf fuel.

28 Son of Binea. 1 Chron. 8:37

29 "I _____ all thy precepts." Ps. 119:128

30 "I cannot dig; to _____ I am ashamed." Luke 16:3

32 "His feet shall stand. . .upon the mount of _____." Zech. 14:4

33 "Ye shall be _____ the Priests of the LORD." Isa. 61:6

34 "The land of Nod, on the east of _____." Gen. 4:16

36 "The glory of the LORD is _____ upon thee." Isa 60:1

37 "The _____ Gabriel was sent from God." Luke 1:26

40 "Grievous words _____ up anger." Prov. 15:1

41 "The spirit _____ him; and he fell." Mark 9:20

43 "Going to and _____ in the earth." Job 1:7

45 Girl's name.

ACROSS

1 "If thou canst _____, all things are possible." Mark 9:23

7 "He took the seven loaves, and _____ thanks." Mark 8:6

8 "We sat _____, yea, we wept." Ps. 137:1

10 In John 19:5 Jesus _____ a crown of thorns.

12 Dam.

14 "Members should have the same _____ one for another." 1 Cor. 12:25

15 Greek letter.

17 "His raiment white as _____." Matt. 28:3

19 "Not _____ of them is broken." Ps. 34:20

20 "_____ the son of Meshullam." 1 Chron. 9:7

22 "_____ blessed Elkanah and his wife." 1 Sam. 2:20

23 Where the gospels can be found: abbr.

24 "The _____ is past, the summer is ended." Jer. 8:20

26 French conjunction.

27 Minister's title: abbr.

28 Age.

29 Judah's firstborn. Gen. 38:6

31 "I _____ him fourfold." Luke 19:8

34 To do the opposite of: prefix.

35 "The dragon that is in the _____." Isa. 27:1

37 Another name for the Parable of the Sower is the Parable of the _____.

38 "Have they not heard? _____ verily." Rom. 10:18

39 "She became a pillar of _____." Gen. 19:26

41 "Cain went out. . .and dwelt in the land of _____." Gen. 4:16

42 "Rulers of fifties, and rulers of _____." Exod. 18:21

43 "I will _____ bread from heaven for you." Exod. 16:4

45 "As the _____ among thorns." Song of Sol. 2:2

46 The Lord said He'd pass over when He _____ blood on the doorposts. Exod. 12:23

48 "I taste bread. . ., _____ the sun be down." 2 Sam. 3:35

49 "_____ the word with joy." Luke 8:13

DOWN

1 "And all _____ him witness." Luke 4:22

2 "The serpent beguiled _____." 2 Cor. 11:3

3 French city: _____ Mans.

4 "The altar _____: for it shall be a witness." Josh. 22:34

5 "_____, and pay unto the Lord your God." Ps. 76:11

6 "Following the _____ great with young." Ps. 78:71

7 "If an ox _____ a man or a woman." Exod. 21:28

9 "Doth he not leave the ninety and _____." Matt. 18:12

10 "The Lord is my shepherd; I shall not _____." Ps. 23:1

11 "Work out your own _____ with fear and trembling." Phil. 2:12

13 Actor's part.

14 "Whosoever shall _____ that Jesus is the Son of God." 1 John 4:15

15 The ark had pitch, which is _____, on the inside and out. Gen. 6:14

16 Suffix meaning "little one."

18 "Do not bear false _____." Luke 18:20

20 They cry to the Lord and He _____ them. Ps. 107:19

21 Consumers.

24 "Every woman shall borrow of _____ neighbour." Exod. 3:22

25 "The great _____ of his right foot." Lev. 14:25

30 "Wilt thou _____ it up in three days?" John 2:20

32 "The _____ of man is Lord." Matt. 12:8

33 "Noah was five hundred years _____." Gen. 5:32

34 "Thou shalt _____ me thrice." Matt. 26:34

36 "They mourned over him saying, _____, my brother!" 1 Kings 13:30

38 "They shall _____ as lions' whelps." Jer. 51:38

40 Row.

42 "Take thee a _____, and lay it before thee." Ezek. 4:1

44 Born.

45 Fifty-four: Roman.

47 Columbia's state: abbr.

48 Tea tree.

ACROSS

1 "They sent _____ Rebekah their sister." Gen. 24:59
5 "Adam and his wife _____ themselves from. . .the Lord God." Gen. 3:8
8 Brother of Shammai. 1 Chron. 2:32
12 Traitor.
13 "The elders, said, We _____ witnesses." Ruth 4:11
14 Son of Eliphaz, duke _____. Gen. 36:15
15 "The _____ of my heart are enlarged." Ps. 25:17
17 Antitoxin.
18 "_____ them about thy neck." Prov. 6:21
19 "He. . ._____ the doors of heaven." Ps. 78:23
21 "If thy _____ eye offend thee." Matt. 5:29
24 Hit.
25 Crude metals.
26 "Thy truth _____ unto the clouds." Ps. 108:4
30 "Smoke as out of a seething caldron (or _____)." Job 4:20
31 "Draw you before the judgment _____?" James 2:6
32 _____ Lanka.
33 "Ye have us for an _____." Phil. 3:17
35 "Hast thou _____ afraid or feared?" Isa. 57:11
36 "They compassed me about like _____." Ps. 118:12
37 "Be ye not unequally _____ together with unbelievers." 2 Cor. 6:14
38 "And thy _____ went forth among the heathen." Ezek. 16:14
41 "Then Martha,. . .went and _____ Him." John 11:20
42 "Isaac blessed Jacob and _____." Heb. 11:20

43 "Let _____ grow instead of wheat." Job 31:40
48 Iceland measure.
49 "Give _____, O my people, to my law." Ps. 78:1
50 "Their _____ is gone out through all the earth." Ps. 19:4
51 Bland.
52 The rams' skins were colored with red _____. Exod. 39:34
53 "The land is as the garden of _____." Joel 2:3

DOWN

1 Islet.
2 "He shall redeem thee. . .in _____ from the power of the sword." Job 5:20
3 "Hast thou not heard long _____?" Isa. 37:26
4 "Even the _____ shall faint and be weary." Isa. 40:30
5 "Lest he _____ thee to the judge." Luke 12:58
6 Wrath.
7 "Kings. . .which built _____ places for themselves." Job 3:14
8 "Israel loved _____ more than all his children." Gen. 37:3
9 "The Creator, who is blessed for ever. _____." Rom. 1:25
10 "I will not _____ speak of any." Rom. 15:18
11 "King _____ the Canaanite, which dwelt in the south." Num. 21:1
16 "The Lord sent fiery serpents. . . and they _____ the people." Num. 21:6
20 Election groups.
21 "Woe unto them that draw. . .sin as it were with a cart _____." Isa. 5:18
22 "He hath. . .cut the bars of _____ in sunder." Ps. 107:16

23 He who _____ wisdom loves his own soul. Prov. 19:8

24 "Thou art worthy to take the book, and to open the _____." Rev. 5:9

26 "No man _____ him of his wickedness." Jer. 8:6

27 "He called the name of the well _____." Gen. 26:20

28 "The fruit of the _____ which is in the midst of the garden." Gen. 3:3

29 "The _____ also calved in the field." Jer. 14:5

31 Diving duck.

34 "That ye may _____ in hope." Rom. 15:13

35 "Every _____ shall be filled with wine." Jer. 13:12

37 "_____, Lord, yet the dogs under the table eat." Mark 7:28

38 Paper measure.

39 Naum's father. Luke 3:25

40 "I will fasten him as a _____ in a sure place." Isa. 22:23

41 "Trodden down as the _____ of the streets." Mic. 7:10

44 "The _____ is withered away." Isa. 15:6

45 "Jehoiada. . .took a chest, and bored a hole in the _____." 2 Kings 12:9

46 Compass point.

47 Elder: abbr.

ACROSS

1 Girl's name.
4 "They lavish gold. . .and _____ a goldsmith." Isa. 46:6
8 "Rejoice for _____ with her." Isa. 66:10
11 Cut of meat.
13 "Thou hast been in _____ the garden of God." Ezek. 28:13
14 "How long _____ ye slack to go?" Josh. 18:3
15 "There was one _____, a prophetess." Luke 2:36
16 "These six _____ of barley gave he me." Ruth 3:17
18 "If it _____ good unto thee to come." Jer. 40:4
19 Play on words.
20 "Thou shalt not _____ the Lord thy God." Matt. 4:7
24 "Let the _____ bring forth the living creature." Gen. 1:24
28 "They have. . .given a _____ for an harlot." Joel 3:3
30 Esrom's son. Luke 3:33
32 "How long will it be _____ ye make an end?" Job 18:2
33 "A wild _____ used to the wilderness." Jer. 2:24
34 "Ye shall be _____ the Priests of the Lord." Isa. 61:6
36 "The son of Abinadab, in all the region of _____." 1 Kings 4:11
37 Greek letter.
38 "To proclaim the acceptable _____ of the Lord." Isa. 61:2
39 "The poor man had. . .one little _____ lamb." 2 Sam. 12:3
40 "A raiser of _____ in the glory of the kingdom." Dan. 11:20
43 "Learn his ways, and get a _____ to thy soul." Prov. 22:25
45 "Go to the _____, thou sluggard." Prov. 6:6

47 "He said, _____, what seest thou?" Amos 8:2
50 If you cast your burdens on the Lord, He _____ you. Ps. 55:22
55 Only.
56 "And _____ did that which was right." 1 Kings 15:11
57 "My mercy will I _____ for him for evermore." Ps. 89:28
58 Hezekiah's descendents, the children of _____. Ezra 2:16
59 Numbers 36:6 says that the daughters of Zelophehad are to marry or _____ whom they think best.
60 Whirlpool.
61 Farming instrument.

DOWN

1 "They mourned. . .saying, _____, my brother." 1 Kings 13:30
2 "There is _____ like me in all the earth." Exod. 9:14
3 They offered _____ _____ rams for burnt offerings. Ezra 8:35
4 "Upon the _____ of it thou shalt make pomegranates." Exod. 28:33
5 Chemical suffix.
6 "They shall _____ the whirlwind." Hos. 8:7
7 "Seek peace, and _____ it." 1 Pet. 3:11
8 Waterpot.
9 Raw metal.
10 "_____, of the Gentiles also." Rom. 3:29
12 "Adam called his wife's _____ Eve." Gen. 3:20
17 One (Spanish).
21 "A _____ of God came unto me." Judg. 13:6
22 "_____ one for another." James 5:16
23 No man _____ the tongue according to James 3:8.

25 "The LORD _____ the soul of his servants." Ps. 34:22

26 "Doth he thank that servant. . . ? I _____ not." Luke 17:9

27 "He said, _____ am I, my son." Gen. 22:7

28 Religious denomination: abbr.

29 Thessaly mountain.

31 "What _____ ye by these stones?" Josh. 4:6

35 Measure: Tripoli.

41 "Therefore shall they _____ of the fruit of their own way." Prov. 1:31

42 In Genesis 3 the devil appeared as a serpent or _____.

44 "In _____ was there a voice heard." Matt. 2:18

46 "An ass _____, and a colt with her." Matt. 21:2

48 Sandwich cookie.

49 Dried.

50 "They _____ it, and so they marvelled." Ps. 48:5

51 "They shall _____ this speech in the land." Jer. 31:23

52 "When ye fast, be not, . . .of a _____ countenance." Matt. 6:16

53 Man's name.

54 "Go and _____ where he is." 2 Kings 6:13

ACROSS

1 "And _____ his son reigned in his stead." I Kings 15:8
4 "Incense from Sheba, and the sweet _____ from a far country?" Jer. 6:20
8 "The king of Israel is come out to seek a _____." I Sam. 26:20
12 One of Paul's letters: abbr.
13 "The space [or _____] before the little chambers was one cubit." Ezek. 40:12
14 "Certain _____ fellows of the baser sort." Acts 17:5
15 Psalm 91:7 says "A thousand shall fall at thy side." Another word for fall is _____.
17 "A time to cast away _____, and a time to gather." Eccles. 3:5
19 "One _____ of gold of ten shekels, full of incense." Num. 7:20
20 "_____ made him a dagger which had two edges." Judg. 3:16
21 "Whose look was more _____ than his fellows." Dan. 7:20
24 Son of Gad. Gen. 46:16
27 "A garment that is _____ -eaten." Job 13:28
29 "He was come _____ to enter into Egypt." Gen. 12:11
31 "As the LORD your God did to the _____ sea." Josh. 4:23
32 "I _____ not able to bear all this people alone." Num. 11:14
33 "We were driven up and down in _____." Acts 27:27
34 Compass point.
35 "I will _____ you out of their bondage." Exod. 6:6
37 "Whither have ye made a _____ today?" I Sam. 27:10
38 "Many of them...used curious _____." Acts 19:19
40 "I would hasten my escape for the windy _____ and tempest." Ps. 55:8

42 "They make _____ to shed innocent blood." Isa. 59:7
44 "Samuel said unto the _____, Bring the portion." I Sam. 9:23
46 "His breath kindleth_____." Job 41:21
49 "I will _____ again unto you." Acts 18:21
51 To deaden.
52 "The words of _____, who was among the herdmen of Tekoa." Amos 1:1
53 "I, _____ I, do bring a flood of waters." Gen. 6:17
55 Actress Gabor.
56 "Drink the _____ blood of the grape." Deut. 32:14
57 "There is no _____ to them that fear him." Ps. 34:9
58 Cleaning cloth.

DOWN

1 "Praise him for his mighty _____." Ps. 150:2
2 Pea _____.
3 "My feet were _____ gone." Ps. 73:2
4 "Is not _____ as Carchemish?" Isa. 10:9
5 "These _____ the generations of Noah." Gen. 6:9
6 Formerly called.
7 "Take thine _____, eat, drink, and be merry." Luke 12:19
8 "Thou didst eat fine _____, and honey." Ezek. 16:13
9 "As with the _____, so with the borrower." Isa. 24:2
10 "Set seven _____ lambs of the flock by themselves." Gen. 21:28
11 Commercials.
16 "They were baptized, _____ men and women." Acts 8:12
18 Abraham's father. Luke 3:34

22 "To _____ the heavy burdens."
 Isa. 58:6
23 "_____ lived seventy years, and
 begat Abram." Gen. 11:26
25 "Grant not, . . .the desires of the
 wicked: . . ._____ they exalt themselves." Ps. 140:8
26 The _____ of March.
27 "Paul stood in the midst of _____
 hill." Acts 17:22
28 Leave out.
30 A Verdi opera.
33 Put on the full _____ of God.
 Eph. 6:11 NIV
36 "Gamaliel, a _____ of the law."
 Acts 5:34
38 Tiny particle.

39 "The _____, and the treader of
 grapes." Amos 9:13
41 "An old lion; who shall _____ him
 up?" Gen. 49:9
43 "The_____ measure that is
 abominable." Mic. 6:10
45 "They _____ that he had spoken
 the parable against them."
 Mark 12:12
47 Bulgarian currency.
48 To catch.
49 Strike.
50 Flightless bird.
51 "The king. . .went in haste unto
 the _____ of lions." Dan. 6:19
54 Richmond's state: abbr.

ACROSS

1 "This is nothing _____ save the sword of Gideon." Judg. 7:14
5 "I will take _____ to my ways." Ps. 39:1
9 "He was _____ at that saying." Mark 10:22
12 Job 14:10 says that man _____ and wastes away.
13 "_____ it, even to the foundation." Ps. 137:7
14 "The great _____ of their right foot." Exod. 29:20
15 "Jesus. . .overthrew. . .the _____ of them that sold doves." Matt. 21:12
17 Thing: Latin.
18 "He shall be guilty in _____ of these." Lev. 5:4
19 "I _____ no pleasant bread." Dan. 10:3
21 "Ye have _____ the people of the LORD." Num. 16:41
23 Simulate.
27 "Ye tithe mint and _____ and all manner of herbs." Luke 11:42
28 "His soul shall dwell at _____." Ps. 25:13
29 "Thou hast _____ our lives." Gen. 47:25
31 One-third yard: abbr.
33 "When he died: his _____ was not dim." Deut. 34:7
34 "The child was _____ from that very hour." Matt. 17:18
35 "We _____ your servants." Josh. 9:11
36 Afterthought in a letter: abbr.
37 "Bind me with seven _____ withs." Judg. 16:7
38 "All the people said, _____, and praised the LORD." 1 Chron. 16:36
39 "Shimei, and _____, . . .were not with Adonijah." 1 Kings 1:8
40 "Peter _____ in himself what this vision. . .should mean." Acts 10:17
42 Kingdoms.

45 Married woman: abbr.
46 "[He]. . .brought him to an _____, and took care of him." Luke 10:34
47 "She _____ beside the reapers." Ruth 2:14
49 One of those who came with Zerubbabel. Neh. 7:7
53 Droop.
54 Son of Eliphaz. 1 Chron. 1:36
56 "There is _____ of you that is sorry for me." 1 Sam. 22:8
57 Compass point.
58 "Elkanah that was _____ to the king." 2 Chron. 28:7
59 Jacob was Esau's _____ brother.

DOWN

1 Sullivan and Wynn.
2 "They. . .abide in the covert to _____ in wait." Job 38:40
3 "As the waters cover the _____." Isa. 11:9
4 "Let the king give her royal _____ unto another." Esther 1:19
5 Part of a day: abbr.
6 "The _____ of the wise seeketh knowledge." Prov. 18:15
7 "He called the name of the well _____." Gen. 26:20
8 "Whatsoever mine eyes _____ I kept not from them." Eccles. 2:10
9 "Let him that _____ steal no more." Eph. 4:28
10 Top quality.
11 "For in very _____, as the LORD God of Israel liveth." 1 Sam. 25:34
16 Holy woman: abbr.
20 "Let him seek peace, and _____ it." 1 Pet. 3:11
22 "They of Persia and of _____ and of Phut were in thine army." Ezek. 27:10
23 "Wizards that _____, and that mutter." Isa. 8:19
24 Beams.

25 Compass point.
26 Paul _____ not speak of what Christ did to make the Gentiles obedient. Rom. 15:18
30 "The cruel _____ of asps." Deut. 32:33
31 "Made _____ from sin, and become servants to God." Rom. 6:22
32 "The thoughts of the diligent _____ only to plenteousness." Prov. 21:5
34 "Though they be red like _____." Isa. 1:18
35 A quantity: abbr.
37 Coagulate.
38 "At home in the body, we are _____ from the Lord." 2 Cor. 5:6

39 "The _____ of the mountains is his pasture." Job 39:8
41 Container.
42 "It shall _____ up wholly like a flood." Amos 9:5
43 "Ahira the son of _____, prince of the children of Naphtali." Num. 7:78
44 "The _____ came to Jesus by night." John 3:2
48 Matthew was a _____ collector. Matt. 9:9
50 "_____ fair is thy love, my sister." Song of Sol. 4:10
51 Numerical: prefix.
52 "They have wandered as blind _____ in the streets." Lam. 4:14
55 Opp. of Lt.

ACROSS

1 "Hear ye me, _____, and all Judah and Benjamin." 2 Chron. 15:2
4 Abysses.
9 "Ye _____ my disciples, if ye have love." John 13:35
12 Kish's father. 1 Chron. 9:39
13 "I suffer not a woman. . .to _____ authority." 1 Tim. 2:12
14 "_____, thou hast nothing to draw with." John 4:11
15 "There he _____ with them, and baptized." John 3:22
17 "_____ sheep I have, which are not of this fold." John 10:16
19 God questions Hagar as to what _____ her. Gen. 21:17
20 "All things indeed are _____." Rom. 14:20
21 "Where I am, there ye _____ _____ also." John 14:3
23 "The child. . .was in the _____ till the day of his showing unto Israel." Luke 1:80
26 "The navy of Tharshish, bringing gold, . . ._____, and peacocks." 1 Kings 10:22
27 "Because of their pains and their _____." Rev. 16:11
28 "I _____ the true vine." John 15:1
29 "There is a _____ here, which hath five barley loaves." John 6:9
30 The lord of that servant will come when he _____ not for him. Luke 12:46
31 One of Benjamin's sons. Gen. 46:21
32 Jose was his father. Luke 3:28–29
33 "The resurrection from the dead, neither _____." Luke 20:35
34 "I will requite thee in this _____." 2 Kings 9:26
35 "With his _____ we are healed." Isa. 53:5
37 Northeastern state.
38 High mountains.
39 James and John were called the _____ of thunder. Mark 3:17
40 "They that cast _____ into the brooks shall lament." Isa. 19:8
42 "John was _____ with camel's hair." Mark 1:6
45 "Let her be as the loving hind and pleasant _____." Prov. 5:19
46 "_____ up a child in the way he should go." Prov. 22:6
48 One of the porters. Ezra 10:24
49 "Which of you. . .can _____ to his stature?" Luke 12:25
50 "Them that had gotten the victory. . .having the _____ of God." Rev. 15:2
51 The men of Shechem were a help or _____ in the killing. Judg. 9:24

DOWN

1 "Go to the _____, thou sluggard." Prov. 6:6
2 "He turned the _____ into dry land." Ps. 66:6
3 "Herod, _____ in royal apparel." Acts 12:21
4 "Behold an Israelite. . .in whom is no _____." John 1:47
5 "Maintain good works for necessary _____." Titus 3:14
6 "I will send those. . .to Tarshish, Pul, and _____." Isa. 66:19
7 Pierre's language: abbr.
8 "Your _____ shall commit adultery." Hos. 4:13
9 "One gate of Gad, one gate of _____, one gate of Naphtali." Ezek. 48:34
10 "The wheat and the _____ were not smitten." Exod. 9:32
11 "Do ye not therefore _____, because ye know not the scriptures?" Mark 12:24
16 "He took one of his _____, and closed up the flesh." Gen. 2:21

18 When you go on someone's property without permission, you _____ pass.
20 Animated.
21 "All the people that came out of Egypt, that were _____." Josh. 5:4
22 "Come ye yourselves _____ into a desert place." Mark 6:31
23 "It is near, even at the _____." Matt. 24:33
24 Sons of Ephraim: Rephah, Resheph, Telah, and _____. 1 Chron. 7:25
25 "I will _____ the shepherd, and the sheep shall be scattered." Mark 14:27
27 "Lazarus, . . .full of _____." Luke 16:20
30 "Every one that _____ of the water with his tongue, as a dog." Judg. 7:5

31 One of David's sons mentioned in 1 Chron. 14:5
33 "Two women shall be grinding at the _____." Matt. 24:41
34 "That _____ after the dust of the earth." Amos 2:7
36 "The heathen _____, the kingdoms were moved." Ps. 46:6
37 "All her mirth to cease, . . .her new _____." Hos. 2:11
39 "Hold up my goings. . .that my footsteps _____ not." Ps. 17:5
40 Son of Jether. 1 Chron. 7:38
41 Bow.
42 Sedan.
43 One of Gad's family. Gen. 46:16
44 "They saw the miracles which he _____." John 2:23
47 Egyptian chief deity.

ACROSS

1 "I have _____ you with milk."
   1 Cor. 3:2
4 "Our rafters of _____."
   Song of Sol. 1:17
7 Don't let him that _____ despise
   the one who doesn't. Rom. 14:3
11 "How _____ the mighty fallen!"
   2 Sam. 1:25
12 Gold was cut into _____.
   Exod. 39:3
13 Mirth.
14 "I have _____ of the Lord that
   which also I delivered."
   1 Cor. 11:23
16 "Then shall the _____ man leap."
   Isa. 35:6
17 "He shall receive the crown of
   _____." James 1:12
18 "He that was spoken of by the
   prophet _____." Matt. 3:3
20 "The fear of man bringeth a
   _____." Prov. 29:25
22 Hindu.
23 Ezra 9:3 says that when he heard
   this thing, he rent (or _____) his
   garment.
24 "_____ from whence thou art
   fallen." Rev. 2:5
28 Common suffix.
29 "The LORD shall _____ their
   strength." Isa. 40:31
30 "Let her be as the loving hind and
   pleasant _____." Prov. 5:19
31 "There is. . .one _____ between
   God and men." 1 Tim. 2:5
33 "All the _____ of the court, shall
   be of brass." Exod. 27:19
34 "For the LORD God is _____
   _____." Ps. 84:11
35 "Thou _____ not see my face."
   Exod. 33:20
36 "Took a _____ in her hand."
   Judg. 4:21
39 Stylishly trim.

40 "Saul and the people spared
   _____." 1 Sam. 15:9
41 "The child shall be a _____ unto
   God." Judg. 13:5
45 Apollo's mother.
46 "_____, the family of Eranites."
   Num. 26:36
47 "Then came David to _____ to
   Ahimelech." 1 Sam. 21:1
48 "The prophecy of _____ the
   prophet." 2 Chron. 15:8
49 Oriental dwelling.
50 "There was again a battle with the
   Philistines at _____." 2 Sam. 21:18

DOWN

1 "That be _____ from thee to do
   after this manner." Gen. 18:25
2 "The flesh was yet between their
   teeth, _____ it was chewed."
   Num. 11:33
3 "I have _____ thy faithfulness."
   Ps. 40:10
4 "Noah was _____ hundred years
   old." Gen. 5:32
5 Fury.
6 "For I know that my _____ liveth."
   Job 19:25
7 "The cry is gone. . .unto _____."
   Isa. 15:8
8 Russian mountain range.
9 "The inhabitants of the land of
   _____ brought water." Isa. 21:14
10 Job 10:4 asks if he _____ as a man
   does.
12 "Shall a man. . .cleave unto his
   _____." Gen. 2:24
15 Ireland.
19 "And _____ famous kings; for his
   mercy endureth for ever."
   Ps. 136:18
20 "There shall come forth a rod out
   of the _____ of Jesse." Isa. 11:1
21 "They shall take away thy _____
   and thine ears." Ezek. 23:25

22 On each board they would put two of these. Exod. 26:17

24 "When he _____, he found them asleep." Mark 14:40

25 "The LORD for _____ them out from the land of Egypt." Exod. 12:42

26 Ages.

27 "Jacob fed the _____ of Laban's flocks." Gen. 30:36

29 "_____ it, even to the foundation thereof." Ps. 137:7

32 "_____ _____ _____, and there is none else." Isa. 45:22

33 "They sold. . .the poor for a _____ of shoes." Amos 2:6

35 A kind of berry.

36 Jesus is sometimes pictured as having a _____ about his head.

37 "Barzillai was a very _____ man." 2 Sam. 19:32

38 "The vultures also be gathered, every one with her _____." Isa. 34:15

39 Russian ruler.

42 Son of Jether. 1 Chron. 7:38

43 "It is _____ heavy for me." Num 11:14

44 Wane.

ACROSS

1 "They shall come from the east, and from the _____." Luke 13:29
4 "Pay me that thou _____." Matt. 18:28
8 William Booth's organization: abbr.
10 "The rich man also _____, and was buried." Luke 16:22
12 Hind.
13 Chess term: _____ passant.
14 "The sons of Judah: _____, and Onan, and Shelah." I Chron. 2:3
16 "_____ we ourselves groan within ourselves." Rom. 8:23
18 "And _____ things of the world, and things which are despised." I Cor. 1:28
20 "All kinds of riches; with silver, iron, _____, and lead." Ezek. 27:12
22 "Him that holdeth the sceptre from the house of _____." Amos 1:5
24 "After I have been there, I must also see _____." Acts 19:21
26 "Solomon's provision for one day was. . .fallow_____, and fatted fowl." I Kings 4:22–23
28 "Let her be as the loving hind and pleasant _____." Prov. 5:19
30 Father of Kish. I Chron. 8:33
31 "I will come and _____ him." Matt. 8:7
32 Son of Merari. I Chron. 24:27
34 Luke was a _____: abbr.
35 "Aaron's _____ that budded." Heb. 9:4
37 Bible book order: Ezra, Neh., _____.
39 "In the night _____ of Moab is laid waste." Isa. 15:1
41 "The longsuffering of God waited in the days of _____." I Pet. 3:20
44 "On him they _____ the cross." Luke 23:26
46 "A vineyard of _____ wine." Isa. 27:2
48 "The wheat and the _____ were not smitten." Exod. 9:32
49 "They made upon the _____ of the robe pomegranates." Exod. 39:24
50 "He moveth his _____ like a cedar." Job 40:17

52 "Why did the heathen _____?" Acts 4:25
54 Benjamin's son. Gen. 46:21
56 "Who. . .meted out the heaven with the _____." Isa. 40:12
58 "Whose waters cast up mire and _____." Isa. 57:20
60 Small fish.
61 "Go _____ now, ye rich men." James 5:1
62 "After the _____ Satan entered into him." John 13:27
64 "I. . .have _____ of nothing." Rev. 3:17
66 "God. . .who giveth songs _____ the night." Job 35:10
67 "The cloak that I left at _____ with Carpus." 2 Tim. 4:13
68 "There is _____ righteous, no not one." Rom. 3:10

DOWN

1 "Who _____ their tongue like a sword." Ps. 64:3
2 Northwestern state: abbr.
3 "_____ them about thy neck." Prov. 6:21
4 "And the prophecy of _____ the prophet." 2 Chron. 15:8
5 "The children of Gad called the altar _____." Josh. 22:34
6 Weep.
7 "He shall eat. . .and _____ their claws in pieces." Zech. 11:16
8 "Their words _____ to them as idle tales." Luke 24:11
9 "Their anointing shall surely be _____ everlasting priesthood." Exod. 40:15
11 "To. . .God our Saviour be glory. . . both now and _____." Jude 25
15 "They _____ upon horses, set in array." Jer. 6:23
17 Father of Salathiel. Luke 3:27
19 "Thou art my _____; this day have I begotten thee." Ps. 2:7
21 "Call ye upon him while he is _____." Isa. 55:6
23 "As yet shall he remain at _____

that day." Isa. 10:32

25 "Be it indeed that I have _____, mine error remaineth." Job 19:4

27 "Adah the daughter of _____ the Hittite." Gen. 36:2

29 "How long will it be _____ thou be quiet?" Jer. 47:6

31 "He that trusteth in his own _____ is a fool." Prov. 28:26

33 "I John. . .was in the _____ that is called Patmos." Rev. 1:9

36 "The son of Abinadab, in all the reign of _____." I Kings 4:11

38 "Neither could any man _____ him." Mark 5:4

40 "Come now, and let us _____ together." Isa. 1:18

42 "The way of an eagle in the _____." Prov. 30:19

43 "The axe _____ fell into the water." 2 Kings 6:5

45 "At that day, saith the Lord, that thou shalt call me _____." Hos. 2:16

47 "_____ thy morsel in the vinegar." Ruth 2:14

49 "A greater than Solomon is _____." Luke 11:31

51 "Ready to be revealed in the _____ time." I Pet. 1:5

53 "Keep me from. . .the _____ of the workers of iniquity." Ps. 141:9

55 "Withal they learn to be _____, wandering." I Tim. 5:13

57 "Fight neither with small _____ great." I Kings 22:31

59 "Sing unto him with. . .an instrument of _____ strings." Ps. 33:2

61 Note of the scale.

63 River in Europe.

65 "I _____ well to be angry, even unto death." Jonah 4:9

ACROSS

1 "Balak. . .brought him up into the high places of _____."
Num. 22:41

5 "Her _____ was to light on a part. . .belonging unto Boaz." Ruth 2:3

8 Latvian coin.

12 "Am I _____ _____, or a whale?" Job 7:12

13 One of Jether's sons. 1 Chron. 7:38

14 Seth's son. Luke 3:38

15 "A very great multitude spread their _____ in the way." Matt. 21:8

17 "Can we find such_____ _____ as this?" Gen. 41:38

18 High school subject: abbr.

19 "He _____ aside into the parts of Galilee." Matt. 2:22

21 "Every city or house divided against itself shall not _____." Matt. 12:25

24 "Did not our heart _____ within us?" Luke 24:32

25 "Lord, what _____ thou have me to do?" Acts 9:6

26 "By faith the harlot Rahab _____ not with them." Heb. 11:31

30 Bronze Roman money.

31 Son of Jahdai. 1 Chron. 2:47

32 "He touched his _____, and healed him." Luke 22:51

33 Yields.

35 Return envelope: abbr.

36 To border on.

37 To spread by scattering.

38 "All the prophets from _____ and those that follow." Acts 3:24

41 "To meet the Lord in the _____." 1 Thess. 4:17

42 "_____ sacrificed unto all the carved images." 2 Chron. 33:22

43 "The Lord make you to _____ and abound in love." 1 Thess. 3:12

48 "I had no _____ in my spirit." 2 Cor. 2:13

49 River island.

50 One of the people who set his seal on the covenant. Neh. 10:17

51 "The _____ are a people not strong." Prov. 30:25

52 Sts.

53 "With what measure ye _____, it shall be measured to you." Mark 4:24

DOWN

1 "Because he was a thief, and had the _____." John 12:6

2 "_____ cried unto the LORD his God." 2 Chron. 14:11

3 Chalice veil.

4 "The kings of the earth. . .shall. . . _____ for her." Rev. 18:19

5 "Lift up the hands which _____ down." Heb. 12:12

6 "Of a truth thou _____ the Son of God." Matt. 14:33

7 "Thy cattle feed in large _____." Isa. 30:23

8 A person _____ from the parable of the fig tree. Matt. 24:32

9 "And _____ with joy receiveth it." Matt. 13:20

10 Musical sound.

11 "Simon, . . . _____ sorcery, and bewitched the people." Acts 8:9

16 "So shall it be in the _____ of this world." Matt. 13:40

20 "There stood up a priest with _____ and with Thummim." Ezra 2:63

21 Trade.

22 Layer.

23 "Which _____ beareth fruit." Matt. 13:23

24 "When thou shalt _____ children." Deut. 4:25

Crossword grid (numbered cells): 1 2 3 4 / 5 6 7 / 8 9 10 11 / 12 13 14 / 15 16 17 / 18 19 20 / 21 22 23 24 / 25 26 27 28 29 / 30 31 32 / 33 34 35 / 36 37 / 38 39 40 41 / 42 43 44 45 46 47 / 48 49 50 / 51 52 53

26 "An holy nation, a _____ people." I Pet. 2:9

27 "What ye _____ in the ear, that preach." Matt. 10:27

28 "Take thine _____, eat, drink, and be merry." Luke 12:19

29 "Simon Peter went up, and _____ the net." John 21:11

31 Country bumpkin.

34 Intimidates.

35 "Against which the _____ did beat vehemently." Luke 6:49

37 "_____, I perceive that thou art a prophet." John 4:19

38 Modern spelling for Abraham's wife's name.

39 "I am alive for evermore, _____." Rev. 1:18

40 "Servants of the _____ high God." Acts 16:17

41 "And his miracles, and his _____, which he did in the midst of Egypt." Deut. 11:3

44 Nest.

45 "They. . ._____ the sacrifices of the dead." Ps. 106:28

46 "He was _____ down on the judgment seat." Matt. 27:19

47 "Sir, come down _____ my child die." John 4:49

CRYPTOSCRIPTURE PUZZLES

by Sharon Y. Brown

Each of the CryptoScriptures is a Bible verse in substitution code. For example, JEHOVAH might become M P X S T Q V if M is substituted for J, P for E, X for H, etc. One way to break the code is to look for repeated letters: E, T, A, O, N, R, and I are the most often used. A single letter is usually A or I. OF, IT, and IS are common two-letter words. Try THE or AND for a three-letter group. The code is different for each CryptoScripture.

1. LRN AI RHF SHRXHBOIN FH
FTKY JHBWN: AMF AI PI
FBLRYXHBOIN AP FTI BIRIJKRC
HX PHMB OKRN, FTLF PI OLP
QBHDI JTLF KY FTLF CHHN, LRN
LSSIQFLAWI, LRN QIBXISF, JKWW
HX CHN.

2. VJK V HZXRP RVYP ZNE ZI EBP
EBLZJP, WVGXJO, SLVXWP ZNL
OZK, VMM GP BXW WPLHVJEW,
VJK GP EBVE IPVL BXY, DZEB
WYVMM VJK OLPVE.

3. MZC VOCFEZC YUOCF OC OL
OPNELLOMWI CE NWIULI FOP: YEH
FI CFUC DEPICF CE RET PZLC
MIWOIGI CFUC FI OL, UST CFUC
FI OL U HIVUHTIH EY CFIP
CFUC TOWORISCWQ LIIA FOP.

4. LQTUYV, ZTQ YUPV'G THOV WG
   OUZ GTUPZQOQV, ZTHZ WZ
   FHOOUZ GHMQ; OQWZTQP TWG
   QHP TQHMX, ZTHZ WZ FHOOUZ
   TQHP.

5. T YTE, DBTQ WUD SZ YTE;
   VWUFZ MRFF R KVVX DBVV: SZ
   KTQF DBRUKDVDB JTU DBVV, SZ
   JFVKB FTAYVDB JTU DBVV RA W
   EUZ WAE DBRUKDZ FWAE,
   MBVUV AT MWDVU RK.

6. QRUJNRZ ANIFJ JNHC FUR EUJN
   IQG PRIAJ JH VRYUFR JNGARFY
   JNRZREUJN: QRUJNRZ ANIFF IQG
   EHSIQ AJIQV PRYHZR I PRIAJ
   JH FUR VHEQ JNRZRJH: UJ UA
   DHQYCAUHQ.

7. SGGJ QGD TKTHB XIQ GQ CYV GAQ DCYQWV, UND TKTHB XIQ ISVG GQ DCT DCYQWV GM GDCTHV.

8. VYC QAOY UOBZB AVC TPEOC QEJA V XGZC FGETO, AO BVEC, HVJAOP, EYJG JAN AVYCB E TGWWOYC WN BSEPEJ: VYC AVFEYR BVEC JAZB, AO RVFO ZS JAO RAGBJ.

9. IDB BEB IDXI LPFTBID XI DYA OXIDBQ, XWR RBAGYABID IP PJBE DYA LPIDBQ, IDB QXSBWA PO IDB SXZZBE ADXZZ GYFT YI PNI, XWR IDB EPNWU BXUZBA ADXZZ BXI YI.

10. MTNS AJHV HFS KVPI HFS
    MKVPG IAS AJHV FTZ JQYS:
    WPTJM QJ VDDSPTJM, QJI OVYS
    WSDVPS FTY: BVPZFTE HFS
    KVPI TJ HFS WSQAHG VD
    FVKTJSZZ.

11. UFZ WRZ WUDG ORTRNRF
    QLOZRN UFZ VFZGKOYUFZLFW
    GMPGGZLFW NVPX, UFZ
    TUKWGFGOO RE XGUKY, GDGF
    UO YXG OUFZ YXUY LO RF
    YXG OGU OXRKG.

12. U BCA QPNI HAXNOC BCA
    CAXNB, U BNK BCA NAUSH,
    AGAS BP TUGA AGANK VXS
    XOOPNIUST BP CUH YXKH, XSI
    XOOPNIUST BP BCA ZNLUB PZ
    CUH IPUSTH.

13. JIT JIOTC PFRTJI XFJ, KWJ CFG
JF ZJTSV, SXH JF DOVV, SXH JF
HTZJGFA: O SR PFRT JISJ JITA
ROYIJ ISBT VOCT, SXH JISJ JITA
ROYIJ ISBT OJ RFGT
SKWXHSXJVA.

14. WHN BSM STXGQRE KX BSM
SMQE HW BSM ZKWM, MLMR
QX OSNKXB KX BSM SMQE HW
BSM OSTNOS: QRE SM KX BSM
XQLKHTN HW BSM GHEV.

15. CKW SII XNSX OD OJ XNB
PKWIA, XNB IEDX KC XNB
CIBDN, SJA XNB IEDX KC XNB
BRBD, SJA XNB LWOAB KC IOCB,
OD JKX KC XNB CSXNBW, TEX
OD KC XNB PKWIA.

16. ZO QPGDD, YXR EXWI PLYP G
    YC MWR: G IGDD ZO OHYDPOR
    YCWXM PLO LOYPLOX, G IGDD
    ZO OHYDPOR GX PLO OYTPL.

17. LO PLYP GQ QDWI PW YXMOT
    GQ ZOPPOT PLYX PLO CGMLPB;
    YXA LO PLYP TFDOPL LGQ
    QHGTGP PLYX LO PLYP
    PYROPL Y JGPB.

18. IZPNP DEPLZTZA, MZTJGR, MZTJGR,
    J PDR NEOW OKZZ, ZSBZVO D
    FDE CZ CWTE WY LDOZT DEA
    WY OKZ PVJTJO, KZ BDEEWO
    ZEOZT JEOW OKZ HJEXAWF WY
    XWA.

19. SJPAAPQ LA BMP ITU BMTB
PUQCYPBM BPIWBTBLVU: OVY
EMPU MP LA BYLPQ, MP AMTJJ
YPRPLDP BMP RYVEU VO JLOP,
EMLRM BMP JVYQ MTBM
WYVILAPQ BV BMPI BMTB JVDP
MLI.

20. GXY XEYD TDX YMFY KJFA RT
EFRJ ZMFQQ YMJ ZXE DK
ANLMYJDXZEJZZ FANZJ VNYM
MJFQNEL NE MNZ VNELZ; FEI
TJ ZMFQQ LD KDAYM, FEI LADV
XC FZ HFQWJZ DK YMJ ZYFQQ.

21. MDL UDP XCTB TDB RFX XDT
FTBD BRC ZDLHP BD WDTPCVT
BRC ZDLHP; EIB BRQB BRC
ZDLHP BRLDIUR RFV VFURB EC
XQNCP.

22. CDAN ZDRHC MAC CRXB CDB
MRUB AJ CDB HAVQ CDT WAQ
OM EROM; JAV CDB HAVQ YOHH
MAC DAHQ DOU WNOHCHBZZ
CDRC CRXBCD DOZ MRUB OM
EROM.

23. GRF ENPVP GVZCP RZE G
AVZANPE CDRBP DR DCVGPI
IDXP MREZ TZCPC, KNZT ENP
IZVF XRPK LGBP EZ LGBP.

24. OLN DMW PTSN YMOPP
NWPUGWS CW HSTC WGWSV
WGUP ITSX, OLN IUPP ESWYWSGW
CW ZLDT MUY MWOGWLPV
XULRNTC: DT IMTC FW RPTSV
HTS WGWS OLN WGWS. OCWL.

25. YS BOAI DATNGYA BOSG NHB
UGZAENHR, NIJ IAWBOAH TSUJ
ISH OSB, W EWUU YXAE BOAA
SGB SQ RL RSGBO.

26. KTI TWY YVZ FKXXLUQF FVWN?
KXLQU, KTI EU EKDFLMUI, KTI
YKQV KYKZ FVZ QLTQ, PKGGLTO
WT FVU TKSU WC FVU GWXI.

27. IZ NSRWW BCWCJZXYWI VZZF
YSZ OQEERXBEZXYN QG YSZ
WQAB IQHA JQB, RXB SCN
YZNYCEQXCZN, RXB SCN
NYRYHYZN, DSCOS SZ SRYS
OQEERXBZB YSZZ.

28. ERPQ YILB XSI PEBC, LRC
KIBMI SVF VR XBHXS TVXS LPP
QEHB SILBX: YEB OERKVCIB SET
DBILX XSVRDK SI SLXS CERI
YEB QEH.

29. TYDYKVPYZYBB CSK VPI UKYGV
QYKALYB' BGEY VPSH JLJBV TSV
HVVYKZI ASTBHQY VPYQ, TSK
CSKBGEY VPYQ; CSK VPSH GKV
G UKGALSHB GTJ QYKALCHZ
USJ.

30. FSB MT GSIM EDFE FYY
EDLSQZ MICG EIQTEDTC JIC
QIIB EI EDTN EDFE YIAT QIB,
EI EDTN MDI FCT EDT VFYYTB
FVVICBLSQ EI DLZ KPCKIZT.

31. KW QUPWZEH ZYP DYRBSDI;
KER SD WNWPG RBSDI KG
CPUGWP UDF JECCHSQURSYD
LSRB RBUDXJISNSDI HWR GYEP
PWVEWJRJ KW TUFW XDYLD
EDRY IYF.

32. ERYRNZ NH TMOR, ZMP PEGP
KR TMORC XMC, LBP PEGP ER
TMORC BH, GZC HRZP ENH
HMZ PM LR PER VYMVNPNGPNMZ
JMY MBY HNZH.

33. EAV WF XEGV QI QWFH ERR,
GY EAO HEA JGRR PIHF EYQFB
HF, RFQ WGH VFAO WGHXFRY,
EAV QENF DM WGX PBIXX
VEGRO, EAV YIRRIJ HF.

34. CAL XWP IGTL YGL VCRL ZAXG
XWP QGDCA, QWCX RV XWRV
XWCX XWGZ WCVX LGAP? CAL
XWP QGDCA VCRL, XWP VPTJPAX
EPYZRIPL DP, CAL R LRL PCX.

35. NIS AKNISDH HIKUU JXN GS
ZEN NX OSKNI AXD NIS
VIQUODSJ, JSQNISD HIKUU NIS
VIQUODSJ GS ZEN NX OSKNI
AXD NIS AKNISDH: STSDF CKJ
HIKUU GS ZEN NX OSKNI AXD
IQH XRJ HQJ.

36. Q CQDD AUOQGX VNXX; KYU
Q OS KXOUKLDDM OHW
CYHWXUKLDDM SOWX:
SOURXDYLG OUX VNM CYUZG;
OHW VNOV SM GYLD ZHYCXVN
UQBNV CXDD.

37. VUP NLLJPNVBJAM BFJ VUQJA IX
BFJ AIKP WLIBJ FNL, DJZVEWJ
FJ QVGJ UIB QIP BFJ QAIKM:
VUP FJ OVW JVBJU IX OIKLW,
VUP QVGJ EC BFJ QFIWB.

38. JDY BGZ AZQUDFP DJ DXY
AQYJQYZ QYZ FDB OQYFQH, EXB
TVRGBN BGYDXRG RDC BD BGZ
UXHHVFR CDAF DJ PBYDFR
GDHCP.

39. AU MANM DYRUEUMA AJI IJHI
IANOO HYM VEYIVUE: TBM
XAYIY DYHWUIIUMA NHL
WYEINCUMA MAUG IANOO ANRU
GUEDS.

40. SOQ XW LVVP KYWSQ, SOQ BSRW
LXSOPG, SOQ KYSPW HL, SOQ
BSRW COLV LXWJ, GSEHOB,
LXHG HG JE KVQE IXHFX HG
BHRWO NVY EVC: LXHG QV HO
YWJWJKYSOFW VN JW.

41. RI YE LBXPJQ'Z PKVZJ BQJ YBIE
YBIZRKIZ: RL RX AJQJ IKX ZK,
R AKVWH PBTJ XKWH EKV. R
NK XK MQJMBQJ B MWBFJ LKQ
EKV.

42. APZ RFX XHXW PA RFX YPZS
ZKE RP DES AZP RFZPKNFPKR
RFX UFPYX XDZRF, RP WFPU
FTGWXYA WRZPEN TE RFX
QXFDYA PA RFXG UFPWX FXDZR
TW VXZAXLR RPUDZS FTG.

43. NSK   FWJ   CRTNS   MNOJ   N   GRS,
    NSK   LNUUJK   WXG   SNTJ   GNTGRS:
    NSK   FWJ   LWXUK   HOJC,   NSK
    FWJ   UROK   MUJGGJK   WXT.

44. EU   ET   NR   UVH   WNIK'T   ZHILEHT
    UVPU   CH   PIH   QNU   LNQTGZHK,
    OHLPGTH   VET   LNZMPTTENQT
    RPEW   QNU.   UVHX   PIH   QHC
    HFHIX   ZNIQEQS: SIHPU   ET   UVX
    RPEUVRGWQHTT.

45. YWF   PKNJ   TVWWUI   EW   LYRLPT
    RSFI   QJLUW,   TWLTKXWM   RSFI
    TLYF,   FILF   PW   GLP   OXKR   IKR
    PW   KNQIF   FK   LXTRWJ   WBWJP
    GLX.

46. CORARQXAR URNWP MDBCNQNRS
UH QVNCO, FR OVER YRVTR
FNCO PXS COAXDPO XDA
KXAS MRBDB TOANBC.

47. SXDBD DJTY BICH UXE, T JP
CUX EXDBEEXZCTHI, JIY CUX
QTWX: UX CUJC KXQTXAXCU
TI PX, CUHBVU UX LXEX YXJY,
NXC DUJQQ UX QTAX.

48. YKJBAOO RKVN BWVHPO KJA PK
WJKPDAN, WJZ LNWR KJA BKN
WJKPDAN, PDWP RA IWR XA
DAWHAZ. PDA ABBAYPVWH
BANUAJP LNWRAN KB W
NECDPAKVO IWJ WUWEHAPD
IVYD.

49. OFH MR SNT ANF, AQ HGNFEGH
    QXUC MEMUPRH ZQ: OFH ENK
    ZQMPH UH FPHN ENNK, HN
    OTUPE HN LMRR, MR UH UR
    HGUR KMA, HN RMXQ ZFIG
    LQNLCQ MCUXQ.

50. YXS VG WFWZP NEFEXA DCEXA
    VG YNN GNWHC, DKV VG WFWZP
    HVZD HCYND DCVB UZEXA
    EXDV DCW YZL, DV LWWT DCWO
    YNEFW KEDC DCWW; DCWP
    HCYNN UW OYNW YXS GWOYNW.

51. KYZ WCR UQBZ NRYW X RAQBR
    WCRI XV ZKV MY K JMUUKB
    QA K EUQDZ, WQ URKZ WCRI
    WCR NKV; KYZ XV YMTCW MY
    K JMUUKB QA AMBR, WQ TMSR
    WCRI UMTCW; WQ TQ XV ZKV
    KYZ YMTCW.

52. HGK AIB AIHEE UZVGY OTZPI
H ATG, HGK PITJ AIHEP SHEE
IVA GHQB MBAJA: OTZ IB
AIHEE AHWB IVA LBTLEB OZTQ
PIBVZ AVGA.

53. SOQXK UTXIQYOXJ TI JNQL
ROPF JNQXK, JNWJ NO BNQUN
NWJN SOKMX W KTTY BTPA
QX FTM BQGG VOPITPE QJ
MXJQG JNO YWF TI COLML
UNPQLJ.

54. KVP OAOPN UPOZHDPO VK EVQ
CL EVVQ, ZYQ YVHBCYE HV WO
POKDLOQ, CK CH WO
POUOCAOQ FCHB HBZYILECACYE.

55. XVLF BS NIRN NIS ELCK IS UZ
QLK: UN UZ IS NIRN IRNI
WRKS JZ, RVK VLN FS
LJCZSEPSZ; FS RCS IUZ YSLYES,
RVK NIS ZISSY LA IUZ
YRZNJCS.

56. EHM KR YJC YVHDORO ZVS VHS
MSJDCFSRCCUVDC, KR YJC
ESHUCRO ZVS VHS UDUIHUMURC:
MKR TKJCMUCRXRDM VZ VHS
NRJTR YJC HNVD KUX; JDO
YUMK KUC CMSUNRC YR JSR
KRJGRO.

57. TU CGB HTWJ QX GTO CGLC
GLCG MUVBPJCLUVTUR DTJVQO
TJ XQMUV: FMC L PQV TJ XQP
CGB FLKZ QX GTO CGLC TJ
SQTV QX MUVBPJCLUVTUR.

58. KIPR QMTW MRBXPZPL, XIMK
HPMR FP KC XPPQ MRL KC
DZPME HSRP IPMZK? ACZ S MH
ZPMLF RCK KC DP DCTRL
CRWF, DTK MWBC KC LSP MK
NPZTBMWPH ACZ KIP RMHP CA
KIP WCZL NPBTB.

59. WFY QT JZR ZWFY DTTHFY JZHH,
KBJ QJ DTT: QJ QN PHJJHC TDC
JZHH JD HFJHC QFJD AQTH
VWQVHY, JZWF ZWUQFE JGD
ZWFYN JD ED QFJD ZHAA, QFJD
JZH TQCH JZWJ FHUHC NZWAA
PH XBHFKZHY.

60. HJQL? SFWH TV FWL LJQL TWNE
XWMT YU LJV LVIOBV WZ LJV
JWBT DJWUL HJYGJ YU YF TWN,
HJYGJ TV JQCV WZ DWM, QFM
TV QEV FWL TWNE WHF?

61. YRWQ NOQZQEPZQ NOS
AQZWGDN GD IDMQZANGDMRDY
OQGZN NP HIMYQ NOS JQPJXQ,
NOGN R KGS MRABQZD
UQNCQQD YPPM GDM UGM:
EPZ COP RA GUXQ NP HIMYQ
NORA NOS AP YZQGN G JQPJXQ?

62. AWERBJ ZBE XRPJQ GXBYE WFH
ZJXC JX NXPBC QW YXRPC, BCH
JX YXRPCXH RC AXYKEBFXT
WCX BCH QJRYQG GXBYE.

63. RNE TRR EYN NTOEY WNTO EYN
RMOF: RNE TRR EYN
HUYTLHETUEX MW EYN QMORF
XETUF HU TQN MW YHJ.

64. EKF YCQKQ QPDO, QKVVCB
UDFFUC JXDUOBCH, PHO
VRBEDO FXCG HRF, FR JRGC
KHFR GC: VRB RV QKJX DQ
FXC MDHLORG RV XCPSCH.

65. IDZ RYVZV MC DWV FDP, QWP
DWV UVPMQRDZ KVRNVVW FDP
QWP UVW, RYV UQW EYZMCR
AVCLC.

66. EGK MXDQ RXSUGQYJKTXS ZG
HTKBXDK RXUGKXDYSGYY; JSW
ZG RXSKGSK HTKB YDRB
KBTSVY JY MG BJUG: OXQ BG
BJKB YJTW, T HTEE SGUGQ
EGJUG KBGG, SXQ OXQYJNG
KBGG.

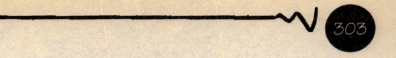

67. HKB WJB UHBY MDY LVQUHUYKM,
HKB BVIVBYB MDY XHMYQG
XDVPD XYQY CKBYQ MDY
LVQUHUYKM LQJU MDY XHMYQG
XDVPD XYQY HRJIY MDY
LVQUHUYKM: HKB VM XHG GJ.

68. SAL INR JWQY ZGRU: SAL RYSM
USY S FMAAHAZ NMAIRG, S PSA
WB INR BHRXL; SAL TSFWJ USY
S KXSHA PSA, LURXXHAZ HA
IRAIY.

69. GE VBDL PUDFHEV UDV FBGV
TE VBH FGM DX VBH EQTYTV,
UDY BDF VBH NDUHE SD OYDF
TU VBH FDJN DX BHY VBGV TE
FTVB ABTCS: HRHU ED VBDL
PUDFHEV UDV VBH FDYPE DX
ODS FBD JGPHVB GCC.

70. NLWGZF, EWGK HAE SHBA, UI
ZGOL; NLWGZF, EWGK HAE SHBA;
EWGK WHYE FGOLY' LILY
CBEWBQ EWI ZGRJY: EWI WHBA
BY HY H SZGRJ GS DGHEY,
EWHE HMMLHA SAGU UGKQE
DBZLHF.

71. ETR BNU MUWWUA BNEB NU
VERU QI LAEH JEW VEYYUR CT
BNU NETR QI BNU DQBBUY: WQ
NU VERU CB EXECT ETQBNUY
MUWWUA, EW WUUVUR XQQR BQ
BNU DQBBUY BQ VEOU CB.

72. QPWUHM PWEIHLHQ PWQ EPUQ,
KMHEEHQ KH VJH WPSH AO
BAQ OAL HRHL PWQ HRHL: OAL
IUEQAS PWQ SUBJV PLH JUE.

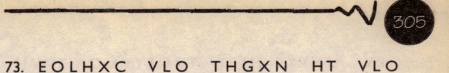

73. EOLHXC VLO THGXN HT VLO
ZBU: THU VLOA NHG YHV,
YOBVLOU CH VLOA UOZR, YHU
IZVLOU BYVH EZUYN; AOV AHFU
LOZKOYXA TZVLOU TOOCOVL
VLOS. ZUO AO YHV SFML
EOVVOU VLZY VLOA?

74. ZGUIU LW MULZGUI BUJ MYI
QIUUV, ZGUIU LW MULZGUI
FYMA MYI XIUU, ZGUIU LW
MULZGUI RPHU MYI XURPHU:
XYI EU PIU PHH YMU LM
KGILWZ BUWDW.

75. EIW GIBWNQASQN POIX
RQWEQVHAG HZLH HZQ KLG IE
HZQ AIWK NI VITQHZ LN L
HZJQE JO HZQ OJUZH.

76. GBV UNVY MYO TVUTYVUO MWH
MUYVR RB HUUZ RMU SYP BG
RMU SBVO, YXO RB OB WR, YXO
RB RUYIM WX WHVYUS HRYRJRUH
YXO DJOKFUXRH.

77. YPCV VUEYP YPX QZIJ LZJ; GZX
CRYZ YPX BZZQEVP DIZDPXYV,
YPUY BZQQZG YPXEI ZGR
VDEIEY, URJ PUOX VXXR RZYPERL!

78. RWM AQHW RRCUW RWM RVV
NQH FQKVMCHW UT KXCRHV
XRA IUXHX, YHQUVM, NQH
XDKW UT QKX TRFH XQUWH;
RWM NQHP AHCH RTCRKM
NU FUIH WKBQ QKI.

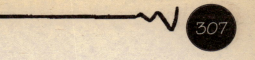

79. RIV MJZH EJRCM CZXL MJL
CZUV MJK YZV BTMJ RCC MJTIL
JLRUM, RIV BTMJ RCC MJK EZHC,
RIV BTMJ RCC MJK OTYJM.

80. RMX XNDNVVUMG UF TF QYN
FUG MR OUQLYLXTRQ, TGJ
FQKDDMXGGNFF UF TF
UGUCKUQI TGJ UJMVTQXI.

81. T JSWL S BLNZLL, KFSK TV
LOLZD BIJTVTIV IY JD WTVQBIJ
JLV KZLJHPL SVB YLSZ HLYIZL
KFL QIB IY BSVTLP: YIZ FL TM
KFL PTOTVQ QIB.

82. UGP DT FURP KGWV WDTL, WUIT
DTTP, UGP MTQUOT VH
BVCTWVKFGTFF: HVO U LUG'F
ZRHT BVGFRFWTWD GVW RG
WDT UMKGPUGBT VH WDT
WDRGXF QDRBD DT SVFFTFFTWD.

83. S XO RMH KSYH, IH XLH RMH
QLXYWMHB: MH RMXR XQSZHRM
SY OH, XYZ S SY MSO, RMH
BXOH QLSYFHRM NALRM OGWM
NLGSR: NAL ESRMAGR OH IH
WXY ZA YARMSYF.

84. EGJ NMRN ZRJO NMO LGSUJ
RQJ RUU NMCQED NMOSOCQ,
DOOCQE NMRN MO CD UGSJ
GW MORFOQ RQJ ORSNM,
JLOUUONM QGN CQ NOZYUOD
ZRJO LCNM MRQJD.

85. IQJ LZO EZSSYKOYJB BNA WZCY JZXUVO QA, NK JBUJ, XBNWY XY XYVY HYJ ANKKYVA, EBVNAJ ONYO DZV QA.

86. BKANAMENA, RZ XAIETAS XNABKNAG, XA ZA WBASMFWB, HGRETAFXIA, FIDFZW FXEHGSQGU QG BKA DENV EM BKA IENS, MENFWRHOK FW ZA VGED BKFB ZEHN IFXEHN QW GEB QG TFQG QG BKA IENS.

87. ZXROYXK YVGX R CQZX NVJT PKQU OYX JQUUVZFUXZO QP YRE ARDE; R YVGX XEOXXUXF OYX MQKFE QP YRE UQIOY UQKX OYVZ US ZXJXEEVKS PQQF.

88. L DGBKTFTN YFHLU GN L PBFYU
KF ZOB ZTNCLUJ: CTK NZO
KZLK HLAOKZ LNZLHOJ GN LN
BFKKOUUONN GU ZGN CFUON.

89. LJC HTQ, T UTMI, CKTJ PMC TJM
ZPCKNM; QN PMN CKN SUPV,
PHI CKTJ TJM DTCCNM; PHI QN
PUU PMN CKN QTMO TZ CKV
KPHI.

90. EQ KREQZ, EQ MUCUWOHP;
EQYOFKQ TRFZ OGMQZKOZT
PNQ GQMUW, OK O ZROZUHC
WURH, XOWSQPN OERFP,
KQQSUHC XNRA NQ AOT
GQMRFZ.

Spotty Headline Puzzles

by Sara Stoker

Fill in the missing letters of each "headline," which relates to a Bible story. Then unscramble the letters you've added to the headline to form a name which is the object of the headline.

NEW TESTAMENT HEADLINES

ASTUTE DOCTOR WRITES
TWO BOOKS OF THE BIBLE

LUKE

BABY JESUS MENTIONED BY
ELDERLY JERUSALEM
TEMPLE LADY TO ALL

ANNA

FAVORITE DISCIPLE
SEES WARRING END TIMES
IN HIS VISION

John

4.

LASU

MAN BOINDED WHILE TROVELING TO PEROECOTE CHRISTIANS

Saul

5.

TEREP

INNOCENO MAN FROED FROM CHAINS AND POISON BY ANSWORED ORAYER

Peter

6.

P · S N

ORIMARY CHRIOTIAO MARTYR SOONOD TO DOATO

T E E XT

Stephen

7.

PHAR●SEE US●S ●EANS OF
RE●SONIN● TO SP●RE
APOST●ES ●IVES

Iemagall Gamaliel

8.

PERS●N BRINGS TO ●IGHT
THE D●STRUCTIVE DIVISIONS
IN A COUR●H

Chloe

9.

M●N S●RVIVES
TERRIB●E SHIPWRECK
AND VI●ER BITE

10.

**ONLY BEING THAT
COMBINE● ●U●T DI●TY
WITH H●MANITY**

11.

**EV●L QUEEN
●EM●NDS EX●CUTION ●F
●IG●TEOU● BAPTIZER**

12.

**D●VOUT MAN
REC●G●IZES BABY AS
THE PRO●I●ED MESS●AH**

13.

RESPEC●ABLE ●ER●ON
●APOIZED ●IS C●USI●
IN ●●E ●ORD●N R●V●R

14.

WRITING ●ETTERS
CONTIN●ES BY
UND●UNTED ●RISONER

15.

DOUB●ING FI●H●●●AN
●ULLS IN ●NOUGH F●SH
TO SI●K B●AT

16.

**●OUNG ●AN
S●RUGGLES T● PAS●OR
FLEDG●NG C●URCH**

17.

**R●NAWAY ●LAV● BEC●●ES
A CHRI●T●A●**

18.

**●ONGU● OF FI●E
SAT U●ON SUDD●NLY
MULTILINGUAL MAN**

19.

CHRISTI●● ●ELIEVED TO ●E
ORDE●ED TO ●CCOMP●NY
EX-PERSECUTOR OF CHRI●TIANS

20.

●ULER SLAUG●TERE● ALL
MALE BABIES IN H●PE OF
●LIMINATING FUTURE KING

21.

●BSENT ●AN D●UB●S
RE●URRECTION T●EORY

22.

MAN DEAD FO● FO●R D●YS
COME● B●CK TO ●IFE
WITH ●EST

23.

●URI●US PHAR●S●E SEEKS
TO●GH AN●WERS IN
●ID●LE OF ●IGHT

24.

F●ITHFUL MAN
●ENER●●SLY HELP●
FELLOW BEL●EVERS

25.

**B●AV● MAN ATTEM●TS ●O
WALK ON WAT●R**

26.

**OV●R FIVE THO●●AND
PEOPLE ARE FED
BY ●U●T MAN**

27.

**A●ROGAN● ●OMINE●RING
MAN REJ●CT●
A●OST●LIC AUT●OR●TY**

28.

ONL● VIRGIN WO●AN
EVER TO GIVE BI●TH
TO B●BY SON

29.

●●EATLY DE●ON-POSS●SSED
WO●A● IS FIN●LL● H●ALED
●ND C●E●NE●

30.

●AREFUL MOTH●R
UNKNOWINGLY PR●PARES SO●
FOR F●TURE MIN●STRY

31.

TR●STED FRIEN●
BETR●Y● ●UST MAN

32.

KING ●PP●RENTLY
LISTENS TO ●RISONE●'S
●RIP●ING TEST●MONY

33.

MA● COMM●●DED TO
B●PT●ZE ●N EX-PER●ECUTOR

34.

MAN WONDERS HOW
BOY'S LUNCH WILL FEED
A CROWD

35.

ANOTHER PLANS FOR
WELL-BEING OF
DISCIPLE BROTHERS

36.

WOMAN DOES INSTANTLY
FOR LYING INCOME AND
KEEPING PART OF PROCEEDS

37.

MAN HOPELESSLY TRIES TO
ERASE BLAME WITH
HAND WASHING

38.

JESUS CALLED
TAX COLLECTOR TO
FOLLOW HIM

39.

SHORT TAX COLLECTOR
HAS RESTFULLY RETURNED
STOLEN GOODS

40.

RULER M●S●●KES JE●US FOR
DE●D ●RISO●ER

41.

●AN IN CROWD
F●RCED TO HELP PR●●●O●ER
CARRY HIS CROSS

42.

JES●S ●●KES ●HE
●L●ND BEGG●● ●E●

43.

●U●T   MAN   T●   WED
●IS   ●REGNANT   FIANC●E

44.

AGGR●VATED   SISTER
●ORE   CONCERNED   ABOUT
CHO●ES   TH●N   WI●H   T●E   GUEST

45.

PERSECUTED   JEWISH   CHR●STI●N
FLEES   ITA●Y   ●●ICKLY   TO
ASSIST   ●POSTLE

46.

TIRE● MISS●●N●RIES
GRACIOUSL● HOUSED
BY WOMAN SE●LER

47.

MAN PROM●TED BY
UNSEEN HO●Y S●IRIT TO
W●TNESS TO AN ET●IOP●AN

48.

H●MBLE MAN WR●TES DOWN
●VERY WORD OF ●OMANS
WHILE APO●●LE DIC●ATES

49.

UN●UST ●INFUL MAN
COMMITS S●ICI●E RATHER THAN
●SK FOR FORGIVENESS

50.

AMID●T ●OYF●L THRONGS
HEAV●NLY KING RIDE● DONKEY
INTO EARTHLY CITY

51.

MAN SLICES OFF EA● OF
ARR●STING SOLDIER WI●H
SOLDI●R'S ●ERSONAL SWORD

52.

MAOSOVE EARTHQUOKE
FREES OESSER-KNOWN MAN
AND OTHERS FROM PRIOON

53.

FIRSO MAO IN ACOAIA
FINALLY BELIOVES IN
GOOOEL'S SOVING MEOSOGE

54.

MAN PROOEEDS TO
EPOESOS AND VERBALLO GAVE
APOSOLE'S OURRENT AFFAORO

55.

BAD PRISONER MAN
CHOSEN TO GO FREE
BY PUBLIC DEMAND

56.

PILATE BECOMES FRIENDS WITH
HATED ENEMY BECAUSE OF
COMMON PRISONER

57.

MAN CAREFULLY INSTRUCTED
IN HOW TO PROPERLY
START A CHURCH

58.

●ROMINENT MAN ●AS
DOC●OR FRI●ND ST●DY
C●RI●T●ANITY TH●ROUGH●Y

59.

R●LER DE●REE● A CENS●●
●O BE T●KEN TH●OU●HO●T
TH● V●●T L●ND

60.

DIETY BECOMES
R●QUIRED ●ACRIFICE FOR
●INFULLY UN●UST H●MANS

BIBLE QUOTATION PUZZLES

by G. Rebecca Shodin

Place the letters in each column into the preceding puzzle grid to form words. The letters may or may not fit into the grid in the same order in which they're given; black spaces indicate the ends of words. When a letter has been used, cross it off and do not use it again. When the grid has been properly filled in, you'll be able to read a Bible verse by scanning the lines of the grid from left to right.

1 John 5:5

C W H T T H T H O N
E O M A L D O U E E
I   I O E E H S V H R
   W F O J I D T S E
   H E R H O A S H T
   L I   T E S B U T
   A H   V E   T   B
   S T   G E
   O

1 John 2:17

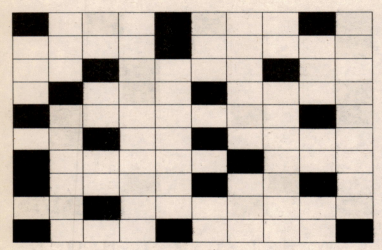

```
O  A  T  D  E  E  D  U  A  E
T  R  H  D  R  I  L  F  R  N
O  W  O  A  E  A  O  H  T  T
D  D  N  H  B  T  T  S  B
U  T  L  E  W  E  H  S  H
   F  O  H  L  H  A  E  E
   H  I  E  T  P  O  F  W
   D     L     A  Y  E  G
         A     Y     V  T
         R
```

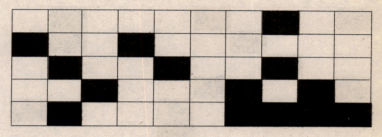

1 PETER 1:16

L	I	C	E	W	S	E	I	T	E
N	Y	H	F	U	R	I	T	I	O
M	E	B	A	L	Y	E		H	T
B		S	O	O	R				A
					R				
					Y				

1 Samuel 12:22

E F I F W T H L K L
G R F S O I L A P N
S T E O A R S O S E
T T H A S P E I M O
U O S S T E A I E P
L E H A K L O A H C
O U H E R E O E E A
O H O M R H H B D L
A R D I L E N S Y D
T P E I T R O E

PHILIPPIANS 1:6

F	I	D	I	N	S	T	N	O	N
T	H	H	L	N	H	A	F	C
R	H	I	I	T	B	E	S	Y	T
L	H	I	J	E	P	D	R	A	O
O	A	E	S	G	G	Y	H	H	I
H	A	I	I	W	T	E	C	U	N
R	F	L	E	O	V	D	D	W	O
H	R	E	S	N	O	U	R	U
T	B	T	H	T	O	U	C	F
W	I		N		U		O	T
	M		H				G	Y
	K		G					

PSALM 18:32

T	T	T	T	E	N	I	R	D	H
T	H	D	M	M	A	W	I	D	E
A	S	Y	C	S	G	G	E	T	E
I	N	A	I	W	A	Y	O	P	H
R	M	E	R	T	.	G	T	T	
	F			E		K		H	

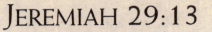

JEREMIAH 29:13

T L N D S Y H K S D
A Y L H D E E I A Y
E M A I T F E N N E
E A E N R H F A L M
A R S U A H L E S H
E   C H W L O R   M
      O   E   L R

PSALM 73:28

M	B	E	T	M	I	O	O	R	L
S	G	C	O	N	R	M	R	A	K
L	E	U	T	A	H	E	O	Y	W
H	N	O	L	Y	Y	D	O	A	G
D	D	R	H	D	G	T	T	E	S
L	U	T	I	O		A	H	R	U
S	T	T	I	R		W	V	R	T
O	O	T	D	I		T	A	I	
P	A		A			F	D	E	
	E					T			

COLOSSIANS 3:2

```
R    O    S    O    E    C    I    N    U    N
     A    F    E    V    H    T    O    G    S
     O    N    F    T    E    Y    O    E    A
     A    N         T    H    I    N    G    R
     O    H         T    I         N    O    T
     T    B                                  S
          N
```

ROMANS 8:5

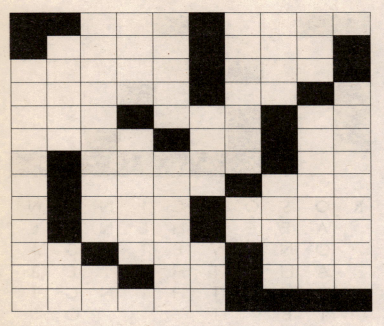

A L H A E O D T T I
F N E E E S E F T E
I G E R E Y F T B M
I F D R R F A H E H
E F A R T T S R E E
T G G R O E A E U
T S F H R T H P R
R I O O I H O A
I F T S T H T Y
N T S H H H
S F T H

PSALM 91:2

```
R   O   R   E   I   U   I   S   L   Y
Y   D   I   M   E   H   G   E   U   O
N   L   L   S   F   L   F   R   R   M
I   D   W   I   L   M   I   S   A   A
T   E   F   N   T   H   T   O   G   T
I       S   H   Y   H   E   M       O
R                       Y           W
D                                   S
```

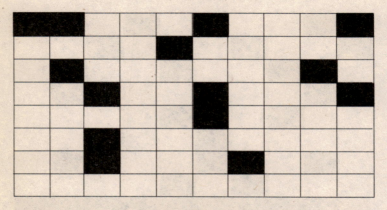

PROVERBS 2:6

L O U O N G O H E O
H H F T N D H V E G
U E S K A D D M N E
G O R O R N T I N T
E R W D F O I O M D
M T A S C L S D
T I H W U E
I I

ROMANS 8:37

```
S   U   T   N   L   L   N   G   O   D
W   O   E   A   H   I   H   M   O   E
E   H   S   T   R   E   O   V   T   N
R   N   U   A   O   L   S   T   H   H
T   E   A   H   H   R       I   S   R
I   U       R   A   N       C   M
Q   E       G   Y   Y           E
        T
```

1 Corinthians 10:31

H	W	R	K	E	V	R	R	A	T
E	O	E	O	F	D	O	E	W	Y
R	I	N	O	T	H	R	R	G	D
A	E	S	E	T	O	E	R		G
E	T	T	E		T	F	E		O
L		R	Y		O	E			Y
L		H	A		O	O			H
D		D				H			L

HEBREWS 11:1

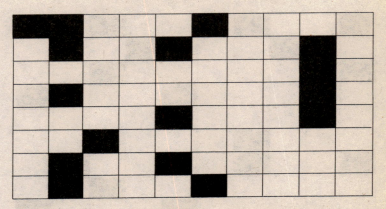

```
H    P    O    O    A    T    O    A    I    O
U    E    N    S    I    O    D    E    N    H
F    B    I    I    T    N    H    E    E    T
H         N    T    W    I    S    S         C
E         T    H    V    T    F    R         T
S         S    F         N    H    E         S
O         E    O         F    C    I         G
              D              G    E         N
              E
```

DANIEL 9:9

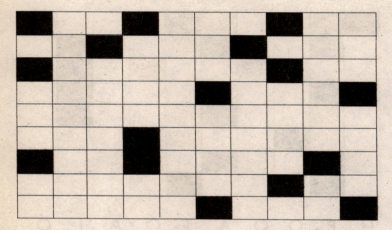

S	T	S	L	S	V	E	I	A	O
A	D	E	E	I	H	H	N	M	D
R	B	E	G	T	E	O	U	L	E
E	C	N	S	L	R	U	G	O	H
F	O	I	O	L	N	G	N	M	S
R	E	E	L	U	H	V	E	E	G
	W	R		H	A	A		G	R
	B	O		O	D	D		D	
	I			T		H			

1 JOHN 5:4

H I O R Y N W G T S
D T V E R H T M R B
D O N H E C E M I T
C F V E E H T O V T
O E T H E C T H R L
O R A V D C I H U T
H F S I T F W A E L
   O O R T W O S O S
      V E R O   O E D
      T N O   R
      E   R   I
      A

JAMES 2:26

O	B	R	S	O	S	S	I	T	H
I	U	O	I	T	L	F	S	S	P
A	R	T	D	A	I	W	A	D	D
H	A	R	K	Y	H	I	T	T	E
W	O	D	T	A	H	E	O	H	T
E	D	I		T		S	U	I	E
F	O	W		S		O			

JOHN 14:6

H W I Y I S H T N O
R U A H U T N E E T
T F B L N M O T B U
H J E N H A O M A I
M E A A T A R D H T
  M U S   F E S H E
  H T U   C   E
    A Y   O   E
      N   E
          M

PSALM 119:73

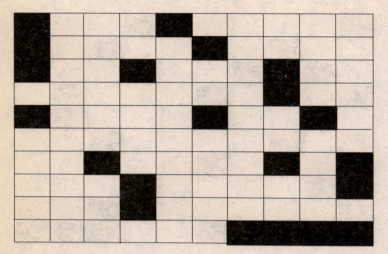

M T E O N O M A F S
S H I V A N M M S
T M I R C E T E I E
N N H E T S M N N A
N G Y V H A N R D N
D D H Y E E M D U E
G A N A M A A U
A Y L E H D I
M E T E D A
H

EPHESIANS 4:2

```
W    E    O    H    N    E    L    L    O    L
O    I    O    I    E    S    I    N    A
N    W    W    M    T    H    R    O    S
H    F    L    N    E    A    L    O    N
E    U    F    N    A    S    E    G
S    S    R    I    B    K    I    N
G         T    R    F    E    L    N         T
G                             L         V
```

PSALM 10:17

H	H	O	R	E	I	H	E	O	O
U	E	A	S	F	E	D	H	A	U
P	E	T	H	L	T	N	H	A	E
S	A	R	O	H	T	T	C	H	R
A	L	E	B	O	T	T	E	R	I
D	R	M	I	D	T	H	E	S	R
R	U	W	E	T		H	H	I	U
U	H	W	A	L			P	H	O
			I	R			E	A	E
			T	L			T		R
			T						

1 Corinthians 14:1

■						■		
	■		■					
	■			■				
		■						
							■	
								■
			■			■		
	■							

```
T    T  E    O    S    C    I    W    R    I    F
Y    L    R    G    D    F    A    E    S    T
R    T    P    L    I    O    D    I    T    I
Y    F    A    T    O    H    .    E    M    Y
A    E    A    N    P    P    T    E    S    B
U    H         R    A    Y    R    S    A    U
                  R    L         H    R    A
                       Y         E
                                 H
```

GALATIANS 3:28

N   I   E   R   R   R   S   F   E   K
N   N   T   E   H   G   R   L   E   S
O   T   O   T   O   E   O   C   B   M
I   E   E   N   I   E   A   U   R   R
M   L   E   H   J   R   I   E   I   O
A   A   L   I   E   R   E   I   L   N
E   S   A   E   T   H   R   S   H   W
E   H   H   R   N   O   E   J   S   Y
T   D   I   R   E   F   R   R   F   E
E   N   T   H   E   N   R   R   S   E
          T   E   E   N

JAMES 2:22

O H I T E S U G S M
T A W O E S K O W U H I D C
A W D R R F H E A N T E T
W U Y E K H W I R F A H
B A Y S F W O R T F H I
A S W P T S

PHILIPPIANS 4:13

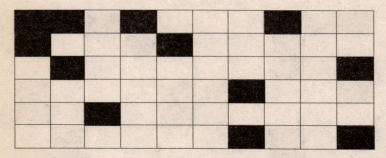

C   H   N   H   T   A   H   W   H   G
H   E   E   I   I   T   U   N   D   T
S   A   R   E   C   O   N   I   E   O
C   H   I   L   S   T   E   M   G   I
        T   S   R   R   G   N
                    H

JAMES 1:19

I L H R R E L O Y
R M Y T W T H R V W
D P B N T E V L E E
S T E A E R A T R A
W M A E K B F O S N
  F T L B A H E E
    S O W E T H
    E   O S E R
          E O
            E

PROVERBS 16:9

W	C	L	A	R	T	T	I	E	R
I	S	T	A	H	H	A	H	S	V
E	H	E	E	B	S	H	N	T	H
	A	Y	E	R	M		D	S	
		E	O	T	U		D	I	
			P	P	D			I	

PROVERBS 3:3

M	K	L	T	T	T	I	O	N	B
T	N	R	T	Y	R	P	E	D	A
A	O	U	T	H	U	N	M	E	H
I	F	R	C	W	H	A	L	T	S
B	A	U	M	T	A	F	E	E	N
E	E	K	T	H	I	N	Y	R	
T	R	E	E	T		E	O	E	
O	C	D	T			E	N		
E	H	E				H	T		
	H	E				B	O		

GALATIANS 6:9

A	A N	Y	O	E	N	G	E	W	S
L	R R	D	L	N	N	E	E	E	E
R	F	I	W	T	N	W	W	I	L
E	A	N	O	L	D	T	A	U	N
H	A	O	T	I	R	E	F	P	S
I	N	L	O	I	E	E		F	S
A		D	N	B	B	E			O
		S							

Philippians 3:14

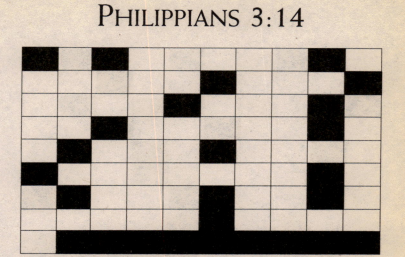

O C T R R F O S G O
M W I K D E Z H E H
H A A P R I H R S O
H R R H T I N E S U
S I A S E N S I T
F E G P R S I G T
F   L R   T N C
    O   J E

ROMANS 12:18

```
I    E    U    I    T         I    M         E    Y    P
U    F    T    I    B         E    A         P    E    S
U    S    L    C    L         L    E         W    I    L
O    M    S    H    L         Y    N         S    A    T
H    E    A    I    H              B         E    N    A
C         A    B    V                                  O
               L
```

JEREMIAH 17:7

W	H	L	R	I	T	A	D	D	I
S	T	T	S	D	N	H	A	P	T
T	L	A	E	E	S	O	U	S	E
I	T	H	H	S	L	M	T	D	E
E	S	O	T	E		R	N	H	
	B	O	E			E	O	N	
	H	O					R		

PSALM 32:11

E	U	A	O	A	E	L	R	R	O
I	N	E	O	I	S	L	A	D	G
D	C	E	Y	A	T	R	F	O	D
H	T	H	E	Y	G	H	L	J	Y
N	J	O	T	U	R	T	A	N	E
I	S	T	N	U	E		T	O	I
		P	H	H	A		L	I	R
		B	R	D	T		E		R
			E		G		A		

MARK 11:24

H I E E R Y F E R E
O E E S A W H O N T
S I T O U A Y U A T
Y T H H N G T E S O
L I E E R E A A D V
E Y V P E Y H H N D
E T H V S E W L B E
     V Y E R M S E A E
     Y E I E H E I T
     A R R T T C N
                     L
                     M

MARK 10:27

E	N	O	E	J	J	G	H	W	P
M	O	T	K	I	E	I	S	O	A
B	N	I	I	H	N	O	L	D	M
B	T	L	G	W	H	S	N	S	S
T	N	R	T	T	E	G	U	U	I
A	P	E	I	H	P	M	F	S	I
A	U	D	S	O	I	T	O	G	R
L	H	O		S	O	I		S	I
O	W	H		N	D	B		E	
I	L			O		T			
	A								
	L								

PROVERBS 24:28

```
W   B   N   N   T   B   T   Y   A   G
A   I   I   S   N   T   S   O   A   A
N   N   T   G   E   U   T   U   Y   E
C   E   E   V   O   O   O   H   T   L
U   P   T   H   A   S   D       C
W   E   I   H   O   N   O       D
W   I   T       H       H       R
I   I   T           O
    S   E           N
        S
```

Matthew 5:16

```
Y   E   H   I   G   O   M   U   O   R
H   S   E   E   N   O   U   O   A   T
L   N   D   E   T   L   I   F   Y   V
H   T   E   E   W   H   H   A   H   G
E   E   G   H   N   R   O   R   A   S
S   L   N   O   Y   Y   S   K   R   F
O   I   D   T   Y   B   E   R   S   T
I   I   Y   U       R   F   A
E   N   R   W       O   C
A   O   M           T   E
```

Psalm 86:2

```
O   O   R   Y   T   Y   S   M   O   U   T
L   L   Y   S   E   O   O   H   S   A   E
M   N   N   T   H   E   A   S   R   V   F
A   R   U   P   R   E   T   E   L   R   O
R   M   M   T   O   S   D   H   E   H   V
E   E   Y   H   G   T   H   U   T   I   N
        Y   T   I   E   T   A   I       V
                    E   A                N
```

PSALM 73:26

A	N	N	U	F	M	L	L	T	H
H	A	T	T	H	A	Y	O	E	E
I	S	G	T	O	P	I	S	E	T
E	N	H	E	H	R	O	F	D	I
Y	R	M	Y	A	R	E	V	A	R
D		M	F	D	E	G	E	S	M
O		B	D	Y	F	T	R	H	R
			Y			O		T	N

MATTHEW 11:28

```
E    E    E    E    E    D    L    A    T    O
 I    T    O    R    A    I    I    A    Y    E
  O    R    L    A    T    S    L    E    R    O
   R    H    H    A    N    L    T    I    A    W
       U    E    A    V    Y    V    L    B    Y
        C         A    G    D    U    N         E
         L                   N             D
          N                   E
```

Mark 9:23

I	V	J	U	E	L	S	O	T	O
M	N	S	F	T	T	H	E	S	A
C	E	I	S	A	V	B	A	H	I
B	A	L	I	S	L	L	T	U	H
I	D	N	M	N	A	R	E	L	I
O	S	E	I	B	U	E	U	T	P
E	H	I	E		T	H	L	T	
		G	S			E	T		

PSALM 119:80

E	T	S	L	A	I	B	T	T	S
O	N	O	R	T	T	N	M	E	H
H	D	A	D	T	A	U	E	A	M
Y	U	H	T	T	T	S	H	Y	E
	E	E	A	E	I	I		B	S
			T						

Proverbs 16:19

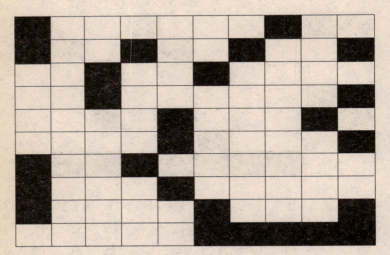

W	B	T	T	H	I	V	I	D	E
O	I	L	E	D	T	P	O	I	L
P	F	O	T	P	T	R	B	E	L
L	E	O	S	T	E	R	U	I	B
O	I	E	H	T	S	T	I	E	
	W	S	A	D	O	H	H	N	
	T	H	U	N	I	H	E	T	
	T	I	N		H	A	M		
	W		Y						
	R								

TELEPHONE SCRAMBLE PUZZLES

by Nancy Bernhard

Each set of telephone push-buttons contains a hidden Bible word—and you'll need to determine which letter of each push-button combination is part of the word.

ALTAR MAKERS

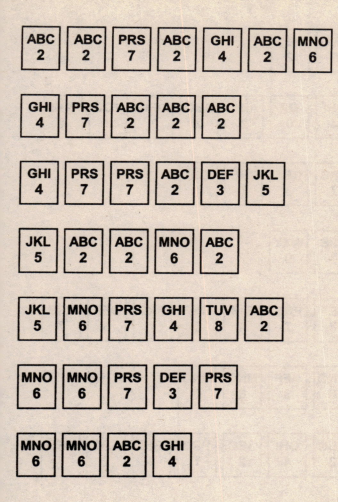

| ABC 2 | ABC 2 | PRS 7 | ABC 2 | GHI 4 | ABC 2 | MNO 6 |

| GHI 4 | PRS 7 | ABC 2 | ABC 2 | ABC 2 |

| GHI 4 | PRS 7 | PRS 7 | ABC 2 | DEF 3 | JKL 5 |

| JKL 5 | ABC 2 | ABC 2 | MNO 6 | ABC 2 |

| JKL 5 | MNO 6 | PRS 7 | GHI 4 | TUV 8 | ABC 2 |

| MNO 6 | MNO 6 | PRS 7 | DEF 3 | PRS 7 |

| MNO 6 | MNO 6 | ABC 2 | GHI 4 |

DIVINE REPORTS OF CHRIST'S BIRTH

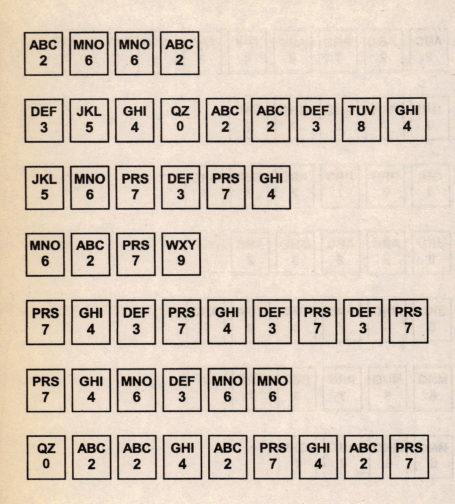

| ABC 2 | MNO 6 | MNO 6 | ABC 2 |

| DEF 3 | JKL 5 | GHI 4 | QZ 0 | ABC 2 | ABC 2 | DEF 3 | TUV 8 | GHI 4 |

| JKL 5 | MNO 6 | PRS 7 | DEF 3 | PRS 7 | GHI 4 |

| MNO 6 | ABC 2 | PRS 7 | WXY 9 |

| PRS 7 | GHI 4 | DEF 3 | PRS 7 | GHI 4 | DEF 3 | PRS 7 | DEF 3 | PRS 7 |

| PRS 7 | GHI 4 | MNO 6 | DEF 3 | MNO 6 | MNO 6 |

| QZ 0 | ABC 2 | ABC 2 | GHI 4 | ABC 2 | PRS 7 | GHI 4 | ABC 2 | PRS 7 |

PEOPLE OF THE NEW TESTAMENT

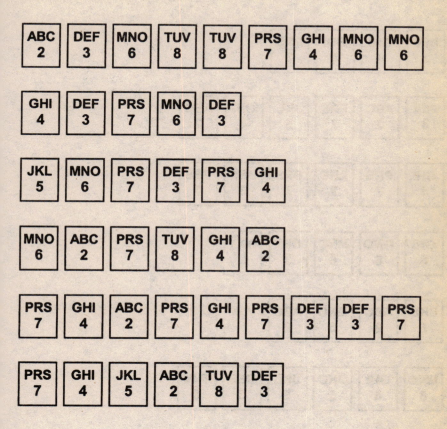

| ABC 2 | DEF 3 | MNO 6 | TUV 8 | TUV 8 | PRS 7 | GHI 4 | MNO 6 | MNO 6 |

| GHI 4 | DEF 3 | PRS 7 | MNO 6 | DEF 3 |

| JKL 5 | MNO 6 | PRS 7 | DEF 3 | PRS 7 | GHI 4 |

| MNO 6 | ABC 2 | PRS 7 | TUV 8 | GHI 4 | ABC 2 |

| PRS 7 | GHI 4 | ABC 2 | PRS 7 | GHI 4 | PRS 7 | DEF 3 | DEF 3 | PRS 7 |

| PRS 7 | GHI 4 | JKL 5 | ABC 2 | TUV 8 | DEF 3 |

FOODS IN THE OLD TESTAMENT

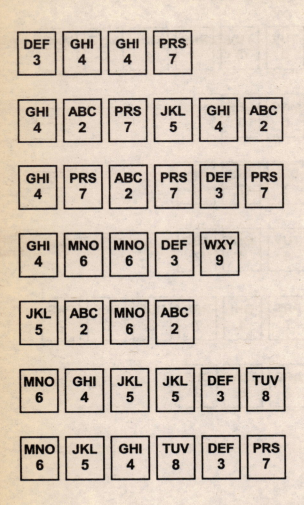

| DEF 3 | GHI 4 | GHI 4 | PRS 7 | | |

| GHI 4 | ABC 2 | PRS 7 | JKL 5 | GHI 4 | ABC 2 |

| GHI 4 | PRS 7 | ABC 2 | PRS 7 | DEF 3 | PRS 7 |

| GHI 4 | MNO 6 | MNO 6 | DEF 3 | WXY 9 | |

| JKL 5 | ABC 2 | MNO 6 | ABC 2 | | |

| MNO 6 | GHI 4 | JKL 5 | JKL 5 | DEF 3 | TUV 8 |

| MNO 6 | JKL 5 | GHI 4 | TUV 8 | DEF 3 | PRS 7 |

APOSTLES

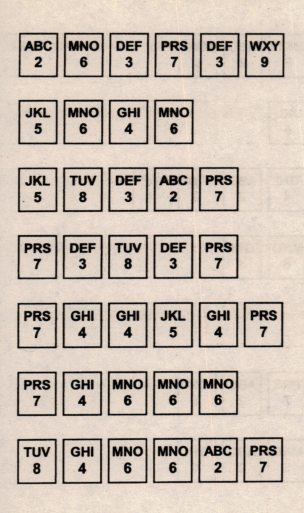

GIANTS

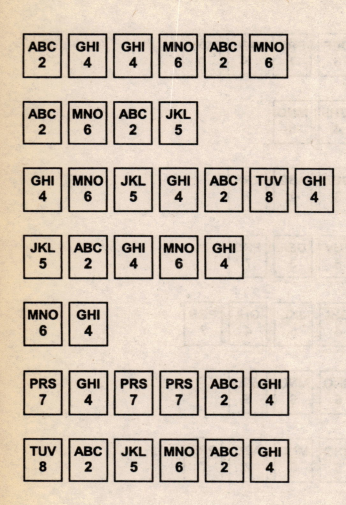

MUSICAL INSTRUMENTS

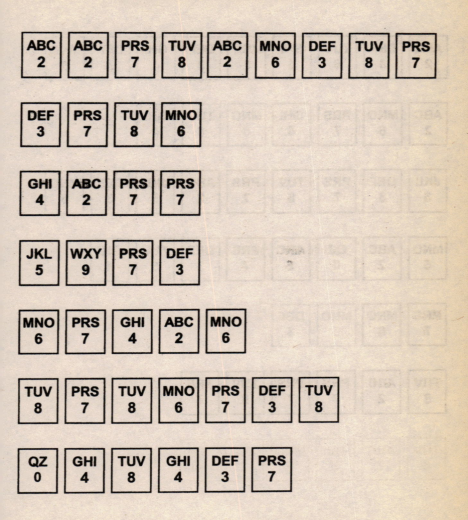

| ABC 2 | ABC 2 | PRS 7 | TUV 8 | ABC 2 | MNO 6 | DEF 3 | TUV 8 | PRS 7 |

| DEF 3 | PRS 7 | TUV 8 | MNO 6 |

| GHI 4 | ABC 2 | PRS 7 | PRS 7 |

| JKL 5 | WXY 9 | PRS 7 | DEF 3 |

| MNO 6 | PRS 7 | GHI 4 | ABC 2 | MNO 6 |

| TUV 8 | PRS 7 | TUV 8 | MNO 6 | PRS 7 | DEF 3 | TUV 8 |

| QZ 0 | GHI 4 | TUV 8 | GHI 4 | DEF 3 | PRS 7 |

Cities in the New Testament

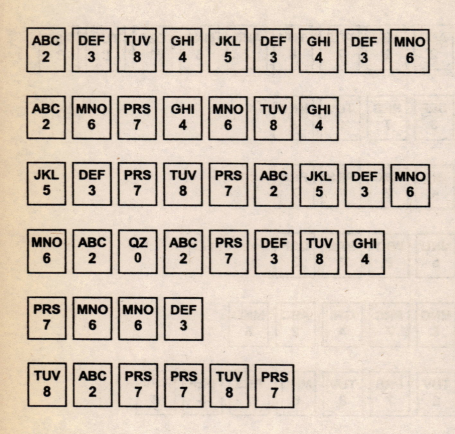

ABC 2	DEF 3	TUV 8	GHI 4	JKL 5	DEF 3	GHI 4	DEF 3	MNO 6
ABC 2	MNO 6	PRS 7	GHI 4	MNO 6	TUV 8	GHI 4		
JKL 5	DEF 3	PRS 7	TUV 8	PRS 7	ABC 2	JKL 5	DEF 3	MNO 6
MNO 6	ABC 2	QZ 0	ABC 2	PRS 7	DEF 3	TUV 8	GHI 4	
PRS 7	MNO 6	MNO 6	DEF 3					
TUV 8	ABC 2	PRS 7	PRS 7	TUV 8	PRS 7			

Conversions in the New Testament

ABC 2	ABC 2	MNO 6	ABC 2	ABC 2	MNO 6	GHI 4	TUV 8	DEF 3
ABC 2	DEF 3	MNO 6	TUV 8	TUV 8	PRS 7	GHI 4	MNO 6	MNO 6

JKL 5	DEF 3	PRS 7	DEF 3	PRS 7

MNO 6	ABC 2	PRS 7	TUV 8	GHI 4	ABC 2

PRS 7	ABC 2	TUV 8	JKL 5

PRS 7	TUV 8	ABC 2	JKL 5	GHI 4	ABC 2	ABC 2	MNO 6

PRS 7	ABC 2	MNO 6	ABC 2	PRS 7	GHI 4	TUV 8	ABC 2	MNO 6

NAMES FOR CHRIST

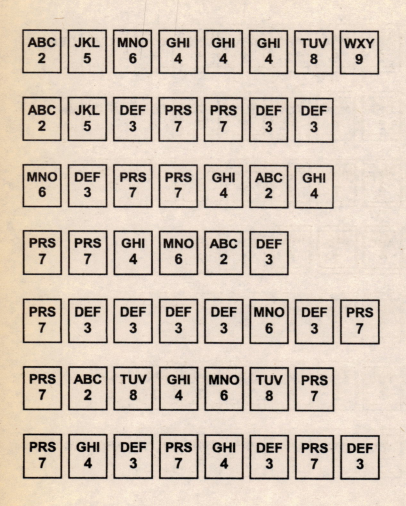

CITIES IN THE OLD TESTAMENT

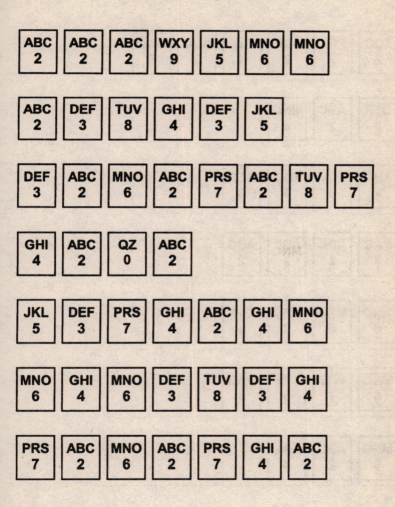

ABC 2	ABC 2	ABC 2	WXY 9	JKL 5	MNO 6	MNO 6
ABC 2	DEF 3	TUV 8	GHI 4	DEF 3	JKL 5	
DEF 3	ABC 2	MNO 6	ABC 2	PRS 7	ABC 2	TUV 8	PRS 7
GHI 4	ABC 2	QZ 0	ABC 2			
JKL 5	DEF 3	PRS 7	GHI 4	ABC 2	GHI 4	MNO 6
MNO 6	GHI 4	MNO 6	DEF 3	TUV 8	DEF 3	GHI 4
PRS 7	ABC 2	MNO 6	ABC 2	PRS 7	GHI 4	ABC 2

CHRIST FIGURES IN THE OLD TESTAMENT

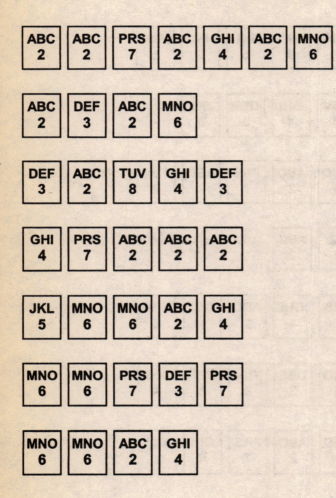

GOD IS. . .

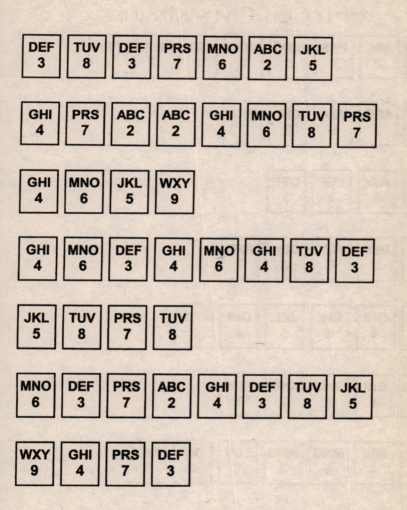

New Testament People with God-Given Missions

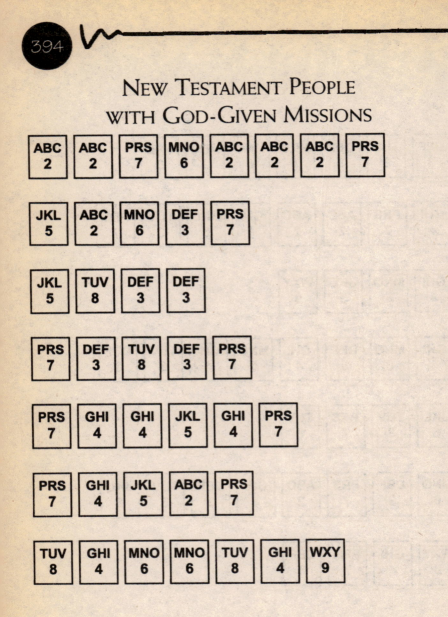

BOOKS OF THE NEW TESTAMENT

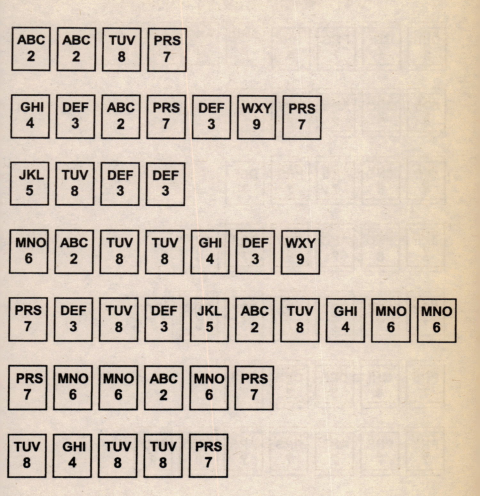

| ABC 2 | ABC 2 | TUV 8 | PRS 7 |

| GHI 4 | DEF 3 | ABC 2 | PRS 7 | DEF 3 | WXY 9 | PRS 7 |

| JKL 5 | TUV 8 | DEF 3 | DEF 3 |

| MNO 6 | ABC 2 | TUV 8 | TUV 8 | GHI 4 | DEF 3 | WXY 9 |

| PRS 7 | DEF 3 | TUV 8 | DEF 3 | JKL 5 | ABC 2 | TUV 8 | GHI 4 | MNO 6 | MNO 6 |

| PRS 7 | MNO 6 | MNO 6 | ABC 2 | MNO 6 | PRS 7 |

| TUV 8 | GHI 4 | TUV 8 | TUV 8 | PRS 7 |

ANIMALS IN THE NEW TESTAMENT

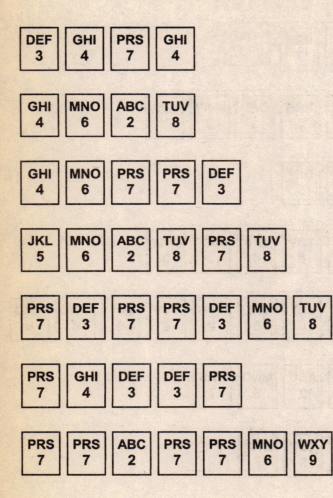

DEF 3	GHI 4	PRS 7	GHI 4

GHI 4	MNO 6	ABC 2	TUV 8

GHI 4	MNO 6	PRS 7	PRS 7	DEF 3

JKL 5	MNO 6	ABC 2	TUV 8	PRS 7	TUV 8

PRS 7	DEF 3	PRS 7	PRS 7	DEF 3	MNO 6	TUV 8

PRS 7	GHI 4	DEF 3	DEF 3	PRS 7

PRS 7	PRS 7	ABC 2	PRS 7	PRS 7	MNO 6	WXY 9

OLD TESTAMENT PEOPLE
WITH GOD-GIVEN MISSIONS

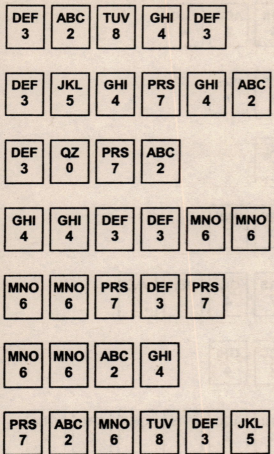

MARTYRS

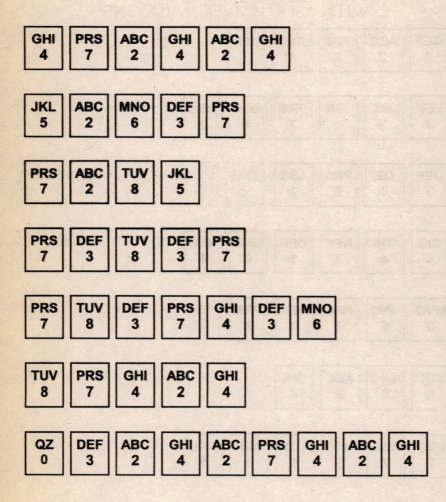

Gifts of the Holy Spirit

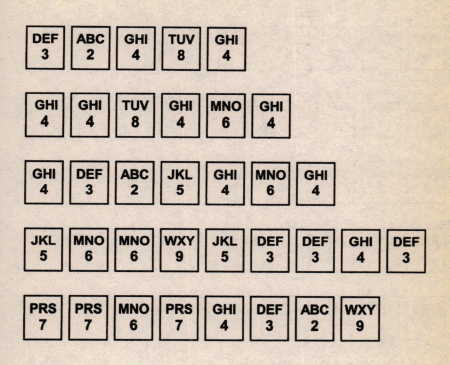

ANAGRAM
PUZZLES

by Paul Kent

Unscramble the letters of the nonsensical message to spell the name of a Bible person, place, or thing. Each letter will be used once.

BIBLE CITIES. . .

A sud scam

_ _ _ _ _ _ _

BOOKS OF THE BIBLE. . .

Undo mere toy

_ _ _ _ _ _ _ _ _

PLACES. . .

Atom is a poem

_ _ _ _ _ _ _ _ _

BAD GUYS. . .

I joust as I card

_ _ _ _ _ _ _ _ _ _ _ _ _

BOOKS OF THE BIBLE. . .

A rich haze

_ _ _ _ _ _ _ _ _

PLACES. . .

O lost movie fun

_ _ _ _ _ _ _ _ _ _ _ _ _

BOOKS OF THE BIBLE. . .

Snag a tail

_ _ _ _ _ _ _ _ _

NEW TESTAMENT PEOPLE. . .

A moot grains ad

_ _ _ _ _ _ _ _ _ _ _

RIVERS/BODIES OF WATER. . .

Reed meant rain

_ _ _ _ _ _ _ _ _ _ _

EVENTS. . .

Not a rice

— — — — — — —

BOOKS OF THE BIBLE. . .

Hi my tot

— — — — — —

NEW TESTAMENT PEOPLE. . .

A brute aims

— — — — — — — — —

Books of the Bible. . .

I jam here

— — — — — — —

Kings. . .

Rob a home

— — — — — —

New Testament People. . .

Mice sound

— — — — — — —

BOOKS OF THE BIBLE. . .

Snail has notes

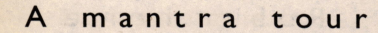

PLACES. . .

A mantra tour

BIBLE CITIES. . .

Hen vine

BOOKS OF THE BIBLE. . .

He no limp

_ _ _ _ _ _ _ _

NEW TESTAMENT PEOPLE. . .

I see harps

_ _ _ _ _ _ _ _

WOMEN OF THE BIBLE. . .

O his dare

_ _ _ _ _ _ _ _

BOOKS OF THE BIBLE. . .

I note last man

— — — — — — — — — —

WOMEN OF THE BIBLE. . .

Arm may end a leg

— — — — — — — — — —

NEW TESTAMENT PEOPLE. . .

A gold prison

— — — — — — — — — —

EVENTS. . .

Joe felt choir tab

_____

BOOKS OF THE BIBLE. . .

See sing

_____

RIVERS/BODIES OF WATER. . .

See a dad

_____

BOOKS OF THE BIBLE. . .

This coin ran

_ _ _ _ _ _ _ _ _ _ _

PLACES. . .

Need of danger

_ _ _ _ _ _ _ _ _ _

NEW TESTAMENT PEOPLE. . .

In more pets

_ _ _ _ _ _ _ _

ANSWERS

Drop Two Puzzles

Revelation:
Quiet, Doing, Grave, Reset, Slice, Chord, Timed, Scans, Plate, Raise, Spins: "A new heaven and a new earth." Revelation 21:1

Ezekiel:
Lanky, Cadet, Spent, Ravel, Piled, Raked, Shear, Raise, Brave, Maine, Local, Broad, Lines: "Blessed be the glory of the Lord." Ezekiel 3:12

Jeremiah:
Heart, Threw, Fable, Scale, Caste, Their, Bread, Fords, Verbs, Least, Trace, Sight, Champ: "Learn not the way of the heathen." Jeremiah 10:2

Romans:
Sheer, Paned, Bated, Grant, Going, Forks, Halos, Brand, Rated, Using, Stomp, Cleat: "For I delight in the law of God." Romans 7:22

Ezra:
Draft, Grain, Robin, Lathe, There, Ether, Banal, Scene, Tiber, Brier, Pains, Cents, Deter: "God, what shall we say after this?" Ezra 9:10

Job:
Stoop, Cello, Leans, Darts, Ruled, Tried, Aping, Droll, Mural, Dined, Cones, Decal, Gleam: "Unto God would I commit my cause." Job 5:8

Ruth:
Cares, Tying, Learn, Sales, Final, Milan, Throe, Maids, Carts, Grain, Singe, Bleat: "Thy people shall be my people." Ruth 1:16

Galatians:
Lease, Clerk, Quint, Seeds, Giant, Sided, Snore, Agent, Warms, Thorn, Court, Drawn: "Bear ye one another's burdens." Galatians 6:2

John:
Croon, Bated, Drain, Caper, Crime, Being, Vials, Lines, Dream, Carts, Skied, Amber, Stile: "Thou hast sent me into the world." John 17:18

Titus:
Teach, Later, There, Heard, Laced, Mayor, Their, Flare, Topic, Dream, Mends, Waste, Toils: "Holding fast the faithful word." Titus 1:9

Genesis:
Grand, Vines, Under, Medal, Frame, Latin, Dread, Write, Slims, Gamin, Boned, Hedge, Stare: "God created man in his own image." Genesis 1:27

Joshua:
Trade, Plant, Tease, Alarm, Refer, Heart, Later, Satin, Tough, Creak, Frees, Amiss, Slain: "For the Lord thy God is with thee." Joshua 1:9

ZECHARIAH:

Meals, Savor, Flora, Bingo, Piece, Names, Chief, Parch, Sheer, Shoal, Cleat, Great, Speed: "I will dwell in the midst of thee." Zechariah 2:10

HAGGAI:

Drone, Stomp, Grain, Eater, Dined, Place, Tardy, Prose, Grate, Moist, Throe: "I am with you, saith the LORD." Haggai 1:13

LUKE:

Leach, Chair, Grade, Trash, Feast, Eaten, Carve, Great, Yeast, Place, Dunes, Singe, Cubed: "Many shall rejoice at his birth." Luke 1:14

HEBREWS:

Steed, Caked, Sales, Tread, Tense, Fling, Soles, Spoil, Elite, Pined, Shape, Borer, Dames: "Now the just shall live by faith." Hebrews 10:38

MALACHI:

React, Trash, Louse, Noble, Topic, Slant, Aping, Timed, Cited, Morse, Prays, Print: "For he is like a refiner's fire." Malachi 3:2

I CORINTHIANS:

Tread, Grips, Treed, Sweet, Brain, Rains, Stork, Hired, Lunge, Drain, Table, Sines: "Charity vaunteth not itself." I Corinthians 13:4

MARK:

Merge, Sleds, Drone, Glean, Strew, Rains, Dirty, Later, Clots, Clean, Frame, Voted, Dense: "And have peace one with another." Mark 9:50

I JOHN:

Shear, Cured, Snare, Reach, Blame, Heart, Drips, Hasty, Acute, Glean, Reign, Scant: "The true God, and eternal life." I John 5:20

Decoder Puzzles

Psalm 4:8
I will both lay me down in peace, and sleep: for thou, LORD, only makest me dwell in safety.

1 Corinthians 9:27
But I keep under my body, . . .lest that by any means, when I have preached to others, I myself should be a castaway.

Psalm 7:17
I will praise the LORD according to his righteousness: and will sing praise to the name of the LORD most high.

Ecclesiastes 1:9
The thing that hath been, it is that which shall be; and that which is done is that which shall be done: and there is no new thing under the sun.

Psalm 20:7
Some trust in chariots, and some in horses: but we will remember the name of the LORD our God.

Philippians 4:13
I can do all things through Christ which strengtheneth me.

Matthew 5:44
Love your enemies, bless them that curse you, do good to them that hate you, and pray for them which despitefully use you, and persecute you.

Proverbs 30:5
Every word of God is pure: he is a shield unto them that put their trust in him.

James 1:5
If any of you lack wisdom, let him ask of God, that giveth to all men liberally, and upbraideth not; and it shall be given him.

Psalm 5:8
Lead me, O LORD, in thy righteousness because of mine enemies; make thy way straight before my face.

1 Corinthians 9:24
Know ye not that they which run in a race run all, but one receiveth the prize? So run, that ye may obtain.

Ecclesiastes 3:1
To every thing there is a season, and a time to every purpose under the heaven.

Romans 12:10
Be kindly affectioned one to another with brotherly love; in honour preferring one another.

Romans 12:20
Therefore if thine enemy hunger, feed him; if he thirst, give him drink: for in so doing thou shalt heap coals of fire on his head.

Psalm 25:7
Remember not the sins of my youth, nor my transgressions: according to thy mercy remember thou me for thy goodness' sake, O LORD.

Psalm 9:2
I will be glad and rejoice in thee: I will sing praise to thy name, O thou most High.

I CORINTHIANS 3:18

Let no man deceive himself. If any man among you seemeth to be wise in this world, let him become a fool, that he may be wise.

TITUS 3:9

But avoid foolish questions, and genealogies, and contentions, and strivings about the law; for they are unprofitable and vain.

I TIMOTHY 6:12

Fight the good fight of faith, lay hold on eternal life, whereunto thou art also called, and hast professed a good profession before many witnesses.

I CORINTHIANS 10:26

For the earth is the Lord's, and the fulness thereof.

ACROSTICS PUZZLES

PSALM 18:2

HIGHSCHOOL	WIGGLE	RECOVERY
FLAVOUR	CALENDER	MARKET

The LORD is my rock, and my fortress, and my deliverer; my God, my strength, in whom I will trust.

PSALM 2:11

JUSTICE	FAVORS	WITHER
BALANCE	DAMAGED	PLURAL

Serve the LORD with fear, and rejoice with trembling.

PSALM 3:7

GUPPY	KINDERGARTEN	CHEF
LOVABLE	ASTRONOMY	NOMINATE

Arise, O LORD; save me, O my God: for thou hast smitten all mine enemies upon the cheek bone.

PSALM 19:14

FARM	HONEYMOON	PGMOVIES
COLANDER	LABYRINTH	OUTGROW

Let the words of my mouth, and the meditation of my heart, be acceptable in thy sight, O LORD, my strength, and my redeemer.

PHILIPPIANS 4:6

PACIFIC	EXTRAVAGANT	HARDWARE
KNUCKLE	QUESTIONABLE	MISSIONARY

Be careful for nothing; but in every thing by prayer and supplication with thanksgiving let your requests be made known unto God.

PHILIPPIANS 2:3

WEEKDAY	PERFECT	EVAPORATE
EMBEZZLE	DUGOUT	FASHION

Let nothing be done through strife or vainglory; but in lowliness of mind let each esteem other better than themselves.

PSALM 19:1

VAT	DESPAIR	MISBELIEF
CHOREOGRAPHY	WORKING	ORIGAMI

The heavens declare the glory of God; and the firmament showeth his handywork.

ROMANS 12:9

WINDOW	VIABLE	GUILTLESS
HINDSIGHT	MARCH	HEADACHE

Let love be without dissimulation. Abhor that which is evil; cleave to that which is good.

ROMANS 12:21

REVENGE	AMPUTATE	FREE
CHAIR	WOODEN	BLAME

Be not overcome of evil, but overcome evil with good.

1 CORINTHIANS 10:31

TICKLE	FOLLY	AGRICULTURE
DRAGON	WISHBONE	PROTECTIVE

Whether therefore ye eat, or drink, or whatsoever ye do, do all to the glory of God.

1 CORINTHIANS 12:13

TUXEDO	ZOOLOGY	PATH
JEWELRY	FABRIC	SUBMARINE

For by one Spirit are we all baptized into one body, whether we be Jews or Gentiles, whether we be bond or free.

I Corinthians 10:33

HURRICANE	MAGIC	VULNERABLE
FITNESS	PERIWINKLE	YONDER

Even as I please all men in all things, not seeking mine own profit, but the profit of many, that they may be saved.

I Corinthians 6:12

TEMPERAMENT	HOWLED	STRATEGIC
EXTRA	UMBRELLA	YOURSELF

All things are lawful unto me, but all things are not expedient: all things are lawful for me, but I will not be brought under the power of any.

I Corinthians 4:10

SUITABLE	INCREASINGLY	WAFFLE
COURTEOUS	DEEP	KHAKI

We are fools for Christ's sake, but ye are wise in Christ; we are weak, but ye are strong; ye are honourable, but we are despised.

Romans 14:11

VALID	GOLF	WORKOUT
CHRISTIAN	HOSPITALITY	BAROMETER

For it is written, As I live, saith the Lord, every knee shall bow to me, and every tongue shall confess to God.

I Corinthians 6:15

IMPERSONAL	BARBECUE	KINGS
OLFACTORY	DAWN	HYPOTHETICAL

Know ye not that your bodies are the members of Christ? shall I then take the members of Christ, and make them the members of an harlot? God forbid.

I Corinthians 5:8

HYPERBOLE	SCARLET	WALK
FAVORITE	COMMUNICATION	PURCHASED

Therefore let us keep the feast, not with old leaven, neither with the leaven of malice and wickedness; but with the unleavened bread of sincerity and truth.

Romans 15:4

FOLLOW	ANONYMOUS	MAVERICK
PREFERENCE	ARCHANGEL	DOMESTIC

For whatsoever things were written aforetime were written for our learning, that we through patience and comfort of the scriptures might have hope.

I Corinthians 2:9

BEWARE	HISTORY	DECEITFUL
FORGIVENESS	IMPROVEMENT	MAINTAIN

But as it is written, Eye hath not seen, nor ear heard, neither have entered into the heart of man, the things which God hath prepared for them that love him.

Romans 14:9

FOREIGNER	MATINEE	HIDDEN
OCTOBER	VENGEFUL	IMPOSSIBLE

For to this end Christ both died, and rose, and revived, that he might be Lord both of the dead and living.

WORD SEARCH PUZZLES

BREAD OF THE PHARISEES

AMONG (8 down, 9 across) BADE (11,10) BASKETS (5,12) BECAUSE (7,13) BEWARE (4,2) BREAD (2,2) BROUGHT (14,1) CONCERNING (1,1) DOCTRINE (12,8) FAITH (1,6) FIVE (11,3) FOUR (1,6) HEED (11,13) LEAVEN (12,6) LITTLE (7,9) LOAVES (14,9) MANY (1,7) NEITHER (12,1) PERCEIVED (5,14) PHARISEES (10,5) REASONED (6,14) REMEMBER (14,2) SADDUCEES (13,9) SAYING (1,8) SEVEN (14,14) SPAKE (1,8) TAKEN (1,10) THEMSELVES (9,5) THEY (1,9) THOUSAND (1,10) TOOK (4,9) UNDERSTAND (4,4)

HIDDEN PHRASE:
He said to them, "O ye of little faith" (Matthew 16:8).

JESUS PAYS TAXES

CAESAR (16,11) CAPERNAUM (6,13) CAST (13,16) CHILDREN (5,6) COUNSEL (11,14) CUSTOM (8,13) EARTH (8,7) ENTANGLE (14,13) FISH (13,1) FREE (2,6) HOOK (16,16) HOUSE (14,3) HYPOCRITES (1,2) IMAGE (5,15) JESUS (1,12) KINGS (13,13) MASTER (7,5) MONEY (7,5) MOUTH (14,5) OFFEND (4,5) OPENED (11,7) PENNY (15,5) PERCEIVED (15,5) PETER (6,16) PHARISEES (11,3) PREVENTED (3,4) RECEIVED (6,15) RENDER (10,16) SIMON (10,12) STRANGERS (2,2) SUPERSCRIPTION (1,4) TEMPT (15,2) THINKEST (9,13) TRIBUTE (7,15) WICKEDNESS (11,11)

HIDDEN PHRASE:
Render to Caesar the things that are Caesar's, and to God the things that are God's (Mark 12:17).

BEING PREPARED

AFTERWARD (2,2) ANSWERED (4,14) AROSE (9,1) BEHOLD (5,1) BRIDEGROOM (10,9) DOOR (7,9) ENOUGH (7,6) FIVE (9,10) FOOLISH (14,8) GIVE (12,10) GONE (5,9) HEAVEN (2,14) HOUR (9,3) KINGDOM (10,1) KNOW (13,1) LAMPS (3,6) LIKENED (13,12) LORD (1,5) MARRIAGE (1,10) MEET (9,14) MIDNIGHT (8,13) NEITHER (7,1) OPEN (6,4) RATHER (4,6) READY (14,7) SAYING (9,6) SELL (8,11) SHUT (14,13) SLEPT (14,2) SLUMBERED (14,13) TARRIED (2,1) TOOK (2,8) TRIMMED (11,13) VESSELS (8,12) VIRGINS (8,2) WATCH (7,11) WISE (10,4)

HIDDEN PHRASE:
Watch ye, stand fast in the faith (1 Corinthians 16:13).

THE TALENTS

ABILITY (3,8) ACCORDING (4,16) AFRAID (3,2) ANSWERED (3,8) AWAY (16,5) CALLED (3,1) CAST (8,5) COMING (3,1) COUNTRY (10,2) DARKNESS (12,13) EARTH (5,5) ENTER (8,11) FAITHFUL (13,4) FIVE (13,11) GAINED (15,16) GATHERING (13,3) GOODS (9,2) HARD (13,12) JOURNEY (13,8) KINGDOM (4,6) LIKEWISE (5,1) LORD (2,16) MADE (1,1) MONEY (16,12) OUTER (15,3) REAPING (15,8) RECEIVED (15,7) RULER (1,4) SAYING (14,1) SERVANTS (14,8) SEVERAL (8,10) SLOTHFUL (13,16) SOWED (14,16) STRAIGHTWAY (6,6) TALENTS (6,3) THINGS (7,15) TRADED (6,3) UNPROFITABLE (12,16) WEEPING (10,15) WICKED (2,11)

HIDDEN PHRASE:
The slothful man saith. . .a lion is in the streets (Proverbs 26:13).

APOSTLES SENT OUT

ABIDE (13,8) ANOINTED (8,9) BEGAN (3,3) BREAD (2,7) CALLED (1,9) CAST (14,1) COATS (12,2) COMMANDED (9,6) DEPART (15,5) DEVILS (9,3) DUST (8,1) ENTER (15,13) FEET (7,9) FORTH (10,11) GAVE (5,13) HEALED (4,8) HEAR (15,4) HOUSE (11,5) JOURNEY (11,12) JUDGMENT (10,13) MONEY (2,10) NOTHING (11,2) OVER (9,1) PLACE (1,2) POWER (2,6) PREACHED (1,2) PURSE (15,12) RECEIVE (14,9) REPENT (15,10) SANDALS (13,5) SCRIP (5,14) SEND (5,14) SHAKE (11,13) SICK (4,10) SPIRITS (3,11) STAFF (4,12) TAKE (9,13) TESTIMONY (2,1) TWELVE (2,1)

HIDDEN PHRASE:
He sent them to preach the kingdom of God (Luke 9:2).

NONE GREATER THAN JESUS

AFRAID (7,15) ANSWERED (16,3) APART (12,8) APPEARED (17,2) BELOVED (16,14) CHARGED (10,4) CLOUD (17,14) DEAD (7,13) EARTH (4,2) ELIAS (6,3) EXCEEDING (9,13) FULLER (3,5) GOOD (17,5) HIGH (5,6) JAMES (15,14) JESUS (5,1) JOHN (15,14) LEADETH (17,13) LOOKED (1,10) MASTER (11,9) MOSES (1,1) MOUNTAIN (7,1) OVERSHADOWED (1,12) PETER (8,13) RAIMENT (11,5) RISEN (11,4) ROUND (16,1) SAYING (12,9) SHINING (3,14) SNOW (5,2) SORE (5,15) SUDDENLY (3,14) TABERNACLES (13,12) TAKETH (6,13) TALKING (17,3) THEMSELVES (8,9) TRANSFIGURED (1,4) VOICE (2,11) WHITE (10,14)

HIDDEN PHRASE:
This is my beloved Son, in whom I am well pleased; hear ye him (Matthew 17:5).

JESUS HEALS A BEGGAR'S EYES
ANSWERED (9,1) BARTIMAEUS (2,10) BEGGING (8,1) BLIND (12,7) CALLED (7,3) CASTING (14,10)
CHARGED (2,3) COMFORT (9,6) COMMANDED (4,2) DAVID (15,6) DISCIPLES (16,10) FAITH (8,10)
FOLLOWED (15,3) GARMENT (9,12) HIGHWAY (10,11) HOLD (5,11) IMMEDIATELY (11,11)
JERICHO (13,10) JESUS (1,8) MERCY (5,1) MIGHT (3,2) NAZARETH (3,6) NUMBER (9,2) PEACE (13,4)
PEOPLE (4,13) RECEIVED (16,8) SAYING (1,6) SIGHT (10,9) STILL (15,13) STOOD (3,5) WHOLE (12,12)
HIDDEN PHRASE:
Tell John. . .how that the blind see, the lame walk (Luke 7:22).

A BELOVED SON IS SENT
ANOTHER (1,8) BEAT (15,11) BELOVED (4,7) BUILDERS (11,6) CAST (12,9) CAUGHT (5,9)
CORNER (6,14) COUNTRY (2,3) DESTROY (3,4) DIGGED (13,12) EMPTY (2,10) FRUIT (15,7) GIVE (5,6)
HANDLED (14,10) HEAD (10,3) HEIR (9,11) HUSBANDMEN (1,4) INHERITANCE (14,1) KILL (15,10)
LORD (11,14) OTHERS (8,8) PLANTED (9,7) RECEIVE (8,4) REJECTED (14,8) REVERENCE (7,2)
SENT (14,11) SERVANT (6,2) SHAMEFULLY (5,14) STONE (15,6) TOWER (1,5) VINEYARD (15,1)
WELL (5,2) WINEFAT (8,13) WOUNDED (4,14)
HIDDEN PHRASE:
What shall I do? I will send my beloved son (Luke 20:13).

TROUBLESOME TIMES
ANOTHER (15,9) ANSWERED (8,12) BEGINNINGS (3,4) BUILDINGS (11,13) CHRIST (4,13)
COME (15,12) DECEIVE (1,12) DISCIPLES (8,11) DOWN (13,11) EARTHQUAKES (13,5) ENDURE (9,7)
FAMINES (12,4) GOSPEL (8,1) HATED (9,5) HEED (7,4) JESUS (4,2) KINGDOM (7,15) KINGS (7,1)
LEFT (13,15) MANNER (11,6) MANY (10,7) MASTER (11,1) NAME (11,11) NATION (8,7)
PUBLISHED (11,7) RULERS (1,4) SAVED (16,3) SHALL (16,15) SORROWS (16,15) STONE (4,8) TAKE (3,3)
TEMPLE (14,9) TESTIMONY (3,14) THROWN (10,6) TROUBLES (2,6) WARS (3,10)
HIDDEN PHRASE:
Heaven and earth shall pass away, but my words shall not pass away (Matthew 24:35).

JOSEPH OF ARIMATHAEA
ALOES (9,8) ALREADY (12,9) ARIMATHAEA (3,1) AWAY (14,11) BEFORE (1,5) BODY (8,9)
BROUGHT (2,8) CALLED (16,10) CENTURION (11,3) COME (14,7) COUNSELLOR (6,14) DEAD (7,14)
DISCIPLE (16,2) DOOR (7,14) DOWN (17,3) EVEN (14,4) FEAR (7,10) GAVE (6,3) HEWN (1,14)
HONOURABLE (11,13) HUNDRED (7,11) JESUS (4,12) JEWS (2,7) JOSEPH (2,7) LAID (17,9)
LINEN (15,2) MARVELLED (2,1) MIXTURE (7,4) MYRRH (6,13) NICODEMUS (17,6) POUND (8,5)
PREPARATION (11,1) ROCK (6,6) ROLLED (12,7) SABBATH (9,6) SECRETLY (15,8) SEPULCHRE (17,13)
STONE (17,13) TOOK (2,14) WRAPPED (3,2)
HIDDEN PHRASE:
Who also himself waited for the kingdom of God (Luke 23:51).

JESUS IN HIS HOMETOWN
ANOINTED (14,3) BLIND (3,8) BOOK (2,1) BROKENHEARTED (1,13) BRUISED (3,8)
CAPERNAUM (11,9) CAPTIVES (18,13) COUNTRY (16,5) DELIVERED (7,10) ESAIAS (13,13) FAME (8,14)
GALILEE (12,8) GLORIFIED (8,11) GOSPEL (14,12) GRACIOUS (4,8) HEAL (11,1) JESUS (4,12)
LIBERTY (3,10) LORD (7,11) MINISTER (8,7) NAZARETH (17,2) OPENED (18,1) PHYSICIAN (18,11)
POOR (10,5) POWER (5,14) PREACH (12,9) PROPHET (17,7) READ (12,1) SABBATH (4,1)
SCRIPTURE (2,5) SIGHT (1,5) SPIRIT (6,6) STOOD (18,4) SYNAGOGUES (6,2) TAUGHT (11,2)
WRITTEN (8,13)

HIDDEN PHRASE:
Ye seek Jesus of Nazareth, which was crucified: he is risen (Mark 16:6).

JESUS TEACHES IN GALILEE
ALL (3,14) CITIES (11,5) DEEP (14,10) ENTERED (7,13) FISHERMEN (9,10) FISHES (2,7) FOLLOWED (1,13)
FORSOOK (8,10) FROM (6,1) GENNESARET (1,10) GONE (2,14) GREAT (7,1) HAVE (13,5) HEAR (6,4)
KINGDOM (15,12) LAKE (13,13) LAND (14,1) LAUGH (3,9) MASTER (9,14) MIGHT (11,8)
MULTITUDE (15,6) NETS (15,2) NOTHING (1,2) OTHER (4,14) PEOPLE (11,11) PREACH (15,1)
PRESSED (5,1) SAID (5,4) SHIPS (11,6) SIMON (5,10) SOUGHT (14,9) SYNAGOGUES (2,5) TAKEN (12,5)
TAUGHT (13,4) THRUST (9,7) TOILED (9,8) WASHING (3,7) WORD (1,1)

HIDDEN PHRASE:
From henceforth thou shalt catch men (Luke 5:10).

THE GOOD NEWS GOES OUT
APPOINTED (1,1) ASHES (11,8) BEHOLD (14,7) BETHSAIDA (7,9) CARRY (10,2) CHORAZIN (13,12)
CITY (15,12) COME (4,1) DRINKING (9,14) EATING (15,11) ENTER (3,9) EVERY (4,5) GREAT (14,8)
HARVEST (12,1) HEAL (4,8) HIMSELF (12,12) HIRE (1,3) HOUSE (15,7) KINGDOM (13,2) LABOURERS (5,7)
LAMBS (11,9) LORD (6,4) MIGHTY (6,15) PEACE (1,13) PURSE (11,15) REMAIN (10,13) REPENTED (8,2)
SACKCLOTH (2,10) SALUTE (2,10) SCRIP (8,15) SEND (7,5) SEVENTY (7,4) SHOES (5,15) SICK (5,15)
TRULY (1,6) WOLVES (2,1) WORKS (5,3) WORTHY (10,14)

HIDDEN PHRASE:
The harvest truly is plenteous, but the labourers are few (Matthew 9:37).

A LOST SON
ALIVE (14,10) BELLY (8,10) BREAD (2,14) CALF (12,15) CITIZEN (16,1) COMPASSION (1,10)
COUNTRY (7,1) DIVIDED (14,4) FAMINE (5,5) FATHER (8,11) FATTED (16,7) FEED (13,14) FIELDS (9,15)
FILLED (9,9) GATHERED (8,13) GOODS (10,2) HEAVEN (11,10) HIRED (1,11) HUNGER (11,11)
HUSKS (4,8) JOURNEY (7,5) KISSED (1,9) LIVING (14,2) LOST (14,2) MERRY (6,11) MIGHTY (7,14)
PERISH (15,15) PORTION (3,7) RING (7,3) RIOTOUS (2,11) ROBE (4,2) SERVANTS (9,10) SHOES (12,8)
SINNED (15,1) SONS (1,1) SPARE (16,8) SPENT (12,7) SUBSTANCE (4,1) SWINE (16,8) WASTED (6,4)
YOUNGER (12,13)

HIDDEN PHRASE:
Son of man is come to seek and to save that which was lost (Luke 19:10).

THE RICH MAN AND LAZARUS
ABRAHAM (12,1) ANGELS (4,10) BEGGAR (10,6) BOSOM (10,6) BURIED (15,4) CARRIED (6,11)
CLOTHED (14,8) COMFORTED (4,3) COOL (4,3) CRUMBS (15,2) DIED (13,7) EYES (5,7) FARED (4,1)
FINGER (9,9) FIXED (12,7) FLAME (12,13) GATE (4,8) GULF (2,8) LAID (4,12) LAZARUS (3,12)
LIFETIME (14,9) LIFTED (11,9) LINEN (11,9) MERCY (6,2) PASS (10,12) PURPLE (7,9) REMEMBER (10,1)
RICH (4,4) SUMPTUOUSLY (14,1) TABLE (5,13) TONGUE (7,14) TORMENTS (7,10) WATER (7,13)

HIDDEN PHRASE:
If they hear not Moses and the prophets, neither will they be persuaded (Luke 16:31).

ZACCHAEUS CLIMBS A TREE TO SEE JESUS
ABIDE (12,15) ABRAHAM (13,9) ACCUSATION (10,5) BEHOLD (2,15) CLIMBED (12,13) COME (9,5)
DOWN (3,7) ENTERED (1,4) FALSE (14,15) FOURFOLD (1,2) GIVE (4,10) GOODS (3,10) HALF (11,15)
HASTE (14,6) HOUSE (11,15) JERICHO (5,12) JOYFULLY (2,4) LITTLE (10,12) LOOKED (7,4) LOST (4,3)
MAKE (3,12) MURMURED (13,3) PASSED (12,7) PLACE (15,8) POOR (15,5) PUBLICANS (6,4)
RECEIVED (13,7) RESTORE (15,2) SALVATION (9,9) SAVE (4,13) SEEK (15,9) SINNER (9,14) STATURE (9,9)
SYCAMORE (11,11) THROUGH (4,5) ZACCHAEUS (5,10)

HIDDEN PHRASE:
I came not to call the righteous, but sinners to repentance (Luke 5:32).

BREAD OF LIFE
ANSWERED (13,13) BELIEVE (15,9) BLOOD (1,8) BREAD (8,5) COMETH (4,9) DESERT (6,6) DRINK (7,5)
ENDURETH (9,9) ETERNAL (13,2) EVERLASTING (9,11) FATHER (15,1) FILLED (15,1) FLESH (12,2)
GIVETH (6,12) HUNGER (2,1) JESUS (1,10) JEWS (13,10) LABOUR (1,5) LIFE (5,12) LOAVES (16,11)
MANNA (2,7) MEAT (14,5) MIGHT (1,1) MIRACLES (12,3) MURMURED (3,11) NEVER (2,9)
PERISHETH (3,5) RAISE (12,7) SEALED (1,2) SENT (6,4) SHALL (12,13) SIGN (16,7) THIRST (12,5)
VERILY (15,7) WORK (4,13)

HIDDEN PHRASE:
This is that bread which came down from heaven (John 6:50).

THE PRINCE OF LIFE
BLESSED (17,3) CHILDREN (4,8) CHRIST (9,12) COVENANT (15,8) DELIVERED (1,9) DESIRED (15,17)
DESTROYED (15,9) FAITH (8,7) FATHERS (7,12) FORETOLD (3,1) FULFILLED (9,8) GLORIFIED (8,5)
GRANTED (7,11) HEAR (7,7) HEAVEN (17,15) HOLY (3,10) IGNORANCE (11,16) INIQUITIES (10,15)
ISRAEL (9,7) JESUS (13,16) LIFE (10,17) MARVEL (17,11) MOSES (13,12) NAME (17,9) PEOPLE (2,3)
PERFECT (11,1) PETER (17,1) PILATE (5,6) POWER (9,6) PREACHED (12,13) PRINCE (1,8) PROPHETS (6,6)
RAISED (16,12) REFRESHING (1,7) REPENT (11,2) RULERS (9,9) SEED (12,4) SOUNDNESS (2,9)
STRONG (2,17) SUFFER (1,15) TURNING (9,10)

HIDDEN PHRASE:
Jesus Christ of Nazareth, whom ye crucified, whom God raised from the dead (Acts 4:10).

BOLD BELIEVERS
BEHOLD (11,4) BOLDNESS (1,7) CAPTAIN (5,3) CORNER (13,9) DEAD (4,10) EARTH (4,5) GRANT (10,9) GRIEVED (9,12) HEAD (13,5) HEAVEN (7,6) JESUS (5,10) LIFTED (6,7) LORD (3,7) MADE (1,14) NAME (2,1) NONE (8,3) OTHER (9,10) POWER (8,2) PRIESTS (14,12) RAISED (4,13) REPORTED (14,14) SADDUCEES (14,2) SALVATION (1,11) SERVANTS (7,8) SPEAK (8,14) STOKE (1,2) THREATENINGS (1,3) VOICE (9,5) WONDERS (12,7) WORD (11,6)

HIDDEN PHRASE:
We were bold in our God to speak unto you the gospel of God (1 Thessalonians 2:2).

WHO SHOULD BELIEVERS OBEY
AGREED (13,5) ANGEL (13,2) ANSWERED (8,10) APOSTLES (3,3) BEATEN (10,6) CALLED (6,1) CANNOT (10,7) COMMAND (8,14) COUNSEL (6,12) DOCTOR (8,8) DOCTRINE (7,14) DOORS (1,9) FEARED (7,6) FILLED (2,14) HIGH (2,7) INDIGNATION (12,1) JERUSALEM (10,4) MORNING (3,12) NAME (10,9) NOUGHT (2,9) OFFICERS (8,13) OPENED (1,8) OVERTHROW (5,3) PETER (14,13) PHARISEE (14,1) PRIEST (14,13) PRISON (3,4) REFRAIN (7,1) SLAY (13,7) TEACHING (2,3) TEMPLE (1,2)

HIDDEN PHRASE:
We ought to obey God rather than men (Acts 5:29).

PAUL PREACHES ABOUT JESUS
AGAINST (12,5) ANANIAS (10,9) AROSE (1,13) CHOSEN (13,2) CHRIST (13,7) CONFOUNDED (12,10) DAMASCUS (3,1) EVIL (4,2) GENTILES (3,8) HARD (4,3) HEAVEN (5,12) ISRAEL (12,8) KICK (13,4) LIGHT (8,13) NEAR (8,9) PERSECUTEST (1,11) PREACHED (2,4) PRICKS (5,8) SAINTS (1,8) SAUL (3,13) SIGHT (13,13) STRAIGHT (13,11) STREET (13,13) TARSUS (4,13) TREMBLING (3,5) VESSEL (1,5) VOICE (3,3) WITHOUT (11,4)

HIDDEN PHRASE:
I am the apostle of the Gentiles (Romans 11:13).

SERVE THE TRUE GOD
ANTIOCH (4,11) BARNABAS (9,8) CHIEF (10,13) DEPARTED (15,4) DISCIPLES (6,10) EARTH (1,15) FAITH (6,14) FEET (13,1) FILLING (11,7) FOOD (11,15) FRUITFUL (3,4) GARLANDS (16,11) GLADNESS (16,2) HEALED (11,10) HEARTS (7,16) HEAVEN (7,16) ICONIUM (3,2) JUPITER (9,12) LEAPED (2,3) LIFTED (2,1) LIKENESS (16,3) LOUD (12,4) LYSTRA (15,16) MERCURIUS (1,3) NATIONS (12,3) OXEN (16,10) PAUL (5,9) PEOPLE (8,14) PRIEST (6,12) RESTRAINED (10,10) SACRIFICE (11,9) SEASONS (14,16) SPEAKER (10,7) STONED (1,11) SUFFERED (14,16) VOICE (4,1) WALKED (6,16) WITNESS (5,10)

HIDDEN PHRASE:
Ye turned to God from idols to serve the living and true God (1 Thessalonians 1:9).

CHRISTIANS UNDER ATTACK
ANOTHER (11,8) BOND (6,13) BRING (2,14) BROTHERS (11,2) CAESARS (2,11) CAUSED (7,7) CHARACTERS (7,1) CITY (12,1) CROWD (6,15) DECREES (3,12) DEFYING (10,11) DRAGGED (10,15) FORMED (8,3) GREEKS (1,7) HOUSE (7,6) JASON (16,15) JEALOUS (10,13) JESUS (15,16) JEWS (16,4) JOINED (16,4) KING (1,4) LARGE (11,15) MARKETPLACE (1,11) NUMBER (15,4) OFFICIALS (15,11) PAUL (7,4) PERSUADED (1,9) POST (7,5) PROMINENT (2,15) RIOT (3,13) ROUNDED (1,2) SEARCH (13,6) SHOUTING (13,10) SILAS (13,6) STARTED (13,2) THROWN (12,12) TROUBLE (2,13) TURMOIL (13,14) WELCOMED (14,2) WOMEN (1,1) WORLD (1,1)

HIDDEN PHRASE:
Blessed are ye, when men shall revile you, and persecute you (Matthew 5:11).

PAUL SPEAKS AT ATHENS
ALTAR (4,5) AREOPAGUS (9,12) ATHENS (4,7) BABBLER (5,1) BEING (15,1) DECLARE (16,1) DEVOTIONS (7,9) DOCTRINE (12,11) EPICUREAN (16,7) GIVEN (3,6) HEAR (4,9) HILL (15,6) IDOLATRY (5,12) IGNORANTLY (4,2) INSCRIPTION (11,8) JESUS (2,2) LIVE (13,4) MARS (4,6) MOVE (2,7) PAUL (9,6) PERCEIVE (16,3) PHILOSOPHER (12,1) PREACH (15,7) STOICKS (9,3) TELL (5,9) UNKNOWN (1,11) WHOLLY (15,10) WORSHIP (6,1)

HIDDEN PHRASE:
God...dwelleth not in temples made with hands (Acts 17:24).

PAUL ARRESTED

AGAINST (1,2) AUDIENCE (9,1) BROUGHT (2,2) CAPTAIN (2,10) CASTLE (7,8) CENTURIONS (10,4) COMMANDED (3,1) CRIED (3,6) CRYING (13,8) ENTERED (6,13) EXAMINED (2,3) FREEBORN (10,1) HEED (9,8) HOLY (10,2) JEWS (13,10) PAUL (13,6) PEOPLE (7,13) PLACE (11,2) POLLUTED (11,2) ROMAN (3,12) SCOURGING (9,11) SPAKE (1,13) STAIRS (9,13) STIRRED (10,13) STOOD (9,13) TAKE (8,11) TEMPLE (8,4)

HIDDEN PHRASE:
So must thou bear witness also at Rome (Acts 23:11).

PAUL ON TRIAL

AGAINST (2,2) ANSWERED (2,2) ANYTHING (8,3) APPEAL (3,4) BROUGHT (13,9) CAESAR (7,9) CHEERFULLY (9,1) CHRIST (6,9) COMMANDED (9,13) CONVENIENT (2,10) DRUSILLA (14,8) FAITH (10,10) FELIX (10,10) FESTUS (7,13) JUDGMENT (12,9) NEITHER (10,4) OFFENDED (14,13) PAUL (11,14) REASONED (11,5) RIGHTEOUS (2,12) SEASON (3,11) SEAT (6,11) TEMPERANCE (10,3) TEMPLE (1,14) TREMBLED (1,6) WIFE (11,4)

HIDDEN PHRASE:
This man doeth nothing worthy of death or of bonds (Acts 26:31).

STORM WARNING

ADVISED (11,11) ALEXANDRIA (10,8) ATTAIN (1,6) AUGUSTUS (1,6) BAND (12,8) BELIEVED (12,4) CENTURION (9,9) CONTRARY (5,2) CRETE (8,2) DAMAGE (13,8) DEPART (13,8) FAIR (11,7) FOUND (2,1) HAVEN (3,13) HURT (7,12) ITALY (9,13) JULIUS (3,1) LIVES (9,8) MASTER (8,1) OWNER (9,5) PERCEIVE (10,10) PRISONERS (2,9) SAILING (1,7) SHIP (2,13) VOYAGE (7,2) WINDS (10,13)

HIDDEN PHRASE:
Once was I stoned, thrice I suffered shipwreck (2 Corinthians 11:25).

PAUL IN ROME

CASTOR (9,6) COURAGE (2,12) DELIVERED (9,5) DEPARTED (7,13) DULL (9,5) DWELL (8,11) DWELT (10,12) EARS (13,7) EXPOUNDED (2,5) GROSS (10,1) HANDS (11,5) HEART (12,9) HIMSELF (1,2) HIRED (12,9) HOUSE (7,14) JERUSALEM (13,11) KEPT (14,11) PAUL (4,7) POLLUX (4,8) PRISONER (12,5) ROMANS (9,9) ROME (5,9) SHIP (4,4) SIGN (9,8) SOLDIER (3,13) SYRACUSE (13,4) THANKED (1,11) WAXED (2,1) WINTERED (2,1)

HIDDEN PHRASE:
All the saints salute you, chiefly they that are of Caesar's household (Philippians 4:22).

PRESSING AHEAD

ALREADY (16,7) APPREHEND (16,7) ATTAIN (10,6) BEHIND (1,8) BRETHREN (13,5) CALLING (4,14) CHRIST (3,5) CONFORMABLE (3,3) COUNT (5,2) DEAD (9,3) DOUBTLESS (9,12) EXCELLENCY (7,13) FAITH (12,7) FELLOWSHIP (2,6) FOLLOW (8,10) FORGETTING (15,1) GAIN (14,2) HIGH (2,13) KNOWLEDGE (11,4) LOSS (7,11) MARK (14,3) MEANS (2,5) MINE (14,3) MYSELF (15,6) PERFECT (4,7) POWER (15,15) PRESS (2,15) PRIZE (15,8) REACHING (5,8) RESURRECTION (14,12) RIGHTEOUSNESS (13,1) SUFFERED (12,10) THINGS (5,12) TOWARD (11,14)

HIDDEN PHRASE:
That I may know him, and the power of his resurrection (Philippians 3:10).

JOHN'S VISION

ALPHA (17,9) ASIA (11,7) BOOK (11,15) BRASS (6,6) BURNED (12,14) CANDLESTICKS (17,3) CHRIST (1,14) CHURCHES (1,13) CLOTHED (16,1) COUNTENANCE (2,3) EPHESUS (10,10) FIRE (15,5) FIRST (12,16) FLAME (16,2) FURNACE (9,7) GARMENT (15,12) GOLDEN (10,5) GREAT (12,12) JESUS (2,12) JOHN (5,12) KINGDOM (17,16) LAODICEA (8,11) LAST (4,1) OMEGA (1,2) PATIENCE (5,1) PATMOS (9,11) PERGAMOS (3,10) PHILADELPHIA (5,14) SARDIS (4,7) SEEN (14,7) SEVEN (16,12) SMYRNA (12,4) SNOW (9,8) SPIRIT (12,15) STRENGTH (16,12) SWORD (6,2) TESTIMONY (13,1) THYATIRA (1,4) TRIBULATION (17,11) TRUMPET (7,15) TWOEDGED (9,13) VOICE (17,4) WHITE (7,6) WOOL (1,1) WRITE (7,6)

HIDDEN PHRASE:
The Son of man shall sit in the throne of his glory (Matthew 19:28).

SCRAMBLED CIRCLE PUZZLES

Jewish men would meet here to talk and do business.   CITY GATE
1. COMPASS 2. CAPTIVE 3. DESOLATE 4. BABYLON 5. GRAVEL 6. SPANNED 7. STRAIT 8. ASHAMED

Another son of David who wanted to be king.   ADONIJAH
1. JEREMIAH 2. DOUBLE 3. BORN 4. HUNTERS 5. DRIVEN 6. JUSTICE 7. CARCASSES 8. ABHOR

A well-known sermon was given here.   The MOUNT of OLIVES
1. FAMINE 2. FORGIVE 3. JUDAH 4. CONTEND 5. VANITY 6. FORSAKEN 7. FILLED 8. INHABIT
9. SALVATION 10. JERUSALEM 11. PRIESTS

These acted as trucks in the ancient times.   CAMELS
1. CHALDEANS 2. SLAIN 3. RUMOR 4. VIOLENCE 5. MULTITUDE 6. JERUSALEM

Another name for Mount Sinai.   MOUNT HOREB
1. SMITE 2. ROUND 3. UNDER 4. INSTRUCTION 5. THICK 6. SIGHT 7. CONSUME 8. SAVIOR
9. REMNANT 10. REBUKE

These two men went to heaven without dying.   ENOCH and ELIJAH
1. EZEKIEL 2. KINGDOM 3. ETHIOPIA 4. CARBUNCLE 5. PHARAOH 6. LIFTED 7. SLAIN 8. TERRIBLE
9. JUDGE 10. REPROACH 11. HEATHEN

This town was known as Jesus' home away from home.   BETHANY
1. BURNING 2. SEASON 3. MATTER 4. THOUSAND 5. PERSIANS 6. SIGNET 7. EARLY

The great devourer as described in Job.   LEVIATHAN
1. PLOWED 2. BETHEL 3. DIVIDED 4. INCENSE 5. IMAGES 6. RETURN 7. BRANCHES 8. DEPART
9. DERISION

Well known as the city of David.   JERUSALEM
1. JUDGMENT 2. HEMLOCK 3. GRAVEN 4. PURSUE 5. MISCHIEF 6. FALLOW 7. TUMULT 8. REAPED
9. MURDER

She was the mother of Ahaziah.   ATHALIAH
1. OBADIAH 2. STUBBLE 3. MIGHTY 4. REMAIN 5. FIELDS 6. THIRST 7. PREVAIL 8. BREACHES

This Roman coin was equivalent in weight to the Hebrew shekel.   DENARIUS
1. DEDICATE 2. WRITTEN 3. GOVERNOR 4. SERVANT 5. RIVER 6. BUILDING 7. UPON 8. SEDITION

An outdoor shelter for holding celebrations.   TABERNACLE
1. LEVITES 2. PASSOVER 3. LAMBS 4. TIMBER 5. RAMS 6. NUMBER 7. DARIUS 8. DECREE 9. KILLED
10. SEVEN

The job of a high government official.   CUPBEARER
1. CUBIT 2. PUBLISH 3. PINE 4. BROUGHT 5. DIVIDE 6. WATERS 7. PORTIONS 8. EGYPT 9. GRIEVED

A letter was written to this believer, the master of a runaway slave.   PHILEMON
1. TROOPS 2. HEAVEN 3. VANISH 4. DELIVER 5. EVIDENT 6. COMMIT 7. POSSESS 8. DISCERN

A method that ancient pagans used to determine the future.   CAST LOTS
1. CONTENT 2. ARROWS 3. TOSSING 4. LOATHSOME 5. CLOTHED 6. COMFORT 7. RETURN
8. REWARDS

Pressed into clay to seal important documents. What was it?   SIGNET RING
1. PERVERSE 2. HIRELING 3. TONGUE 4. IMAGINE 5. TOKENS 6. WRATH 7. DECLARE 8. INCREASE
9. BLOWN 10. ANGER

A tall plant that grows in swamps and rivers and is used to make heavy paper.
1. PURITY 2. HASTEN 3. CAPTIVITY 4. NEEDY 5. TRUST 6. MOUTH 7. PERISH

Special words from Jesus on the Mount of Olives.   <u>BEATITUDES</u>
1. BURDEN 2. SMOOTHER 3. DRAWN 4. ATTEND 5. SACRIFI CE 6. DESTROY 7. BUTTER 8. WANDER
9. DECEIT 10. ENEMIES

Another name for Satan.   <u>BEELZEBUB</u>
1. LAMB 2. BLESSED 3. CORRECT 4. FOLLOW 5. ZION 6. BEAUTY 7. BURN 8. JUDGE 9. BELIEVE

Chosen to replace Judas as one of the twelve apostles.   <u>MATTHIAS</u>
1. MEDITATE 2. WAVES 3. RIGHT 4. TREMBLE 5. HANDMAID 6. MINE 7. STATUTES 8. CURSED

It's not about reading the future but about speaking the Word of God.   <u>PROPHECY</u>
1. OPPRESSOR 2. SHOULDER 3. THRONE 4. PRIDE 5. EARTH 6. DIMNESS 7. JUSTICE 8. SYRIA

The governing council of the Jews.   <u>SANHEDRIN</u>
1. DISTRESS 2. DREAM 3. NOISE 4. THUNDER 5. EMPTY 6. DEBATE 7. DRINK 8. CHILD 9. TURN

Rules made by people that may not have anything to do with God's requirements.   <u>TRADITIONS</u>
1. SERVANT 2. RETURN 3. BACKWARD 4. SHEPHERD 5. VANITY 6. SHOUT 7. BUILT 8. FOOLISH
9. DOWN 10. SPRING

A story that teaches a lesson.   <u>PARABLE</u>
1. PORTION 2. MARRY 3. FORGET 4. BEAUTY 5. REMEMBER 6. SPRINKL E 7. GRIEF

It was because of this that Paul ended up on the island of Melita.   <u>SHIPWRECK</u>
1. THIRST 2. SHOWERS 3. ARISE 4. PLANT 5. AWAY 6. REJECT 7. PROSPER 8. CHANGE 9. KINGS

A celebration to help us remember all that the Lord has done for us.   The <u>LORD'S SUPPER</u>
1. BLOOD 2. WIDOW 3. SWEAR 4. DUST 5. FALSELY 6. STAND 7. CAUSE 8. PLAYING 9. PEOPLE
10. EXECUTE 11. ROUND

An important Roman army officer.   <u>CENTURION</u>
1. INCENSE 2. AMEND 3. GLEAN 4. REVOLT 5. BURNED 6. RAPTURE 7. NATION 8. WHOLLY
9. FRIEND

Flowers that grow wild all over Galilee.   <u>LILIES</u> of the <u>FIELD</u>
1. GILEAD 2. VIOLENCE 3. KINDLE 4. WORSHIP 5. ENTER 6. ROOFS 7. FARTHER 8. FIRE 9. LIFE
10. LEBANON 11. ABIDE

He smelled bad, but he did live again.   <u>LAZARUS</u>
1. BEHOLD 2. WATCH 3. ZEALOUS 4. ESCAPE 5. BROOK 6. FURY 7. ASHES

A kind of magic.   <u>SORCERY</u>
1. GNASH 2. PROPHET 3. SECRET 4. COVERED 5. DRUNKEN 6. MISERY 7. DESTROY

A place where Jewish people gathered to worship each Sabbath day.   <u>SYNAGOGUE</u>
1. STONE 2. ENEMY 3. YOUNG 4. ARROW 5. AGAINST 6. SHOUT 7. GRAVEL 8. SOUGHT 9. QUIVER

Paul's long preaching caused this one to fall out of a window.   <u>EUTYCHUS</u>
1. FAMINE 2. UNDER 3. TAUNT 4. NINETY 5. COUNTRY 6. HIGH 7. STATUTES 8. SIEGE

This trade was learned by every Jewish boy.   <u>TENTMAKER</u>
1. DEBTOR 2. BEGET 3. BRANCH 4. MIDST 5. EMINENT 6. TOWARD 7. TAKEN 8. BROKEN 9. POOR

Paul was kept under arrest for two years by these two Roman governors.   <u>FELIX</u> and <u>FESTUS</u>
1. FLESH 2. MANNER 3. DEALT 4. PERISH 5. EXECUTE 6. FALLEN 7. STRETCH 8. DESIRE 9. DESPITE
10. MOURN 11. WASHED

A person is made this way because of Christ's sacrifice on the cross. **RIGHTEOUS**
1. PROFANE 2. FRONTIERS 3. GLORY 4. HEATHEN 5. STATELY 6. BONES 7. VOICE 8. DUMB
9. PROPHESY

A blind man was given sight in this city. **DAMASCUS**
1. SWORD 2. EXALT 3. AMONG 4. SCATTER 5. SPEAK 6. STRETCH 7. RUIN 8. RIVERS

Well-to-do Greek children were accompanied everywhere by these. **GUARDIANS**
1. GROAN 2. CHESTNUT 3. LAMENT 4. SPREAD 5. HAND 6. SLAIN 7. GARDEN 8. BOUND
9. SHADOW

A new commandment to live by. **LOVE ONE ANOTHER**
1. GALLERIES 2. POSTS 3. LEAVEN 4. BETWEEN 5. STORIES 6. HUNDRED 7. THREE 8. NARROW
9. NORTH 10. BROAD 11. CUBIT 12. HEAD 13. CHAMBER 14. ARCHES

Jesus was fond of saying this in greeting. **PEACE BE UNTO** you
1. PALM 2. MASTER 3. FAIR 4. ACCORD 5. HEWN 6. BURN 7. CORNET 8. TROUBLE 9. DOMINION
10. HEIGHT 11. WHOM

"God is with us." Another name for the coming Messiah. **IMMANUEL**
1. DIVERSE 2. TIME 3. FLAME 4. ANCIENT 5. GARMENT 6. PLUCKED 7. EXCEEDING 8. WHEELS

Enemies of Israel who lived in Palestine. **PHILISTINES**
1. TROOPS 2. HARVEST 3. WICKED 4. LIES 5. WINE 6. ROBBERS 7. CONSENT 8. MIDST 9. KNOW
10. FORMER 11. SOUR

A dark and scary place for this prophet. The **LIONS DEN**
1. CLEAN 2. PUBLISH 3. WITHHOLD 4. WANDER 5. FOREST 6. DRINK 7. PALACE 8. HOLINESS

They believe our lives are controlled by something other than God. **ASTROLOGERS**
1. CEDAR 2. SPOILED 3. LOATHED 4. BROKEN 5. FLOCK 6. GOODLY 7. CORNER 8. KING
9. VINTAGE 10. DEPART 11. SMITE

They had a lot to say in the Old Testament. **PROPHETS**
1. PRAY 2. REWARD 3. OTHER 4. OPENLY 5. GATHER 6. BETTER 7. ALTAR 8. SPIN

Old or new, it's almost the same thing. **COVENANT**
1. CONCERN 2. WONDER 3. LOAVES 4. BREAD 5. MORNING 6. BEWARE 7. SOLOMON 8. FAITH

Jerusalem had thirty-seven of these cut into the rock under the city. **CISTERNS**
1. PERCEIVED 2. DISCIPLES 3. SEVEN 4. DEPART 5. MEAT 6. ROOTED 7. FAINT 8. FISHES

An ancient early warning system. **WATCHMEN**
1. WAVES 2. SAYINGS 3. SUBTLETY 4. CAIAPHAS 5. HUNGER 6. SLUMBER 7. SCRIBES 8. ANGEL

To the world, something to be avoided—but to God, it is a valuable character trait. **MEEKNESS**
1. FAMINE 2. REVILE 3. DEVOUR 4. KINDLE 5. OPENED 6. RAVENS 7. SAMARITAN 8. SEPULCHRE

Place known for its beauty and riches. **BABYLON**
1. BEFORE 2. CAPTAIN 3. BOLDNESS 4. EARLY 5. COUNCIL 6. POWER 7. CANNOT

An ancient method to communicate a call to worship or war. **TRUMPET**
1. SAFETY 2. IGNORANCE 3. HUMOR 4. MIGHTY 5. UPROAR 6. DAMSEL 7. TEACH

A title given by Jesus to this evil one. **PRINCE** of the **EARTH**
1. PAUL 2. GRAVEN 3. CRIED 4. LANDED 5. ACCORD 6. ADJURE 7. EPHESIANS 8. ACHAIA 9. FERVENT
10. TRAVEL 11. THREE

The Jewish people were not allowed to wear this. FOREIGN CLOTHES
1. FEARING 2. CENTURION 3. SCARCE 4. CRETE 5. TACKLING 6. GODLY 7. FIFTEEN 8. CHEER
9. COLOR 10. SHOULD 11. TESTIFY 12. FORTH 13. TRIBES 14. SAILED

A person of authority then, and still today. MAGISTRATE
1. MARRIED 2. SAVED 3. ANGER 4. CHARITY 5. SHAVEN 6. PRESENT 7. NATURE 8. ABIDE 9. TRUTH
10. BAPTIZE

Springs of water bubbling from the earth. FOUNTAINS
1. HENCEFORTH 2. COMMON 3. ABUNDANT 4. CONCORD 5. DEATH 6. DARKNESS 7. FAINT
8. RENEWED 9. ROSE

A word on everyone's lips at the end. APOCALYPSE
1. CONTAINED 2. DEPTH 3. LOVE 4. CHRIST 5. CAUSE 6. FAMILY 7. HEAVENLY 8. POWER
9. GENTILES 10. MINISTER

He stands opposed to Jesus Christ. ANTICHRIST
1. WALK 2. MANIFEST 3. STRIVING 4. PATIENCE 5. CONSIST 6. HOPE 7. MYSTERY 8. MINDED
9. GOSPEL 10. REQUESTS

To obey and follow the One above. SUBMIT
1. SCYTHIAN 2. QUARREL 3. BRETHREN 4. COMFORT 5. EPISTLE 6. TURNED

This man was the people's only way to be forgiven, before Jesus.
HIGH PRIEST
1. CHERISH 2. WRITE 3. AMONG 4. EXHORT 5. PROVE 6. OVERTAKE 7. ABSTAIN 8. ESTEEM
9. BESEECH 10. QUIET

Another "monster" from the book of Job. BEHEMOTH
1. REBUKE 2. BRAWLERS 3. HEIRS 4. BELLIES 5. BLAMELESS 6. BISHOP 7. SUBVERT 8. CHARITY

They were always ready to have Jesus as their guest. MARY and MARTHA
1. MEEKNESS 2. PECULIAR 3. SAVIOR 4. GAINSAYER 5. MAGISTRATES 6. GRACE 7. LOVER 8. EXHORT
9. HAND 10. APPEARED

CROSSWORD PUZZLES

Puzzle #218

```
S A L E M · B L A D E
S T R O V E · E A T I N G
E R E · E L D A D · D O R
E O · N O I S E · · U O
S K I P · N E T · T U G S
T E N O N S · S M I T H S
· N U N · · A R T · · ·
O P E N E D · W H E E L S
W O R D · E A I · D R A W
N O · H A D S T · P O ·
E R R · E L O T H · A P R
R E T I R E · Y E L L E D
· R E F E R · E N T E R ·
```

Puzzle #222

```
F A R · G R A P E · L A Y
O W E · A I D E D · E T E
R E V I V E · A G A T E S
· · O L E · S C E N T · ·
R O L L · U L E · G E B A
O U T · E S E · H E R E S
O G · S W E E T E R · R S
T H R E E · P A W · S E A
S T E W · B E G · S T A Y
· · S E V E R · B A R · ·
C H I D E S · H A T E T H
R E S · N O M A D · E R E
Y E T · T R O D E · T I N
```

Puzzle #220

```
· P L A N T · G R A N T ·
C O V E R · L O R D · E
A H · A T E · E A R · T N
N A G · S A · A R A R A T
S H O E · D A N · Y E A R
T A B L E · L E T · D R Y
· · · S L I D E · · · ·
E O S · T I E · N A D A B
N A I L · E N D · S A M E
S T R A I T · A T · Y E A
U S · I S H · G A D · N S
E · E S L I · O R E B · T
· A S H E N · N E B A T ·
```

Puzzle #224

```
J A H · G A T E · M A N
A X I L · O H A D · E W E
E L S E · D A U G H T E R
L E S S · · · T E E · ·
· · C A L E B · S W E E T
A S A · A N E R · N N E
C O L · D A G O N · T O N
H O E · N A M E · E S D
E N S U E · N E V E R ·
· · · S A W · · A T A D
T H R E S H E D · R A C E
W O E · E E R Y · S I R E
O D D · S N E E · N E D
```

Puzzle #226

A	H	A	B		H	A	M		E	L	S	E
C	A	V	E		A	G	O		R	O	A	D
T	R	O	W		D	E	N		R	O	L	E
S	E	W	A	R	D		T	H	O	M	A	S
		R	O	I		H	U	R				
R	E	N	E	W	E	D		E	S	H	E	K
I	R	E		D	I	E		E	V	I		
P	A	R	E	D		G	L	E	A	N	E	D
		L	I	E		E	A	T				
L	I	L	I	E	S		C	R	O	W	N	S
E	N	O	S		T	A	T		N	E	A	T
W	I	S	H		E	W	E		E	A	S	E
D	A	T	A		R	E	D		D	R	A	M

Puzzle #232

L	A	D	E		D	O	T	E		D	A	B
A	S	I	A		U	R	I	M		E	G	O
P	A	S	T	O	R		M	E	L	T	E	D
		T	E	M	A		N	E	E	D	Y	
S	H	I	N	E		M	E	D	E	S		
A	I	L		G	R	A	Y		S	T	O	P
U	R		A	I	D	E	S			R	E	
L	E	S	T		P	O	S	T		S	E	R
		T	A	K	E	N		O	P	H	N	I
S	T	A	I	N		T	R	U	E			
N	O	B	L	E	S		H	E	L	E	P	H
A	L	L		E	A	S	E		S	T	O	A
G	E	E		S	T	A	Y		E	S	P	Y

Puzzle #228

			A	C	C	U	S	E	D			
	D	O	D	A	I		A	B	O	D	E	
	U		D	R	E	A	M	E	R		C	
A	M	T		E	L	I	U	D		R	O	E
D	A	R	N		E	R	E		S	E	L	A
I	H	E	A	R	D		L	A	T	T	E	R
V		L	V	I		M	A	R		T		
I	S	L	E	E	P		F	I	N	I	S	H
N	A	I	L		E	S	E		D	E	L	L
E	D	S		S	W	E	L	L		D	A	Y
	O		A	T	T	A	L	I	A		V	
	C	H	L	O	E		E	N	S	U	E	
			P	A	R	A	D	E	S			

Puzzle #234

			K	I	N		S	O	N			
	C	H	I	D	E		O	V	E	N	S	
	L		D	O		A		E	R		N	
W	E	N		L	E	P	E	R		S	A	P
H	A	T	E		W	E	T		S	T	I	R
O	N		N	N	E		C	A	N		L	O
		E	T	A		D	A	Y				
A	T		E	Y	E		H	O	R		N	O
S	E	E	R		A	R	E		E	N	A	N
A	N	D		S	T	O	R	E		S	H	E
	O		H	A		T		A	S		U	
R	E	A	L	M		P	S	A	L	M		
			S	E	E		G	E	T			

Puzzle #230

F	L	E	W		O	D	E	D		I	M	P
A	I	A	H		B	A	R	E		N	O	R
N	D		O	P	E	N		I	N	T	O	
		S	L	A	Y		H	A	D		E	D
L	O	W	L	Y		J	A	D	O	N		
I	M	A	Y		S	A	V	E		E	W	E
S	E	R		L	E	P	E	R		E	E	R
A	R	M		E	R	A	N		E	D	E	N
	S	E	V	E	N		G	L	E	D	E	
A	T		R	I	D		S	A	I	D		
N	O	N	E		D	A	Y	S		A	H	
O	N	O		S	L	O	W		H	A	T	E
N	E	T		H	O	R	N		A	M	E	N

Puzzle #236

		H	E	M	A	N		J	E	S	U	S
C		R	A	T	E		E	V	E	R		N
L	T		Y	E	T		S	I	T		S	E
E	A	T	E	R		S	L		H	E	W	
A	P	E	S		A	R	E		D	U	L	L
R	E	S	T	O	R	E		E		S	A	Y
		T		I	T	A	L	Y		B		
E	L	I	L		L	E	E	W	A	R	D	
S	O	F	T		A	M	T		A	N	E	R
H	A	Y		E	L		I	N	D	I	A	
E	D		H	A	T		G	O	T		N	W
K		W	I	S	E		I	T	E	M		N
	R	I	D	E	R		N	A	D	A	B	

Puzzle #238

D	E	N		A	S	I	D	E		A	W	E
A	V	I	M		A	D	E		S	T	A	Y
M	E		A	P	P	O	I	N	T		S	E
	R	I	D	E		L		E	A	C	H	
M		M	E	E	T		H	E	R	A		M
A	S	P		P	R	O	U	D		E	R	A
Y	O	U	R		I	N	S		A	S	O	K
B	U	T		W	E	E	K	S		A	T	E
E		E	Y	E	D		S	O	A	R		R
	E	D	E	N		N		M	I	S	T	
S	D		A	T	T	I	R	E	D		E	A
A	G	U	R		O	N	O		E	V	E	N
Y	E	S		S	W	E	E	T		A	N	D

Puzzle #244

L	A	M	B	S		B		A	M	B	E	R
O	S	E	E		T	E	A		E	A	S	E
A	S	A		F	O	L	D	S		T	E	N
F		D	R	A	W		D	A	R	T		D
	D	O	E	R		W		M	E	L	T	
R	O	W	S		S	A	D		N	E	A	R
A	T		P	H	E	N	I	C	E		B	E
W	E	R	E		A	T	E		W	A	L	L
	D	E	C	K		S		H	E	R	E	
A		S	T	I	R		S	I	D	E		W
L	O	T		N	E	C	K	S		T	W	O
A	N	E	M		D	A	Y		H	A	I	R
S	O	D	O	M		B		H	A	S	T	E

Puzzle #240

G	A	T		I	S	L	E	S		A	R	A
O	W	E	D		T	A	R	E		R	E	D
D	E	N		B	O	Y		N	A	M	E	D
	T	R	A	P		A	S	K		D		
A	S	H	E	R		G	L	E	A	M		A
B	E		S	N	A	R	E		N	A	A	M
R	A	W		S	M	A	R	T		D	I	M
A	M	E	N		E	N	T	E	R		D	O
M		T	A	U	N	T		L	I	N	E	N
	D		I	N	D		M	E	D	E		
W	O	R	L	D		R	A	M		S	A	T
A	D	O		E	W	E	S		S	T	I	R
D	O	E		R	A	I	S	E		S	L	Y

Puzzle #246

D	E	B	T		M	E	L	T		B	A	N
A	R	A	H		E	V	E	R		A	R	E
N	E	A	R		N	E	V	E	R	S	A	W
			E	N	D			M	O	I		
B	R	O	A	D		L	A	B	A	N	O	N
L	E	A	D		W	O	R	L	D		F	I
E	A	R		S	H	A	M	E		B	A	G
S	C		S	E	A	T	S		S	A	G	E
S	H	I	N	E	T	H		U	N	D	E	R
			M	O	M			A	S	A		
F	O	R	W	E	C	A	N		R	E	S	T
E	R	A		T	H	I	N		E	L	S	E
B	A	H		H	I	D	E		S	A	W	N

Puzzle #242

P	A	S	T	O	R		B	O	A	S	T	
A		H	I	M		B	E	G	E	T		M
I	N		P	A	D	A	N		R	O	S	E
N	E	H		R	I	S	E	S		P	E	D
E	R	A	N		D	E	A	L	S		V	A
D		N	O	T		S	T	A	I	N	E	D
	P	A	R	A	H		H	I	L	E	N	
S	E	N	S	U	A	L		N	A	G		
A	N		E	N	D	O	R		S	E	B	A
I	C	E		T	H	O	R	N		V	E	T
T	E	L	L		E	S	S	A	Y		L	H
H		S	Y	E	N	E		M	E	N		A
	S	E	E	N	O		R	E	T	U	R	N

Puzzle #248

M	I	N	T		A	S	S		D	A	N	
A	C	R	E		B	I	T		O	R	E	
Y	E	A	R		S	N	O	W		V	E	X
		R	O	T		P	R	I	E	S	T	
	S	H	O	H	A	M		O	R			
A	T	E	R		I	E		T	I	R	E	D
S	E	A		S	N	A	R	E		O	W	E
A	P	R	O	N		N	U		A	M	E	N
	N	O		S	N	O	R	E	S			
S	A	V	O	U	R		N	E	A			
E	R	E		T	A	R	E		R	A	G	E
L	E	I		N	O	S		A	G	U	E	
F	A	N		G	E	T		T	O	R	N	

431

Puzzle #250

R	A	W			S	A	W		F	L	A	W
O	N	O		P	A	R	E		A	E	R	O
D	A	N		A	V	A		F	R	A	M	E
E	N	D	U	R	E		A	L	M	S		
		E	S	T		M	E		T	E	N	
A	C	R	E		L	E	A	N			D	O
P	A	S	S		M	E	N		A	B	E	T
E	R		T	H	A	T		B	O	N	E	
S	E	A		E	D			B	A	R		
	B	O	R	E		M	I	L	D	E	W	
B	R	I	B	E		F	I	R		E	L	I
A	I	D	E		L	O	R	D		R	A	N
D	E	E	D		A	R	E			S	H	E

Puzzle #256

				G	A	A	L				
			G	O	S	P	E	L			
		L	U	D		P	A	I	N		
	O	A	R		B	E	R	E	A	N	
A	R	M		L	E	A	N		T	O	W
S	P	E	C	I	A	L		T	I	R	A	S
P	A		E	A	R		F	R	O		N	U
S	H	E	A	R		P	L	A	N	E	T	S
S	O	S		S	E	E	P		L	E	I	
	N	E	P	H	E	W		H	A	D	
		D	R	O	P		D	A	M		
		O	N	E	W	A	Y				
			E	D	E	N					

Puzzle #252

C	A	N	E		N	A	Y		H	A	H	A
A	M	O	N		I	R	E		A	N	A	N
B	O	A	T		N	E	T		G	O	L	D
	S	H	E	E	T	S		W	A	N	T	
			R	A	H		H	E	R			
O	T	H	E	R		L	U	D		T	H	E
L	O	A	D		A	I	R		S	I	O	N
D	R	Y		E	N	E		E	W	E	R	S
			S	L	Y		A	G	E			
	T	A	P	E		A	N	G	E	L	S	
D	O	V	E		A	M	I		T	A	T	E
A	R	E	A		D	E	S		E	N	O	N
M	A	R	K		O	N	E		R	E	A	D

Puzzle #258

				C	H	O	P		A	G	U	R
	A	R	E	L	I			L	E	P	E	R
T	R	E	A	D	S		T	A	S	S	E	L
A	D	A	R		O	M	A	R		A	S	A
L	O	T		A	N	E	R		F	L	E	D
K	N	E	E	L		T		C	R	E	T	E
			L	A	W		T	O	E			
P	R	E	S	S		B		A	T	O	N	E
E	A	S	E		R	E	A	L		L	A	D
A	P	T		S	I	G	N		T	I	M	E
T	H	E	F	T	S		G	R	A	V	E	N
	A	E	R	I	E		E	A	R	E	D	
		M	O	R	N		L	E	E	S		

Puzzle #254

N	O	W		E	A	R	N		B	A	N
A	D	A	M		F	R	E	E		E	N	E
M	E	T	E		T	E	A	C	H	E	T	H
E	D	E	N			P	H	I				
			R	E	M	I	T		O	T	H	E	R
D	U	E		E	R	A	N		E	L	I	
E	N	D		T	O	L	A	D		R	O	B
A	D	S		N	E	A	R		I	N	S	
D	O	T	E	D		S	M	A	R	T	
		A	R	T			E	A	S	E		
R	E	S	T	O	R	E	D		A	G	E	S
A	D	O		P	U	R	E		L	E	A	P
M	E	N		S	E	E	N		S	T	Y	

Puzzle #260

			B	E	L	I	E	V	E
	G	A	V	E		D	O	W	N
W	O	R	E		S		W	E	I	R
C	A	R	E		T	A	U		S	N	O	W
O	N	E		S	A	L	L	U		E	L	I
N	T		H	A	R	V	E	S	T		E	T
F		R	E	V		A		E	O	N		N
E	R		R	E	S	T	O	R	E		D	E
S	E	A		S	O	I	L	S		Y	E	S
S	A	L	T		N	O	D		T	E	N	S
	R	A	I	N		N		L	I	L	Y	
	S	E	E	S		T	I	L	L			
		R	E	C	E	I	V	E				

Puzzle #262

```
A W A Y   H I D     J A D A
I A G O   A R E     O M A R
T R O U B L E S   S E R A
      T I E   O P E N E D
R I G H T   S L A P
O R E S   R E A C H E T H
P O T   S E A T S   S R I
E N S A M P L E   B E E N
    B E E S   Y O K E D
R E N O W N   M E T
E S A U   T H I S T L E S
A L I N   E A R   L I N E
M I L D   D Y E   E D E N
```

Puzzle #268

```
E L S E   H E E D   S A D
D I E S   R A S E   T O E
S E A T S   R E S   O N E
    A T E   K I L L E D
P R E T E N D   R U E
E A S E   S A V E D   F T
E Y E   C U R E D   A R E
P S   G R E E N   A M E N
    R E I   D O U B T E D
R E A L M S   M R S
I N N   S A T   N E H U M
S A G   O M A R   N O N E
E N E   N E X T   T W I N
```

Puzzle #264

```
A N N   H I R E   J O Y
L O I N   E D E N   A R E
A N N A   M E A S U R E S
S E E M   P U N
    T E M P T   E A R T H
B O Y   A R A M   E R E
A S S   N A M E D   D O R
P S I   Y E A R   E W E
T A X E S   S N A R E
    A N T   A M O S
S U S T A I N S   M E R E
A S A   K E E P   A T E R
W E D   E D D Y   H O E
```

Puzzle #270

```
A S A   G U L F S   A R E
N E R   U S U R P   S I R
T A R R I E D   O T H E R
    A I L S   P U R E
M A Y B E   D E S E R T S
A P E S   S O R E S   A M
L A D   L O O K S   E H I
E R   M A R R Y   P L A T
S T R I P E S   M A I N E
    A L P S   S O N S
A N G L E   C L O T H E D
R O E   T R A I N   U R I
A D D   H A R P S   A I D
```

Puzzle #266

```
A S A   C A N E   F L E A
C O L   A R E A   L E W D
T U M B L E   S T O N E S
S P O O N   E H U D
    S T O U T   A R E L I
M O T H   N E A R   R E D
A M   A D R I A   S E
R I D   R O A D   A R T S
S T O R M   H A S T E
    C O O K   C O A L S
R E T U R N   D A M P E N
A M O S   E V E N   E V A
P U R E   W A N T   R A G
```

Puzzle #272

```
F E D   F I R   E A T S
A R E   W I R E   G L E E
R E C E I V E D   L A M E
    L I F E   E S A I A S
S N A R E   T E L I
O R E   R E M E M B E R
E S E   R E N E W   R O E
M E D I A T O R   P I N S
    A S U N   C A N S T
H A M M E R   T R I G
A G A G   N A Z A R I T E
L E T O   E R A N   N O B
O D E D   D A R   G O B
```

Puzzle #274

W	E	S	T	■	O	W	E	S	T	■	S	A
H	■	■	D	I	E	D	■	D	O	E	■	E	N
E	R	■	E	V	E	N	■	B	A	S	E	■
T	I	N	■	E	D	E	N	■	R	O	M	E
■	D	E	E	R	■	R	O	E	■	N	E	R
H	E	A	L	■	I	B	R	I	■	D	R	■
E	■	R	O	D	■	■	E	S	T	■	E	■
A	R	■	N	O	A	H	■	L	A	I	D	■
R	E	D	■	R	I	E	■	H	E	M	S	■
T	A	I	L	■	R	A	G	E	■	E	H	I
■	S	P	A	N	■	D	I	R	T	■	I	D
T	O	■	S	O	P	■	N	E	E	D	■	L
I	N	■	T	R	O	A	S	■	■	N	O	N	E

Puzzle #276

B	A	A	L	■	H	A	P	■	L	A	T	U
A	S	E	A	■	A	R	A	■	E	N	O	S
G	A	R	M	E	N	T	S	■	A	O	N	E
■	■	E	N	G	■	T	U	R	N	E	D	■
S	T	A	N	D	■	B	U	R	N	■	■	■
W	I	L	T	■	P	E	R	I	S	H	E	D
A	E	S	■	R	E	G	E	M	■	E	A	R
P	R	O	D	U	C	E	S	■	S	A	S	E
■	■	A	B	U	T	■	S	T	R	E	W	■
S	A	M	U	E	L	■	A	I	R	■	■	■
A	M	O	N	■	I	N	C	R	E	A	S	E
R	E	S	T	■	A	I	T	■	A	T	E	R
A	N	T	S	■	R	D	S	■	M	E	T	E

CryptoScripture Puzzles

1. Romans 12:2—And be not conformed to this world: but be ye transformed by the renewing of your mind, that ye may prove what is that good, and acceptable, and perfect, will of God.

2. Revelation 19:5—And a voice came out of the throne, saying, Praise our God, all ye his servants, and ye that fear him, both small and great.

3. Hebrews 11:6—But without faith it is impossible to please him: for he that cometh to God must believe that he is, and that he is a rewarder of them that diligently seek him.

4. Isaiah 59:1—Behold, the LORD's hand is not shortened, that it cannot save; neither his ear heavy, that it cannot hear.

5. Psalm 63:1—O God, thou art my God; early will I seek thee: my soul thirsteth for thee, my flesh longeth for thee in a dry and thirsty land, where no water is.

6. Leviticus 18:23—Neither shalt thou lie with any beast to defile thyself therewith: neither shall any woman stand before a beast to lie down thereto: it is confusion.

7. Philippians 2:4—Look not every man on his own things, but every man also on the things of others.

8. Luke 23:46—And when Jesus had cried with a loud voice, he said, Father, into thy hands I commend my spirit: and having said thus, he gave up the ghost.

9. Proverbs 30:17—The eye that mocketh at his father, and despiseth to obey his mother, the ravens of the valley shall pick it out, and the young eagles shall eat it.

10. 1 Chronicles 16:29—Give unto the LORD the glory due unto his name: bring an offering, and come before him: worship the LORD in the beauty of holiness.

11. 1 Kings 4:29—And God gave Solomon wisdom and understanding exceeding much, and largeness of heart, even as the sand that is on the sea shore.

12. Jeremiah 17:10—I the LORD search the heart, I try the reins, even to give every man according to his ways, and according to the fruit of his doings.

13. John 10:10—The thief cometh not, but for to steal, and to kill, and to destroy: I am come that they might have life, and that they might have it more abundantly.

14. Ephesians 5:23—For the husband is the head of the wife, even as Christ is the head of the church: and he is the saviour of the body.

15. 1 John 2:16—For all that is in the world, the lust of the flesh, and the lust of the eyes, and the pride of life, is not of the Father, but is of the world.

16. Psalm 46:10—Be still, and know that I am God: I will be exalted among the heathen, I will be exalted in the earth.

17. Proverbs 16:32—He that is slow to anger is better than the mighty; and he that ruleth his spirit than he that taketh a city.

18. John 3:5—Jesus answered, Verily, verily, I say unto thee, Except a man be born of water and of the Spirit, he cannot enter into the kingdom of God.

19. James 1:12—Blessed is the man that endureth temptation: for when he is tried, he shall receive the crown of life, which the Lord hath promised to them that love him.

20. Malachi 4:2—But unto you that fear my name shall the Sun of righteousness arise with healing in his wings; and ye shall go forth, and grow up as calves of the stall.

21. John 3:17—For God sent not his Son into the world to condemn the world; but that the world through him might be saved.

22. Exodus 20:7—Thou shalt not take the name of the LORD thy God in vain; for the LORD will not hold him guiltless that taketh his name in vain.

23. Deuteronomy 34:10—And there arose not a prophet since in Israel like unto Moses, whom the LORD knew face to face.

24. 2 Timothy 4:18—And the Lord shall deliver me from every evil work, and will preserve me unto his heavenly kingdom: to whom be glory for ever and ever. Amen.

25. Revelation 3:16—So then because thou art lukewarm, and neither cold nor hot, I will spue thee out of my mouth.

26. Acts 22:16—And now why tarriest thou? arise, and be baptized, and wash away thy sins, calling on the name of the Lord.

27. Deuteronomy 6:17—Ye shall diligently keep the commandments of the LORD your God, and his testimonies, and his statutes, which he hath commanded thee.

28. 1 Samuel 12:24—Only fear the LORD, and serve him in truth with all your heart: for consider how great things he hath done for you.

29. Nehemiah 9:31—Nevertheless for thy great mercies' sake thou didst not utterly consume them, nor forsake them; for thou art a gracious and merciful God.

30. Romans 8:28—And we know that all things work together for good to them that love God, to them who are the called according to his purpose.

31. Philippians 4:6—Be careful for nothing; but in every thing by prayer and supplication with thanksgiving let your requests be made known unto God.

32. 1 John 4:10—Herein is love, not that we loved God, but that he loved us, and sent his Son to be the propitiation for our sins.

33. Luke 9:23—And he said to them all, If any man will come after me, let him deny himself, and take up his cross daily, and follow me.

34. Genesis 3:13—And the LORD God said unto the woman, What is this that thou hast done? And the woman said, The serpent beguiled me, and I did eat.

35. Deuteronomy 24:16—The fathers shall not be put to death for the children, neither shall the children be put to death for the fathers: every man shall be put to death for his own sin.

36. Psalm 139:14—I will praise thee; for I am fearfully and wonderfully made: marvellous are thy works; and that my soul knoweth right well.

37. Acts 12:23—And immediately the angel of the Lord smote him, because he gave not God the glory: and he was eaten of worms, and gave up the ghost.

38. 2 Corinthians 10:4—(For the weapons of our warfare are not carnal, but mighty through God to the pulling down of strong holds.)

39. Proverbs 28:13—He that covereth his sins shall not prosper: but whoso confesseth and forsaketh them shall have mercy.

40. Luke 22:19—And he took bread, and gave thanks, and brake it, and gave unto them, saying, This is my body which is given for you: this do in remembrance of me.

41. John 14:2—In my Father's house are many mansions: if it were not so, I would have told you. I go to prepare a place for you.

42. 2 Chronicles 16:9—For the eyes of the LORD run to and fro throughout the whole earth, to shew himself strong in the behalf of them whose heart is perfect toward him.

43. Judges 13:24—And the woman bare a son, and called his name Samson: and the child grew, and the LORD blessed him.

44. Lamentations 3:22-23—It is of the LORD's mercies that we are not consumed, because his compassions fail not. They are new every morning: great is thy faithfulness.

45. Colossians 4:6—Let your speech be always with grace, seasoned with salt, that ye may know how ye ought to answer every man.

46. Romans 5:1—Therefore being justified by faith, we have peace with God through our Lord Jesus Christ.

47. John 11:25—Jesus said unto her, I am the resurrection, and the life: he that believeth in me, though he were dead, yet shall he live.

48. James 5:16—Confess your faults one to another, and pray one for another, that ye may be healed. The effectual fervent prayer of a righteous man availeth much.

49. Genesis 50:20—But as for you, ye thought evil against me; but God meant it unto good, to bring to pass, as it is this day, to save much people alive.

50. Genesis 6:19—And of every living thing of all flesh, two of every sort shalt thou bring into the ark, to keep them alive with thee; they shall be male and female.

51. Exodus 13:21—And the LORD went before them by day in a pillar of a cloud, to lead them the way; and by night in a pillar of fire, to give them light; to go by day and night.

52. Matthew 1:21—And she shall bring forth a son, and thou shalt call his name JESUS: for he shall save his people from their sins.

53. Philippians 1:6—Being confident of this very thing, that he which hath begun a good work in you will perform it until the day of Jesus Christ.

54. 1 Timothy 4:4—For every creature of God is good, and nothing to be refused, if it be received with thanksgiving.

55. Psalm 100:3—Know ye that the LORD he is God: it is he that hath made us, and not we ourselves; we are his people, and the sheep of his pasture.

56. Isaiah 53:5—But he was wounded for our transgressions, he was bruised for our iniquities: the chastisement of our peace was upon him; and with his stripes we are healed.

57. Proverbs 10:13—In the lips of him that hath understanding wisdom is found: but a rod is for the back of him that is void of understanding.

58. Acts 21:13—Then Paul answered, What mean ye to weep and to break mine heart? for I am ready not to be bound only, but also to die at Jerusalem for the name of the Lord Jesus.

59. Mark 9:43—And if thy hand offend thee, cut it off: it is better for thee to enter into life maimed, than having two hands to go into hell, into the fire that never shall be quenched.

60. 1 Corinthians 6:19—What? know ye not that your body is the temple of the Holy Ghost which is in you, which ye have of God, and ye are not your own?

61. 1 Kings 3:9—Give therefore thy servant an understanding heart to judge thy people, that I may discern between good and bad: for who is able to judge this thy so great a people?

62. 2 Chronicles 34:1—Josiah was eight years old when he began to reign, and he reigned in Jerusalem one and thirty years.

63. Psalm 33:8—Let all the earth fear the LORD: let all the inhabitants of the world stand in awe of him.

64. Matthew 19:14—But Jesus said, Suffer little children, and forbid them not, to come unto me: for of such is the kingdom of heaven.

65. 1 Timothy 2:5—For there is one God, and one mediator between God and men, the man Christ Jesus.

66. Hebrews 13:5—Let your conversation be without covetousness; and be content with such things as ye have: for he hath said, I will never leave thee, nor forsake thee.

67. Genesis 1:7—And God made the firmament, and divided the waters which were under the firmament from the waters which were above the firmament: and it was so.

68. Genesis 25:27—And the boys grew: and Esau was a cunning hunter, a man of the field; and Jacob was a plain man, dwelling in tents.

69. Ecclesiastes 11:5—As thou knowest not what is the way of the spirit, nor how the bones do grow in the womb of her that is with child: even so thou knowest not the works of God who maketh all.

70. Song of Solomon 4:1—Behold, thou art fair, my love; behold, thou art fair; thou hast doves' eyes within thy locks: thy hair is as a flock of goats, that appear from mount Gilead.

71. Jeremiah 18:4—And the vessel that he made of clay was marred in the hand of the potter: so he made it again another vessel, as seemed good to the potter to make it.

72. Daniel 2:20—Daniel answered and said, Blessed be the name of God for ever and ever: for wisdom and might are his.

73. Matthew 6:26—Behold the fowls of the air: for they sow not, neither do they reap, nor gather into barns; yet your heavenly Father feedeth them. Are ye not much better than they?

74. Galatians 3:28—There is neither Jew nor Greek, there is neither bond nor free, there is neither male nor female: for ye are all one in Christ Jesus.

75. 1 Thessalonians 5:2—For yourselves know perfectly that the day of the LORD so cometh as a thief in the night.

76. Ezra 7:10—For Ezra had prepared his heart to seek the law of the LORD, and to do it, and to teach in Israel statutes and judgments.

77. Ezekiel 13:3—Thus saith the LORD GOD; Woe unto the foolish prophets, that follow their own spirit, and have seen nothing!

78. Exodus 34:30—And when Aaron and all the children of Israel saw Moses, behold, the skin of his face shone; and they were afraid to come nigh him.

79. Deuteronomy 6:5—And thou shalt love the LORD thy God with all thine heart, and with all thy soul, and with all thy might.

80. I Samuel 15:23—For rebellion is as the sin of witchcraft, and stubbornness is as iniquity and idolatry.

81. Daniel 6:26—I make a decree, That in every dominion of my kingdom men tremble and fear before the God of Daniel: for he is the living God.

82. Luke 12:15—And he said unto them, Take heed, and beware of covetousness: for a man's life consisteth not in the abundance of the things which he possesseth.

83. John 15:5—I am the vine, ye are the branches: He that abideth in me, and I in him, the same bringeth forth much fruit: for without me ye can do nothing.

84. Acts 17:24—God that made the world and all things therein, seeing that he is Lord of heaven and earth, dwelleth not in temples made with hands.

85. Romans 5:8—But God commendeth his love toward us, in that, while we were yet sinners, Christ died for us.

86. I Corinthians 15:58—Therefore, my beloved brethren, be ye stedfast, unmoveable, always abounding in the work of the Lord, forasmuch as ye know that your labour is not in vain in the Lord.

87. Job 23:12—Neither have I gone back from the commandment of his lips; I have esteemed the words of his mouth more than my necessary food.

88. Proverbs 12:4—A virtuous woman is a crown to her husband: but she that maketh ashamed is as rottenness in his bones.

89. Isaiah 64:8—But now, O LORD, thou art our father; we are the clay, and thou our potter; and we all are the work of thy hand.

90. I Peter 5:8—Be sober, be vigilant; because your adversary the devil, as a roaring lion, walketh about, seeking whom he may devour.

SPOTTY HEADLINE PUZZLES

	MISSING LETTERS	HIDDEN NAME		MISSING LETTERS	HIDDEN NAME
1.	UEKL	Luke	31.	UDASJ	Judas
2.	NNAA	Anna	32.	AAPRGPI	Agrippa
3.	OJNH	John	33.	NANAIAS	Ananias
4.	LASU	Saul	34.	ARNEDW	Andrew
5.	TEREP	Peter	35.	MALESO	Salome
6.	PSNTEEH	Stephen	36.	AIARSHPP	Sapphira
7.	IEMAGALL	Gamaliel	37.	PTEALI	Pilate
8.	OLEHC	Chloe	38.	EATTWHM	Matthew
9.	AULP	Paul	39.	HACCAZUSE	Zacchaeus
10.	SJSEU	Jesus	40.	ITASAPN	Antipas
11.	IDAEORHS	Herodias	41.	MOISN	Simon
12.	EONMSI	Simeon	42.	UMATBIARSE	Bartimaeus
13.	TPSBTHONTHJAIE	John the Baptist	43.	JSOHPE	Joseph
14.	LUAP	Paul	44.	AMRATH	Martha
15.	TSERMPEINO	Simon Peter	45.	IALQUA	Aquila
16.	YMTOTIH	Timothy	46.	DIAYL	Lydia
17.	USEOMSIN	Onesimus	47.	PLPIHI	Philip
18.	TERPE	Peter	48.	UIERSTT	Tertius
19.	ANBBRAAS	Barnabas	49.	JSUDA	Judas
20.	RHDOE	Herod	50.	SJUES	Jesus
21.	AMOTSH	Thomas	51.	RETEP	Peter
22.	RUASALZ	Lazarus	52.	SIALS	Silas
23.	COIEUSMDN	Nicodemus	53.	TNHESPASA	Stephanas
24.	AGUSI	Gaius	54.	CHUYTCIS	Tychicus
25.	REPTE	Peter	55.	BSARBUBA	Barabbus
26.	EUSJS	Jesus	56.	ORDHE	Herod
27.	RTDEESPOHI	Diotrephes	57.	ITSTU	Titus
28.	YMRA	Mary	58.	PHTEUHSIOL	Theophilus
29.	GRMEMNAYEALAD	Mary Magdalene	59.	UCSUSTARGUEASA	Caesar Augustus
30.	CEENUI	Eunice	60.	ESSJU	Jesus

Bible Quotation Puzzles

I John 5:5—Who is he that overcometh the world, but he that believeth that Jesus is the Son of God?

I John 2:17—And the world passeth away, and the lust thereof: but he that doeth the will of God abideth for ever.

I Peter 1:16—Because it is written, Be ye holy; for I am holy.

I Samuel 12:22—For the LORD will not forsake his people for his great name's sake: because it hath pleased the Lord to make you his people.

Philippians 1:6—Being confident of this very thing, that he which hath begun a good work in you will perform it until the day of Jesus Christ.

Psalm 18:32—It is God that girdeth me with strength, and maketh my way perfect.

Jeremiah 29:13—And ye shall seek me, and find me, when ye shall search for me with all your heart.

Psalm 73:28—But it is good for me to draw near to God: I have put my trust in the Lord God, that I may declare all thy works.

Colossians 3:2—Set your affection on things above, not on things on the earth.

Romans 8:5—For they that are after the flesh do mind the things of the flesh; but they that are after the Spirit the things of the Spirit.

Psalm 91:2—I will say of the Lord, He is my refuge and my fortress: my God; in him will I trust.

Proverbs 2:6—For the Lord giveth wisdom: out of his mouth cometh knowledge and understanding.

Romans 8:37—Nay, in all these things we are more than conquerors through him that loved us.

I Corinthians 10:31—Whether therefore ye eat, or drink, or whatsoever ye do, do all to the glory of God.

Hebrews 11:1—Now faith is the substance of things hoped for, the evidence of things not seen.

Daniel 9:9—To the Lord our God belong mercies and forgivenesses, though we have rebelled against him.

I John 5:4—For whatsoever is born of God overcometh the world: and this is the victory that overcometh the world, even our faith.

James 2:26—For as the body without the spirit is dead, so faith without works is dead also.

John 14:6—Jesus saith unto him, I am the way, the truth, and the life: no man cometh unto the Father, but by me.

Psalm 119:73—Thy hands have made me and fashioned me: give me understanding, that I may learn thy commandments.

Ephesians 4:2—With all lowliness and meekness, with longsuffering, forbearing one another in love.

Psalm 10:17—Lord, thou hast heard the desire of the humble: thou wilt prepare their heart, thou wilt cause thine ear to hear.

I Corinthians 14:1—Follow after charity, and desire spiritual gifts, but rather that ye may prophesy.

Galatians 3:28—There is neither Jew nor Greek, there is neither bond nor free, there is neither male nor female: for ye are all one in Christ Jesus.

James 2:22—Seest thou how faith wrought with his works, and by works was faith made perfect?

Philippians 4:13—I can do all things through Christ which strengtheneth me.

James 1:19—Wherefore, my beloved brethren, let every man be swift to hear, slow to speak, slow to wrath.

Proverbs 16:9—A man's heart deviseth his way: but the Lord directeth his steps.

Proverbs 3:3—Let not mercy and truth forsake thee: bind them about thy neck; write them upon the table of thine heart.

Galatians 6:9—And let us not be weary in well doing: for in due season we shall reap, if we faint not.

Philippians 3:14—I press toward the mark for the prize of the high calling of God in Christ Jesus.

Romans 12:18—If it be possible, as much as lieth in you, live peaceably with all men.

Jeremiah 17:7—Blessed is the man that trusteth in the Lord, and whose hope the Lord is.

Psalm 32:11—Be glad in the Lord, and rejoice, ye righteous: and shout for joy, all ye that are upright in heart.

Mark 11:24—Therefore I say unto you, What things soever ye desire, when ye pray, believe that ye receive them, and ye shall have them.

Mark 10:27—And Jesus looking upon them saith, With men it is impossible, but not with God: for with God all things are possible.

Proverbs 24:28—Be not a witness against thy neighbour without cause; and deceive not with thy lips.

Matthew 5:16—Let your light so shine before men, that they may see your good works, and glorify your Father which is in heaven.

Psalm 86:2—Preserve my soul; for I am holy: O thou my God, save thy servant that trusteth in thee.

Psalm 73:26—My flesh and my heart faileth: but God is the strength of my heart, and my portion for ever.

Matthew 11:28—Come unto me, all ye that labour and are heavy laden, and I will give you rest.

Mark 9:23—Jesus said unto him, If thou canst believe, all things are possible to him that believeth.

Psalm 119:80—Let my heart be sound in thy statutes; that I be not ashamed.

Proverbs 16:19—Better it is to be of an humble spirit with the lowly, than to divide the spoil with the proud.

TELEPHONE SCRAMBLE PUZZLES

ALTAR MAKERS
- ABRAHAM
- ISAAC
- ISRAEL
- JACOB
- JOSHUA
- MOSES
- NOAH

DIVINE REPORTS OF CHRIST'S BIRTH
- ANNA
- ELIZABETH
- JOSEPH
- MARY
- SHEPHERDS
- SIMEON
- ZACHARIAS

PEOPLE OF THE NEW TESTAMENT
- CENTURION
- HEROD
- JOSEPH
- MARTHA
- PHARISEES
- PILATE

FOODS IN THE OLD TESTAMENT
- FIGS
- GARLIC
- GRAPES
- HONEY
- LAMB
- MILLET
- OLIVES

APOSTLES
- ANDREW
- JOHN
- JUDAS
- PETER
- PHILIP
- SIMON
- THOMAS

GIANTS
- AHIMAN
- ANAK
- GOLIATH
- LAHMI
- OG
- SIPPAI
- TALMAI

MUSICAL INSTRUMENTS
- CASTANETS
- DRUM
- HARP
- LYRE
- ORGAN
- TRUMPET
- ZITHER

CITIES IN THE NEW TESTAMENT
- BETHLEHEM
- CORINTH
- JERUSALEM
- NAZARETH
- ROME
- TARSUS

CONVERSIONS IN THE NEW TESTAMENT
- CANAANITE
- CENTURION
- LEPER
- MARTHA
- PAUL
- PUBLICAN
- SAMARITAN

NAMES FOR CHRIST
- ALMIGHTY
- BLESSED
- MESSIAH
- PRINCE
- REDEEMER
- SAVIOUR
- SHEPHERD

CITIES IN THE OLD TESTAMENT
- BABYLON
- BETHEL
- DAMASCUS
- GAZA
- JERICHO
- NINEVEH
- SAMARIA

CHRIST FIGURES IN THE OLD TESTAMENT
- ABRAHAM
- ADAM
- DAVID
- ISAAC
- JONAH
- MOSES
- NOAH

GOD IS...
- ETERNAL
- GRACIOUS
- HOLY
- INFINITE
- JUST
- MERCIFUL
- WISE

NEW TESTAMENT PEOPLE WITH GOD-GIVEN MISSIONS
- BARNABAS
- JAMES
- JUDE
- PETER
- PHILIP
- SILAS
- TIMOTHY

BOOKS OF THE NEW TESTAMENT
- ACTS
- HEBREWS
- JUDE
- MATTHEW
- REVELATION
- ROMANS
- TITUS

ANIMALS IN THE NEW TESTAMENT
- FISH
- GOAT
- HORSE
- LOCUST
- SERPENT
- SHEEP
- SPARROW

OLD TESTAMENT PEOPLE WITH GOD-GIVEN MISSIONS
- DAVID
- ELISHA
- EZRA
- GIDEON
- MOSES
- NOAH
- SAMUEL

MARTYRS
- ISAIAH
- JAMES
- PAUL
- PETER
- STEPHEN
- URIAH
- ZECHARIAH

GIFTS OF THE HOLY SPIRIT
- FAITH
- GIVING
- HEALING
- KNOWLEDGE
- PROPHECY

ANAGRAM PUZZLES

Bible Cities: Damascus
Books of the Bible: Deuteronomy
Places: Mesopotamia
Bad Guys: Judas Iscariot
Books of the Bible: Zechariah
Places: Mount of Olives
Books of the Bible: Galatians
New Testament People: Good Samaritan
Rivers/Bodies of Water: Mediterranean
Events: Creation
Books of the Bible: Timothy
New Testament People: Bartimaeus
Books of the Bible: Jeremiah
Kings: Rehoboam
New Testament People: Nicodemus

Books of the Bible: Thessalonians
Places: Mount Ararat
Bible Cities: Nineveh
Books of the Bible: Philemon
New Testament People: Pharisees
Women of the Bible: Herodias
Books of the Bible: Lamentations
Women of the Bible: Mary Magdalene
New Testament People: Prodigal Son
Events: Battle of Jericho
Books of the Bible: Genesis
Rivers/Bodies of Water: Dead Sea
Books of the Bible: Corinthians
Places: Garden of Eden
New Testament People: Simon Peter

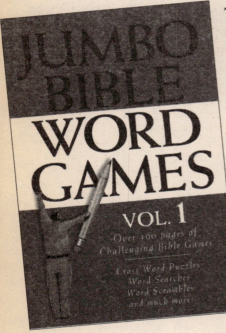